Because of a Fishbone

Because of a Fishbone

Written by
Monica Kocsmaros

Story by Janči David Teschner

Copyright © 2013 by Monica Kocsmaros.

Library of Congress Control Number:		2012923639
ISBN:	Hardcover	978-1-4797-6798-4
	Softcover	978-1-4797-6797-7
	Ebook	978-1-4797-6799-1

All rights reserved. No part of this book may be reproduced or transmitted in any form or by any means, electronic or mechanical, including photocopying, recording, or by any information storage and retrieval system, without permission in writing from the copyright owner.

This book was printed in the United States of America.

Rev. date: 08/06/2013

To order additional copies of this book, contact:
Xlibris Corporation
1-888-795-4274
www.Xlibris.com
Orders@Xlibris.com
122524

CONTENTS

Foreword...9
No Allies..13
Gypsy Music, September 10, 1933..........................20
A Hard Lesson, 1935......................................35
Schnitzel Sandwich, 1936.................................62
Vanilla Cookies, Summer 1937.............................84
Gone Fishing, 1938......................................103
Because of a Fishbone, December 1938....................126
The Wrong Way, March 1939...............................133
Žid, 1940...149
A Train Ride, 1942......................................163
Glorious Fruits, 1943...................................177
Cuckoo Clocks, 1944.....................................186
Going Home, June 1945...................................245
A New Life Awaits, Spring 1947..........................259
Afterword...269

This book is dedicated with love and fond memories to my dear wife, Ruth, and all my family and friends—those who are with me today and those who did not have the chance to tell their own stories. I hope my words will honor their spirit and do justice to their tremendous courage. Through the pages of this book, the light of your lives will shine forever.

Janči David Teschner

FOREWORD

GRANDPARENTS ARE SPECIAL people—*the true* heroes of our generation. The word "hero" itself has undergone transformation over the years. The qualities that would merit the title fifty years ago are not necessarily the same qualities possessed by today's role models.

Two short generations ago, men and women displayed the kind of strength of character that took them through world wars. In our history's darkest moments, it was their commitment to survive that allowed them to emerge from the atrocities of concentration camps. Growing up and listening to stories of events that seem so far away made those experiences real for me. In my life, I have been fortunate to have living heroes nurture and guide me. They are my grandparents.

The bond between grandparents and their grandchildren is precious and unique. As a grandchild with loving grandparents to whom I have been extremely close all my life, I have come to realize more each day how powerful they have been in shaping and influencing the man that I am becoming. My grandparents have been a living, breathing history book that has taught me about my roots as a Jew; they have brought to life the history of my family and created for me an "internal lens" for insight into who I am as a human being. I have been blessed to live my young life hearing my grandparents tell their stories: my Saba's struggle to survive the Nazi regime as they invaded the former Czechoslovakia; my Savta's fleeing from the then USSR to Romania; my Zaidie's days, trying to keep his family together as the threat in Poland loomed just over his shoulder; my Bubie's childhood in the Ukraine, living on rations.

I always thought that my Saba's stories resembled the kind one would see in a Hollywood film—a tale of adventure, with the added elements of adversity, sorrow, and accomplishment. But his were not the tales of a big-screen writer. They are the real days of his childhood, interrupted by tragedy. They are the words of a young boy who came face-to-face with the kind of horror that imagination cannot create but reality cannot bring to an end. They are the real memories—all that is left from what was taken from him.

With each new time I hear his stories, I learn more about these great men and women—these heroes. Today, I live in a world where hard work and dedication to a dream can translate into the realization of one's aspirations. I have seen the glow in my grandparents' eyes when I tell them of my accomplishments and what I hope to achieve. I know that in the pivotal moments of their battles to live, my family's future generations were saved.

The love of my life wrote this book. Monica has been my heart and soul ever since we met in grade seven. As a result, she has grown up around my family and has shared in those special Friday nights, when my Saba will often share a glimpse into his past.

My Saba's tales of struggle have always struck Monica profoundly. This book was her idea, her undertaking, and has become a source of pride for my whole family. She had the fortunate ability to check her facts with my Saba and bounce her ideas off my family when she wished. I can only hope that I provided her with enough support while she wrote. I cannot thank her enough for what this book has done—in these pages lies the history of my family, now commemorated forever and brought to life. But even more importantly, herein lies the kind of story that inspires future generations.

This is the kind of story that ensures we will "never forget." But I have always been of the view that remembering is simply not enough.

While it is true that passing these stories from one generation to another is in and of itself an important responsibility, we must do more.

Let our history teach us not only the importance of remembrance but serve as an impetus for each of us to become ambassadors for justice, truth, and peace for all.

Ryan Teschner

NO ALLIES

WE'VE CREATED OUR own prison, stuck in a hole somewhere below the ground, and I don't even know if we'll ever get out of here. Ironically, this place was meant to protect us.

Winter is rapidly setting in, ready to smother us at any unexpected moment. Through a funneled route, the cold creeps into our dismal hideaway, preventing any warmth from reaching us. Quietly, it slithers through, gracefully entwining itself with our bodies to the point we can't be untangled, reminding me of a time when Apu[1] pointed out a spruce tree on one of our walks. As tall as Goliath, the grandeur of the tree was breathtaking, especially to me, a boy a fraction of its height. Staring up at it, my neck craned back, I couldn't help but feel sorry for it despite its sublime impression. From the roots to the branches, a canker disease seeping large drops of gray-colored sap had infected the entire tree. Constricting its life by cutting off water flow, the fungus was suffocating the innocent tree with an unrelenting malice, the spruce needles decaying brown or already dead. Surrendering to the fact that nothing could save this spruce, I just helplessly stood there, marveling at the forces of nature. Then it was time to continue walking along to the next fascinating scene. Curious at that time to know what it must feel like to have no control over something that's taken control of you—I think I finally know.

Extreme weather of this magnitude is not something we are prepared for or can even recall in recent memory. Time did not enable us to pack heavier. Even if it did, most of the items would've been lost along the

---

[1] *Apu* means "father" in Hungarian.

way, strewn about the roads and trails—my gray turtleneck here, some wool socks Babka[2] spent hours knitting there—the extra weight of clothing not bearing enough significance to lug with us. Trying to picture what I would've packed had it made it all the way here, nothing comes to mind that would be warm enough. Even my rust-colored warm winter jacket may only have given my extremities a superficial sense of heat, completely ignoring the needs of my internal organs that feel like they are slowly freezing to death. Only a meager long-sleeved cotton T-shirt, shorts, and canvas shoes clothe me. My shivering body is left without proper protection from the bitter wind that cunningly blows through any crack it can find, chilling me to the bone. Goose bumps cover the entire surface of my skin and won't disappear no matter how hard I rub them, desperately trying to generate warmth. I have come to the conclusion that they are now a permanent addition to my body.

Shifting my thoughts to something warmer, I picture myself lying by the pool at Zelená Žaba,[3] while rays of the sun beat down, hitting every inch of me. Pausing for a moment from my thoughts, I try to see if I feel warmer. I don't.

I look down at my shoes, the soles shedding off like skin. Walking kilometers in forests and mud paths, I did my best to salvage the rubber soles, evidently an impractical undertaking. Eventually, I admitted that my shoes were not going to survive this unforgiving terrain. Hiking boots with insulated lining would've been more appropriate for an expedition like this, cradling my feet like pieces of gold that need to remain untouched to preserve their value. I didn't have time to put them on.

Lifeless solitude down here is not what we bargained for.

---

[2] *Babka* means "grandmother" in Slovak.

[3] *Zelená Žaba* means "green frog."

Instead, we should be back home in Trenčianské Teplice,[4] nuzzled at the foot of the Western Carpathian Mountains. In our spacious home built by Opapa[5] for Mamička[6] and Apu when they got married, we would sit around the oak dinner table handcrafted by a local artisan in the city. Lighthearted conversation would fill every corner in the dining room. Words would weave around doorways, flowing into the kitchen and venturing upstairs, wanting to share the familial spirit. A plateful of chicken *paprikash* would sit in front of us. I can still taste the tender chicken covered in a rich golden sauce spiced with paprika and firm dumplings of just the right consistency, a feat Mamička has mastered. Now I have grown used to the taste of stale bread with plum butter.

In my former reality, on a full stomach, we would then lounge in the living room, drinking hot mint tea to digest our savory meal. Casting a warm glow over us, the fire would crackle, lit using logs laboriously cut by Apu's two left hands on the days he'd be home from work. Marta would work on a drawing hunched over the coffee table, sitting cross-legged on the floor, engrossed in her new masterpiece. Mamička would kneel beside her, her long brown hair parted in the middle and pulled back in a tight bun, maintained by weekly visits to the hairdresser, encouraging Marta's artistic hand. In the mahogany leather recliner, Apu would sit reading the local newspaper, filling his mind with more knowledge of current events.

Snapshots of what life used to be like are my only sense of security now. Those are the relaxed surroundings I yearn for during the day and dream about each night. But nostalgia is a double-edged sword, removing

---

[4] *Teplice* pronounced in Czech is TEP-LI-TSE.

[5] *Opapa* means "grandfather" in German.

[6] *Mamička* means "mommy" in Slovak.

me from my current pain, while at the same time taunting me with what is out of reach.

All we have now are tree roots and dirt surrounding us to the point of claustrophobia. Nothing homey can be found anywhere down here. Carefully straightened paintings aren't hanging on the walls. Carpets aren't on the floors cushioning feet treading upon them. No treasured belongings of mine sit proudly on display. Barren and monochromatic are our makeshift home. For how long, we don't know. An eternity already seems to have passed. How slow time moves when waiting for your inevitable fate, like pieces on a board game with a predestined outcome. When I think back and actually take the effort to make my mind count, it has been seventeen days. Seventeen days of my life vaporized.

My mind doesn't instinctively react to the signals I send up to it anymore, telling me that parts of my brain are starting to atrophy. Each day has become one and the same, a blur because I can't tell them apart. Wednesday could be Friday; Thursday could be Monday. It doesn't matter anymore. Insignificant details like having plum butter on bread or frozen apples from the trees outside are the only ways I can differentiate one day to the next. Losing track of time like this astonishes me. Each day in my room at home, I was able to look at the calendar on my wall, marking important days like birthdays or Boy Scout meetings. I especially used to get excited toward the end of the month when I would be able to flip the calendar and see what plane awaited me next. Not that there was a shortage of planes in my bedroom. Suspended from the ceiling and neatly placed on my dresser, these flying inventions would sit in positions I spent hours perfecting. Habits I cultivated for almost fourteen years that gave me a sense of a scheduled lifestyle are long gone. Sunrise and sunset don't exist in my world anymore. I can't enjoy the warmth of the sun while playing soccer outside because the only time I can climb above the bowels of where we are is to obtain food for my family's survival. What used to be a simple task is now a dangerous adventure.

All our days are filled with dread, not knowing what is to come. Dangerously, our minds wander to possible outcomes of our situation. Bad ones always outnumber the good. Amazingly, there are several different versions of terrible endings I can visualize. With this kind of imaginative mind, I should spend more time writing. At least then, it would be fiction.

Uneasiness around here feels as thick as the stale air we're breathing, too thick to cut even with the sharpest of knives from Baračka.[7] Always unsure if we will have enough food to eat or if we are hidden well enough, making it through each day only gives us more time to brood over our circumstance and wonder.

I look over at Apu, a crumpled heap in the corner. Helpless and unable to react to his environment, this is not the man I know. Simply, it is his withering body. Blood quickly soaks through Mamička's wool scarf that is stuffed in Apu's belly wound. Nothing else around here is thick enough to saturate the constant flow. At first, the blood was a bright red color. Now it has become brown with none of that visual appeal. Each day, his condition deteriorates further. Weakness has become a lead weight bearing down on him in every direction. Mamička softly whispers in his ear with a soothing voice, gently rocking him in her arms. I am hopeful that her voice enters some part of Apu's conscience, comforting him in his pain. Watching Apu, I know he is unable to make any rational decisions at this time, which causes my own mind to struggle in figuring out what our next move should be. We can't stay here forever.

Although engrossed in my thoughts, I still watch Marta silently sit in the corner with no toys to play with, her large blue eyes drably watching

---

[7] *Baračka* is pronounced BAR-ACH-KA.

the ground. I move over to her and pull her close to me. Orienting herself, she finds a sweet spot somewhere in the grooves of my chest and closes her eyes, placated for the time being. Knowing she will temporarily escape into her dreams, I can continue to think.

Wheels in my mind are spinning, a constant motion of contemplations swirling throughout, not properly dissolving. If we don't leave soon, we will be discovered. Logically, I deconstruct our dour situation and acknowledge that knowing where we are works to our advantage. Navigating through the mountainous terrain of the Carpathians in the deep snow will not pose a challenge to me. Getting my parents and Marta through it will. Apu can barely stand, let alone trek through feet of snow in the coldest winter we've seen; and my sister, so petite and fragile, I'm scared we'll lose her along the way in these treacherous conditions.

Minutes or even hours pass, and my frenzied deliberations finally begin to settle. Leaving soon is imperative. I can feel it somewhere deep within my gut, a persistent feeling I can't ignore. Change is rapidly rolling through outside. I feel the uneasy shift—people not willing to offer us as much information; villagers in Kšinná looking the other way when we arrive to get food. Suspicions are rising, and movement in this direction must be getting closer. I don't want any unforeseen circumstances to prevent our escape. In the past, that has led to disaster.

Looking to see if I can gather any allies around here, I hang my head. I can't trust these people with anything, not even a slice of bread. They have already proven their callousness to me. Asking for their help would only jeopardize my family's survival.

How we got here is a story unto itself. I didn't think we'd make it out alive. Somehow, we managed, but I know not everyone was as fortunate as us. I watched as they fell. Silently, I pray that if I get knocked over as

I've seen happen to countless others, I'll be able to get back on my feet and lead my family to a place where life can resume normalcy, a place where we can replant our roots and let them grow.

This is my story.

GYPSY MUSIC, SEPTEMBER 10, 1933

THE DOORBELL RINGS, echoing loudly off the walls and disrupting a household already on edge. A beware sign should be placed on their front door, warning any unexpected visitors about the state of what lies inside. "Enter at your own risk," it should say. Omama[8] Gabriela, or Ella as everyone calls her, hurries to open the door. Her grey hair, neatly pinned up only moments ago, is looking disheveled, and her frantic round face is flustered at having to leave her post down the hall. A deliveryman expectantly stands on the other side, Omama's stocky frame overpowering his meager height. Random white strands of hair sporadically sprout from his bald head. Behind him, a white horse-drawn buggy is parked. The embroidered patch on his navy uniform informs his customers that his name is Victor from Rose's Flowers. Without giving him the chance to introduce himself, Omama begins instructing him on where to put the flowers, wanting this intermission terminated quickly, so she can resume her more important duties. He nods in overwhelmed understanding and quietly heads back to his buggy, desperately trying to remember all the directions given to him.

Getting flowers today is a surprise to Janči.[9] Everyone seems too busy to think of such a trivial indulgence. But this unanticipated event entertains him as he watches Victor get swallowed up behind the back of the buggy. Walking down the garden path for a better view, Janči sees Victor fumbling about inside the buggy, filling his arms with as many

---

[8] *Omama* means "grandmother" in German.
[9] *Janči* is pronounced YAN-TCHI.

white and yellow mums they can hold. Cautiously, he makes his way back toward the house, more vigilantly on the stairs and then victoriously reaching the top. He lowers the flowers before his trembling arms drop them. Omama sweeps a load of them in her arms to speed things up, every second too precious to waste. Victor begins placing the flowers in vases already standing at attention. As the process of displaying the flowers continues, it reaches the point where one piece of furniture is barely distinguishable to the next, each piece modified into a fashionable flowerpot.

Frantically, Omama calls for backup reinforcements. Jožka, Janči's nanny, materializes with bountiful long light brown hair flowing behind, a red flowered apron tied around her tiny waist, the cape of a super hero ready to save the day. Her twenty-year-old youthful exuberance, contained in a small and slim body, supplies enough energy to expedite the job.

After half an hour, Victor has made three weary trips to the buggy, bringing in an endless stream of flowers. Sweat patches form under his arms, and beads of perspiration glisten off his forehead. Exhausted and ecstatic, he notifies Omama that no more flowers are left. She nods her head in satisfaction and thanks him while looking around the house at the final result. With that stamp of approval, he is free to go. Relief washes over his face, and he dashes out before another word can be directed his way.

Gazing around, Janči sees the new visitors have beautifully invaded their house, implanting themselves on every available surface—on the coffee table with legs engraved in an ornate pattern; in the window sills where all kinds of decorations have been shoved aside to accommodate the temporary guests; on the dining room table, they encircle the glass vase filled with hydrangeas; and on the hexagonal shaped table in the foyer with the table cloth looking like a large doily. Wherever an ounce of space can accommodate them, the flowers are there, adding their pleasant company to an overwrought house. Janči's eyes were filled with a cheerful sea of white and yellow, Mamička's favorite colors.

Of course, Apu is the genius behind this. Commuting home from his job in Basel, Switzerland, is a tiring ordeal that is usually done once a week, but special occasions like this warrant an extra trip. Being a scientific advisor at Wonder Pharmaceuticals, he helps develop new products like Ovaltine, orange tins of it even more prevalent in the house than the flowers.

Commotion of this magnitude has never crossed the threshold of their house. Janči finds it a bit rankling because it doesn't revolve around him. It is all about his new sibling who is supposed to enter the world today. The aroma of *pörkölt*[10] and sounds of laughter must have pervaded their way through Mamička's stomach, reaching the baby, making it desperate to arrive in their world. Now Janči will have to share all those things, the idea not sitting well with him.

Around the house, the hustle and bustle combined with the excitement almost makes it feel like a holiday; although the difference is Janči's not being doted on, there are no presents for him to unwrap, and none of his favorite meals have been prepared. Instead, an impenetrable wall has been erected in front of him. His age, even though almost three, limits the amount of information he receives and the level of involvement he is entitled to, which has hindered his ability to participate in the action of the house. He has been banished to the living room, where Jožka has brought down toys from his room, wooden planes and cars, marbles and Meccano, creating a pity pile for him.

Omama is still running from room to room, the scent of her floral perfume with a hint of jasmine lingering in the air behind her blending

---

[10] *Pörkölt* is a Hungarian veal stew.

in with the overpowering bouquet of the mum's. She carefully rearranges the flowers which continue to look the same with all the fussing, trying to keep herself busy until she is required back in the bedroom, excused for the time being. Fortunately, Babka Helena hasn't made it here yet, having to abide by the train schedule from Beluša, or else she'd be in the same hyperactive state.

Opapa periodically comes to the living room, nervously pacing back and forth, readjusting his bowtie, taking off his glasses and rubbing his nose, running his hands through his white hair, his round friendly face knitted in angst, and then going back down the hall to continue pacing. There he meets Apu pacing the hall as well, anxiously wringing his hands, unable to stand still.

Being shut out from all this action only ignites Janči's curiosity more. He inches his way to the hallway, trying to uncover any new details. Prompting his right foot to take the next step toward the unknown adult world, he is interrupted.

"Janči, it's not time yet. You have to wait here until the baby is born."

Caught off guard at her sneaky appearance, he turns to face Omama who now decides to pay attention to him. Disappointed that his journey has already ended, he resorts to compassionate protesting.

"I want to know how Mamička's doing. I haven't seen her all day."

"Don't worry, Jančika.[11] You'll see her soon." And with that, she hightails back into the living room to find another chore to keep her occupied.

Janči crosses his arms and stomps his foot on the ground to demonstrate his annoyance. Already he can see the beginnings of how much more attention this baby is going to get. With a big huff, one that

---

[11] When adding a "ka" at the end of a name in Hungarian, it is a term of endearment.

loses all its effect with no one to witness it, he goes back to the living room and picks up one of his airplanes. On the beige carpeted tarmac, he taxis it along, preparing for takeoff. Masterfully, he flies it above his head with a technique that would make any trained pilot proud.

Apu makes an appearance in the living room, his lean body in a grey suit, settling into his favorite armchair. Anxiously, his smooth hands flip through the daily newspaper, but his deep brown eyes can't stay on the page. The slight dimple in his chin becomes more pronounced as he purses his perfectly shaped lips. Opapa shortly follows him in his usual three-piece suit, this one a camel color with a white kerchief sticking out the left breast pocket. His quickly receding sheer white hair is such a contrast against the thick black frames he wears, but even those can't hide his squeezable pudgy cheeks. His hefty body plunks down next to Janči. Shocked, Janči hands him a plane before he relapses into his fretful state. Half-heartedly, Opapa flies it around, but his distracted glances toward the hallway, and feigned interest prove his mind is elsewhere. Watching Opapa lost in his thoughts makes Janči to think about Dedko,[12] Apu's father, who isn't here to share in the festivities, dying a year before Janči was born. All Janči knows about him is that he was the principal of an elementary school in Beluša.

"Just keep playing, Janči. I'll be right back," Opapa tells him, getting up from the couch. Apu follows him out.

Diving hard into the floor, Janči's plane makes a crash landing and is discarded back in the pile it came from. No one has the time to spend with him now. Is this what his life is going to become? Playing with his airplanes by himself while everyone else is fussing about the baby? What can he do to possibly stop this from happening? He wonders. He can't compete with being cuter or smaller or needing more attention.

---

[12] *Dedko* means "grandfather" in Slavic.

Resigning himself, he knows the baby will rule the household, a basic fact that cannot be rewritten.

Most of the main floor practically empty, Jožka, the only one left, clambering in the kitchen, preoccupied with preparing a special meal for tonight, one that Janči was not consulted about. He has been deserted, a feeling he believes he should start getting used to.

Throughout the living room, walls are plastered with paintings of countryside, horses and wagons, and bowls filled with fruits. Glass cabinets framed by a rich cherry wood line the walls. On display are all of Mamička's treasured items. About twenty decorative antique Dresden porcelain figurines pose through the glass to onlookers. A lady standing in a ruffled white dress, another one in a green and pink lace dress, and a pair of birds make up the front row. A collection of crystal figurines and vases are on another shelf along with silver teaspoons and matching saucers, too nice to ever serve coffee in. Ornamental china bowls are the final addition with elaborate hand painted floral and gold work. Many were gifts from her wedding and subsequent anniversaries, birthdays, and some she bought simply for her love of them. Janči can relate to Mamička's appreciation for her collection as he takes great pride in his own toys. He wonders if might be able to showcase his planes in these glass cabinets beside Mamička's Dresden porcelain dolls.

Creeping over to the hallway, he peers down at it again, unsure if he should try his stint once more, fearing that he will be reprimanded harshly if he does. Mamička and Apu's room is the first one on the right. Omama rushes out of it. His heart beating fast, Janči quickly moves out of her view, back pressed firmly against the wall, trying to blend into it as much as possible, although his red shirt doesn't camouflage well against the cream background. He can hear Opapa asking "What? How is Mitzka?"

A minute later, she runs back in with a wet white towel. Trying to make sense of what he just saw, he only has more questions without answers. What is that towel for? Do they have to clean the baby with it? Is the baby already born because he doesn't hear any crying? Distraught at his blameless ignorance, he wanders to the kitchen to see if he can amuse himself with something in there, perhaps some food.

Warm air outside allows most of the windows in the house to be open. Sunlight flows through, washing the house in a honeyed haze. A slight breeze sweeps in every now and again, refreshing, not unpleasantly cool. Before he even reaches the kitchen, sounds of Hungarian gypsy music start up outside, falling into his ears, note by note, filling them with a sweet melody. Intrigued, he follows the sounds through an unseen yet exhilarating trail to investigate. Chords lead him to the front door. Standing by his parent's bedroom window on the perfectly manicured green lawn is the gypsy band from the family's restaurant, another gift from Apu to Mamička. The band members are wearing colorful Folkloric costumes, navy trousers cut in Hungarian style adorned with black stripes and fringes and red dolmans. Distinct dark features, their eyes, hair, and even the shade of their skin, sun kissed to the most extreme degree, compliment their middle-aged appearance. Between their instrumental pieces, they wave at Janči with large grins.

Intently, he focuses on the musicians. An ensemble of sounds drifts into the air, a harmonious blend of instruments that are independently indistinguishable. Methodically, the sounds break down as each player spontaneously explores their own mood, spawning innovative notes, each one taking turns to play the oomh-paa parts, each one a prodigy player in their own right. Among them, the energy is contagious, the music accelerating, louder and more thrilling as the solos are passed back and forth, their bodies working feverishly to keep up with the fast-paced rhythms they've established for themselves.

His eyes can barely keep up with the arm of the violin player, the instrument smartly tucked under his chin. It becomes a blur at the speed it moves back and forth. Underneath Janči, his feet take on a life of their own, unable to resist the infectious sounds. He sways back and forth, jumps around, anything to keep his body in motion, the music becoming adrenalin rushing through his veins. They are playing the unmistakable Csárdás.[13] Recognizable by its variation in tempo, the music starts out slow, tempting you with its romance. Before you even have the chance to notice the change, the beat has morphed into a very fast pace, inviting your feet to join. And you do. Enraptured, he listens attentively, his ears fully immersed in the chords freely flowing out of all the instruments, a magical recipe of sounds merging together perfectly. Finishing their first two songs, the band sets down their instruments for a break. Janči would like to give them a cue to continue, but he doesn't have such authority. With his form of entertainment ending, he aimlessly meanders back in the house.

Time is ticking by, and he can't find enough things to amuse himself with. Toys punctuate the floor, abandoned like him. His stomach is doing small turns, concerned about what's going on in the bedroom. Each second feels like an hour. His ears perk up, not to the sounds of the band outside, but to a faint crying in the distance. That has to be the baby. Nothing else could make that howling noise, although he is unable to discern if it's a boy or girl. Either could produce that high wailing pitch. Unsure about whether he will be welcomed in the bedroom yet, he decides it would be safer to sit at the edge of the hallway. Miserably, he plunks his chin into his hands. Until someone decides to get him, he will sit here, dejected, and continue to wait. He bets he has already become a memory that is slowly fading and difficult to make out in their minds.

---

[13] *Csárdás* is a traditional Hungarian folk dance.

He envisions them crowding around the bed, staring wondrously at the baby, cooing at its incomparable cuteness. Fighting with each other about who gets to hold and cuddle the bundle first, none of their thoughts will shift to Janči alone. Once content with their indulgence of the baby, perhaps they'll remember the lone family member has been excluded from this entire progression.

Footsteps softly make their way toward him, the unmistakable creaking of the worn out floor giving them away. Gently, a hand is placed on his shoulder.

"Jančika," Omama says behind him, "come and meet your new sister."

A sister? The word sounds like a foreign language to him. Hearing it repeated in his head, he immediately forgets about his sulking just seconds ago. A bewildering transformation overtakes him as he cultivates strategies on how to be a good big brother since he *is* the only brother she has. Enthusiastically, he takes Omama's weathered and worn hand.

Her grasp does not deny the power it still holds after helping to raise six brothers and one sister, the youngest of them the same age as Mamička. With Omama being the oldest, she assumed this responsibility after their parents died at a very young age. Even after marrying Opapa Leopold, or Poldi as everyone calls him, she insisted her siblings, Miki, Turi, Robert, Palko, Geza, Adi, and Kamila live with them. Opapa never argued but rather helped them establish themselves, sending them to school and personally teaching them the pastry- and chocolate-making business. It was only Robert who didn't follow this path, choosing to practice law instead.

Unconventional chocolate classes were set up where Opapa's tutelage began with the tastes and attributes of different types of chocolate, each one differing in taste due to the varying amounts of cocoa butter and chocolate liquor they contain. In great detail, he went on to define their traits. Each type of chocolate was sampled to ensure full understanding of the subtleties. Lectures continued about filled chocolates, which Opapa would make them taste as well. "When tasting these, the texture should not leave any grain on the tongue. Keep the chocolate in your mouth for a few seconds to taste the base and flavors, and then chew it to get a dose of the filling. Note how long the flavor lingers on the tongue."

Creating chocolate with rich flavor and texture was the next step as was mastering the skill of tempering. Opapa pressed on in his discourse while their faces crumpled in a combination of confusion and concentration, inconsequential to their lecturer. Various cast iron and tin moulds made by master craftsmen were shown to the avid learners, Opapa declaring that each one was to be hand filled.

After the intensive sessions on chocolate making, without any break, Opapa steered them directly into pastry making with several tips to impart on his students. "Always ensure ingredients are measured exactly. Sieve the flour at least three times. Work the pastry as lightly as possible as if handling a snowflake. When rubbing in the butter in short pastries, use your fingertips and lift them into the air. Allow the pastry to rest for at least an hour each time it is handled." Then the gamut of dough's was discussed, from short crust to *štrudel* filo.

By the end of it all, each of Omama's brother's could barely stand, the information bearing down on them. Hesitantly, they all began preparing their own chocolates and pastry dishes to show Opapa what they had learned and to prove they were ready to tackle this elaborate business. With the generous skills and guidance Opapa shared, the four of them began toward successful careers in this trade, settling in Teplice surrounded by mountains and tranquility or the cosmopolitan city of Trenčín. Turi and Adi built their own pastry shop, while Geza and Miki continue to run Opapa's.

Omama and Janči walk to the bedroom he's been craving to enter the entire day. Finally, he has been granted permission, the gate has been unlocked, and he is welcomed among the adults again. Inhaling oxygen into his lungs, he prepares himself for this moment. The door to his parents' bedroom takes on an enticing aura, beckoning him to walk through it. After having spent a day trying to know what was happening on the other side, it almost appears mystical out of a fairytale. Omama reaches above his head and pushes it open for him. Closing his eyes, he conceptualizes the scene that will unfold on the other side—a carnival with carousels, ponies, ice cream, and cute little babies. Blankly standing at the doorstep without attempting to take another step forward, Omama offers him a slight push from behind.

Breaking his reverie, he opens his eyes, startled that the scene before him is starkly different from the idyllic one that was in his head before taking the step across the threshold. Dr. Szephazi, their family doctor, stands to the side of the bed. His tall frame is not daunting as a warm look dances in his eyes. Wrinkles contour his face, but his wire-framed spectacles do a good job at taking the attention off them. A stethoscope hangs around his neck, a toy that Janči mischievously eyes. In his left hand, he is holding a small black leather bag, probably to stash more of his invaluable toys. Beside the doctor stands a plain looking middle-aged woman with a pale complexion. She carries a heavyset frame with shoulder-length dark blonde hair tied back in a simple ponytail. Her big brown eyes stare back at Janči, her face gleaning a drained expression, although he does see the glint of a smile breaking through.

Janči then sees Apu beaming with happiness, standing beside Mamička who is lying on her bed with the notorious white towel around her forehead. Her face is ghostly white, and she looks more somnolent than he's ever seen, deathly ill in fact. Her brown hair is matted to her head, and the glow of sweat covers her bare skin. Tears stinging his eyes, Janči rushes over, doing his best not to cry because he needs to be brave at a time like this. One escapes and trickles down his cheek, the saltiness hitting his taste buds.

"Mamička, are you okay?" he asks with the most amount of valor he can gather from his feeble storage, the inventory of it quickly depleting.

"I'm more than okay, Jančika," she says, smiling. The smile reassures him because it is so recognizable, a comfort blanket he can cuddle in to protect him. Seeing the tears brimming around his eyelids, she takes her free hand out of the bed, and lovingly wipes them away.

"Don't cry, honey. I'm fine and so is your new sister. Her name is Marta.[14] Come closer so you can meet her."

Cautiously, Janči leans in further, holding all his limbs still, not wanting to create any noise that might make her cry. Wrapped in a pastel pink blanket, it's hard to believe the tiny bundle in Mamička's arms is an actual person. She is sleeping soundly, not what Janči would expect after the wailing sounds that reached his ears minutes ago. A little tuft of blonde hair covers her head, and she has the face of an angel. Janči can't disguise the elation he feels, a permanent smile painted on this face. Marta has gained his approval in a matter of seconds and pushed any unpleasant thoughts about her out of his mind. Gingerly, he looks down at her and becomes amazed at her narrow nose, smooth skin, little eyes, and miniscule eyelashes. She even smells loveable as he nuzzles his face into her.

"She's so small."

"You were just as small when you were born."

He doesn't believe it.

"And just as cute."

---

[14] Marta is named after Apu's younger sister who died of pneumonia at the age of eighteen, a year before Janči was born.

This time, Janči smiles. Maybe this whole notion of sharing things with someone else can work. He leans over to give her a deserving and tender kiss. *I will be the best brother ever*, he thinks to himself. All his feelings of jealousy over her birth fade into nothingness as his sister opens her soft blue eyes.

After all the excitement of the day, Janči is ready to retire to bed, exhausted. Only minutes after his eyes close, they are jolted open again from the sound of thunder rumbling in the distance. Anxiously, he counts to three when the lighting illuminates the black sky outside. Rain is already pounding down and heavily pattering on the windows of the house. With his eyes wide open, Janči pulls the navy comforter up to his chin, ensuring his body is well protected underneath. A flash of light outside causes him to frenetically jump. A crash of thunder follows, rolling through the valley between the mountains, loudly echoing from one side to the next. He can say he gave it an honest try, but there is no way he will make it through the night alone in his bedroom with the raging storm so close to his head. It's also a good excuse to be able to spend the night with Marta.

Dragging his comforter behind him, he runs downstairs to his parents' bedroom where they are already expecting him. In the corner, the mauve couch becomes Janči's refuge where he covers himself with an abundance of pillows. The elements outside still keep him on edge, the noise too disruptive for him to sleep. He puts pillows on the double windows trying to block out the sound.

"Lie back down, Janči, and I'll read to you," Mamička proposes. "Hopefully, that will put you to sleep. Marta will listen too from her crib."

And so the story of "Hansel and Gretel" begins. Sounds of the storm curtail, and Janči begins dreaming about bread.

—⋙—

Apu begins taking Janči on walks into the forest, feeling that at the age of four, he can begin to grasp simple concepts about nature. These walks turn into ritualistic expeditions where Apu uses the outdoors as a classroom to teach his son, pointing things out like trees, meadows full of colorful flowers and birds. These outings are not only their special time together as father and son, but also as friends. Janči enthusiastically waits for these days when Apu is home from work and sets time aside, always seemingly unlimited, to teach his son and watch him grow.

"In the spring time, you'll see lots of bees because the flowers are blooming, and they need the flowers to make honey."

As the years go on, the conversations evolve into more advanced subjects, the basics of nature not challenging enough for Janči's inquisitive mind anymore. Apu earnestly introduces new subjects or tokens of information into Janči's lexicon that quickly get absorbed by his son.

"Janči, if you look at the position of the sun, you can figure out what time it is. The sun rises in the east and sets in the west, so if you picture it like an arch, if it's in between, it would be around noon." Apu's hand moves his coffee colored hair out of his eyes and shields his narrow face from the sun as he looks up. Only a week later, when asking Janči to estimate the time based on what he was taught the previous week, Janči immediately looked up toward the sun, moved his head from east to west noticing the position of the sun in the middle of that arch and predicted, "I'd say just after three o'clock." Apu looked at his watch, and it said 3:15pm.

Traversing through the meadows and woods, Janči and Apu follow differently marked paths on each outing, one time blue, the next yellow, and then green, every color leading them on a new trail and thrilling adventure. Even when they have to repeat trails, there is still pleasure in rediscovering them as if travelling them for the first time. It seems there is always something fresh to see, hear, or smell, whether a beech, deer, or chamomiles, nothing escaping Apu's prying senses.

Over the years, their walks never wane, and the conversations between them reach a level of candid sophistication. Apu is always open to discuss any topic, whether politics, technology, or sports, never one to limit his son's knowledge. For him, knowledge is wisdom, a bold and simple statement he always lives his life by. Apu imparts his own liberal views on politics and religion, not one for orthodoxy rituals, yet never judging those who do or don't practice them, making it effortless for Janči to learn the meaning of tolerance and acceptance. Apu analyzes and dissects political parties, their leaders and motives. Janči reciprocates with his own thoughts, never afraid of divulging what he's thinking, Apu always intrigued by the way his son's mind is maturing.

A HARD LESSON, 1935

LITTLE HANDS GRASP Janči's pants, bunching fabric as an anchor and tugging on it to pull herself up off the floor onto her unsteady feet. She'll grab onto anything that will support her—the couch, the coffee table, but this time, he is the closest thing in reach. Slightly fearing to let go but more curious about the world of walking, she ventures off, arms still outstretched, ready to hold on to the next nearest object when needed to brace herself. At points, her walk is more of a run, and he nervously waits, thinking she will tumble forward any second with her uneven balance. If she does fall, as long as no one makes a fuss, she'll be right back up stumbling to another area of the room. Every nook and cranny is explored by her voracious senses and craving to have free rein over this new world she is claiming as her own. Crawling into spaces and dark labyrinths, the sense of fear so apparent in adults, is nonexistent in her exploration. Everything needs to be carefully audited in her hands, and then as if her hands were deceiving her, directly placed into her mouth to verify its physical existence.

From the kitchen, Mamička's watchful eye is on Marta, giving Janči the opportunity visit Omama at the other end of the house on the main floor, the layout of their home unlike any other in the neighborhood. A year before Janči was born, when his parents got married, Opapa bought a piece of land where two houses were situated, each with its own lot, facing back-to-back with a narrow passage between them. He converted the two houses into one, number 17/18 Suché Mlýny.[15] Across the street

---

[15] *Suché Mlýny* means "dry mill."

is the train station, and in front of the house is the small river Teplička, flowing into the large river Váh. River Teplička wasn't brawny enough to power the flour mill, giving rise to the street name.

Upstairs, there are four bedrooms, one bathroom, and one kitchen, while downstairs are a living room, dining room, master bedroom, two smaller bedrooms, two bathrooms, and a kitchen. Having a kitchen on each floor becomes extremely useful when an influx of refugees stream through in the years to come. A circular flower room filled with rattan furniture and a large window offers a sanctuary away from the regular buzz of the house. Daffodils, radiant yellow carnations, tranquil blue and pink hyacinths, deep purple irises, intense red tulips, and pure white orchids confidently let their rainbow of colors dazzle their beholder, tempting even the shrewdest gardener to smell their enchanting bouquet. Each flower is meticulously planted from cuttings, becoming prized possessions once they start to flourish.

Opening Omama's door, the familiar air, stale from the lack of change, reaches Janči. An inert tone has filled the room, the stark white walls looking more bear now than they ever used to except for the lone painting of fruit in a beautifully crafted porcelain bowl framed by an ornate polished gold frame. Hearing him enter, Omama turns her stare from the window to the door with a tremendous amount of effort, causing Janči to wince in pain on her behalf.

"Hi, Janči," she greets him with warmth, her face lighting up, appreciative for the company. "How are you and little Marta doing today?"

"She's moving around a lot. She gets everywhere."

Omama smiles weakly. She looks down solemnly at her own legs that she now regards as intrusive objects. For the past month, they haven't been able to properly function, unable to get her out of bed. No amount of struggling and forcing them to bear weight has worked. Beneath her, they buckle, demonstrating their preference of simply lying comatose on the mattress, at ease against the white sheets, not caring about the inconvenience they are causing.

"You need to bring her next time. Not that I'll be much fun. I can't chase her around everywhere."

"I'll bring her later today. She loves seeing you. How are you feeling?" Janči asks.

"As good as I can be." Her words are a partition to the truth.

"You'll be better soon."

"You're right. I will." He can tell she's not convinced. "So tell me, how is Eli doing?"

Eli, Fiorella's nickname, is one of his best friends. Apu is good friends with her father, Mr. Fried, and Mamička close with her mother, Maria, both coincidentally having the same name. Her family owns a large clothing and shoe store, located among other stores inside a two-story castle where Apu always buys his shoes. On one seemingly insignificant day, Janči accompanied Apu on a shoe purchase.

That day, Eli, with stunning Italian features of olive-colored skin and a thick mane of shoulder-length chocolate brown hair and dark scrutinizing eyes, happened to be in the store. Although two years younger than Janči, the two of them became inseparable. Living so close to each other only helped fuel the friendship. Her sizeable home, with a burnt red roof, light yellow outer walls—as if ceaselessly enfolded by sunshine—and dotted by numerous windows, is implanted into the side of a mountain, backing onto the woods slightly above Janči's home.

And so the detailed stories begin, what games they played in the forest, what berries they picked, what Janči ate at Ali's bakery, the ramblings of her five-year-old grandson could entertain her for hours on end. Beyond the focused eyes, however, is an aloneness no one understands—an isolation of not being able to chase your grandchildren around the house or take them for walks outside and buy them candy, of being confined to a bed, a place she doesn't seek for rest anymore but rather a place she yearns to escape.

"That sounds like a lot of fun." An energetic aura that was once exuded from Omama has been replaced with melancholy. Hiding in the corners of the room are the shadows of death, waiting for the right moment to swoop in.

"You better go back to Mamička. I'm sure she'll have dinner ready soon."

He gives her a kiss on the cheek that is sinking further in. She turns to look back out the window.

Each evening, Opapa prepares Omama's dinner, carefully setting the food on a red, yellow, and blue royalty patterned chintz tray. A single rose that is regularly changed sits in a small crystal vase. He takes it to her bedroom where he first lovingly adjusts her in the bed, fluffing and rearranging the goose feather pillows behind her, permitting the tray to comfortably rest on her lap. Once she is settled and ready to eat, he then sits at the small wooden table beside the bed and they both begin their dinner together. Sometimes, their conversations are endless, Opapa talking about his day and the business, and other times, they just eat, not needing words to interrupt their uncomplicated silence. Simple glances at each other are charged with a love that never needs recharging even after decades of marriage.

Opapa and Janči head into town the next afternoon for a special treat for Omama. It's a place where potato sugar is manufactured. The white sign with black block letters simply advertise "Starch and Potato Sugar." Any other superfluous descriptors would be unnecessary. The owner, a slim-built man the height of Opapa, has an extremely round face with rosy cheeks always looking as if he's just run up a flight of stairs. His bald head shines in the light. Small talk is instigated, and without having to tell him their specific order, he hands over a small brown paper bag filled with a special kind of sugar made from potatoes. This is the only way Omama can savor the sweet taste of anything, real sugar being her body's lethal enemy.

Back in her bedroom, they produce the recognizable brown bag. Enthusiastically, she takes out a cube and puts it in her mouth, thrilled by the treat like a small child would be. Sweet flavor overwhelms her mouth, and her hand is quickly rummaging in the bag for another one, not wanting the moment to end. She looks over at Janči smiling—the light in her eyes brighter than yesterday—and offers him one. He never takes one from her no matter how many times she pushes the bag in front of him. It is only for her.

Over the following months, Janči sees the rapid deterioration of Omama, her body becoming smaller and frailer each day. His visits become more frequent, a gnawing fear they may end sooner than they should always with him. After visiting her each day, sometimes several times a day, he feels emotionally drained, never getting used to seeing Omama in that condition. It's getting harder for her to keep up a conversation, doing more listening than talking. She barely has the energy to lift her head or hands to eat. Under the blanket, her body is disappearing. Helpless, all he can do is tell her he'll back soon and gently close the door behind him, leaving her to rest.

After hours of playing outside with Eli, Janči bursts through the front door, excited for another visit with Omama with much to tell her. He immediately heads straight toward her bedroom.

"Janči," Mamička calls out to him as he passes the living room. Swollen red eyes and a flushed face make it obvious that she's been crying.

A foreboding feeling about what she needs to tell him overtakes Janči's body, incapacitating all its normal functions, bringing everything to a standstill except for the ball of iron in the pit of his stomach.

"Oh, Janči, my honey. Come here," she says, opening her arms.

Maybe if he doesn't go to her and doesn't listen to what she has to say, it won't be true. Maybe if he just shuts everything out around him and goes down the hall, he'll be able to sit down on the edge of Omama's bed and spend hours talking to her, telling her the funny joke he learned today and listening to all of her stories. Maybe he can go with Opapa to buy her potato sugar again today. Janči's head begins moving slowly side to side, denying the truth that is about to be revealed to him, a cover yanked off him when he's not ready to get out of bed, the chill making him want to crawl back under the snugness of ignorance.

Omama is dead at the age of forty-nine. His chest is tightly being squeezed by a racking despondency. Holding back the dam of tears that are about to gush out, he runs up to his room, slamming the door behind him. His pillow is instantly wet from the tears that won't stop falling. Uncontrollable convulsions take over his body as he cries for the unfairness of this. How can they go on living the rest of their lives when hers has stopped? Omama wasn't ready to go. There was still too much life left in her. Burying his head back in his pillow, he hopes it will drown out his thoughts. Only three months from now, they were going to celebrate her fiftieth birthday.

Opapa takes her death harder than any of them. He enters a state of robotic motions, numbing himself to the pain he can't handle. He does his best to put on a happy face for everyone's sake, but his lifeless eyes reveal his true condition. Losing the will to deal with life, let alone with business, he decides to sell his successful beer warehouse, an easy sale to a businessman from Hungary. Complete ownership of his pastry shop in

Trenčín, Conditoria Weiss, is also passed on to Uncle Miki, who renames it Conditoria Weil.

Janči has a hard time coping with the fact that everyone outside the family is still going about their normal routine as if nothing ever happened. Don't they know he just lost his Omama? Why aren't they crying, in shock, and unable to function? It doesn't make any sense to him, but as time goes by, Janči slowly learns a hard lesson, one he thought could never be true—even in the face of death, life does manage to go on, one foot in front of the other, one day at a time.

―⚮―

Whoever says never do business with family just hasn't learned the proper way of doing it. Uncle Geza and Opapa have worked together amicably for years. The two of them run the family restaurant, Baračka, situated in an expansive garden with mountains rising in the background. It's in the village of Omšenie, near Trenčianské Teplice.

Rising over the trees, the sun casts giant shadows on the grass, periodically shining beams of light through the dense foliage. Motorbikes are zooming by, heading to their different destinations. Janči is on the lookout for one car in particular, a big black six-seater Praga with a heavy rear end where the engine is mounted, driven by Martin, Opapa's driver. It was not an ostentatious decision to get a driver but rather a practical one with Opapa running three businesses—the pastry shop, restaurant, and, until recently, the beer warehouse. Instead of being hassled at finding ways to get from one place to another in a hurry, it made more sense to have someone he could always rely on. Martin was so dependable that he became Opapa's right-hand man at the beer warehouse before it was sold.

Normally, the trio, Janči, Marta, and Mamička would make the half-hour walk to the restaurant through the park. Before Marta could walk, Janči would insist on pushing her in the pram, delicately designed with ornate spoke wheels featuring small hubcaps, a working parking brake, and adjustable sun and sleep shield he was always careful to pull down when necessary. Detailed mini opera windows decorated the sides, and Marta would happily coo in the light pink wicker bassinet when he looked through them. Even now, she sometimes gets tired out before they reach the restaurant, so Janči or Mamička end up carrying her. When Mamička can't go with them or they don't feel like walking, Martin kindly picks them up and takes them to Baračka or Conditoria Weil—whatever they're in the mood for.

Conditoria Weil is the epitome of heaven for Janči, offering a plethora of tantalizing napoleons and *dobos tortes* that are eternally at his disposal, causing his sweet tooth to spiral out of control. Only one difficulty ever confronts him at the pastry shop—choosing what to treat himself to. Uncle Miki always cuts off Janči's favorite part of the cake, the burnt pieces from the sides that are filled with cream.

"He's eating too much," the other bakers warmly warn Uncle Miki who avidly agrees but replies with "let him eat. He will get sick of it," but Janči never does.

Christmas is Janči's favorite time to be there. Theirs is the only bakery that makes the special *Szaloncukor*[16] that get hung on every Christmas tree in the area. Wrapped first in white paper with fringes on the side, they are then twisted over with shiny foil in a rainbow of colors like blue, red, yellow, or green. One end has a small piece of string with a loop or small metal hooks that get hung on the tree. Janči's small fingers have tried to tie the string on the candy leaving a sufficient loop for the

---

[16] *Szaloncukor* means "parlor candy" in Hungarian.

hanging process, but they are not nimble enough. Instead, he watches Uncle Miki who has efficiently mastered this procedure. Inside these wrappers is a treat made of fondant and covered by chocolate with different flavor-filled centers waiting to be discovered—strawberry, vanilla, raspberry, orange, or lemon—a sweet surprise for children eating them once the tree comes down.

Martin comes around the bend, pulling to a stop in front of Mamička. Still lingering with a few drops of water, the car is sparkling clean, never to be seen with a trace of dirt on it, just like Martin will never be seen with a scuff on his shoe or wrinkle in his pants, taking great care in his appearance almost as much as Opapa. Swiftly, Martin gets out wearing a crisp black suit and chauffeur hat covering an expanse of grey hair. Janči always asks to try on the hat, each time, hoping his head has grown, but it never does as the hat slides down over his eyes.

Martin's brown eyes crinkle into a warm smile as he opens the back door to let them in. Janči crawls in first to the spacious interior, always coveting the window seat. Marta follows in the middle, and then Mamička. When it's only Marta and him going up to Baračka, they get the privilege of sitting in the front with Martin, like honorary guests, and offered caramel candies that always get stuck in their teeth.

They start off along the winding road of the mountain. Coming to a gradual stop, recognizable sounds and smells let them know they have arrived. Low hanging trees spill leaves into the small Lake Baračka, and swans fill the water, flocking here to swim peacefully yet attracting throngs of spectators who invade their privacy. Sweet sounds of a violin drift into Janči's ears, a classical piece by Karol Szymanowski. Music here changes as often as the meals on the tables. Depending on what time of day you choose to dine, you can be hastily led to the dance floor with something upbeat playing in the early afternoon or enveloped by the tunes of a gypsy band at five o'clock.

Janči jumps out of the car, Mamička carrying Marta behind him. An empty table waits for them by one of the large windows. Every diner looks outside onto a picturesque painting. Mountains trace across the background, touching the sky. Lush green forest fills the foreground as far as the eye can see. A final touch to this masterpiece is the lake, painted a deep blue. The contrast of all these colors, the perfection of their shapes and proportions, and the gentleness of their curves all gives the illusion of a fictitious backdrop. A few steps outside and the mirage is still authentic. Several tables lazily lounge under enormous linden trees which offer shade to anyone fleeing the heat with their glossy, dark green heart-shaped leaves. Small, yellowish summer flowers are not easily detected on this tree, but their scent is overwhelming, sweet like honey, perfect for making herbal tea.

Inside, the restaurant is a fair size, packed with almost a hundred and fifty tables, usually all occupied by guests. Pine furniture finished with a white lacquer fills the room, and patterned table clothes protect them. Impeccably constructed, the high quality craftsmanship is timeless, creating a rustic charm that fits into this countrylike surrounding. Designs are relatively simple, letting the outdoor landscape be the main attraction. Windows encase each side of the restaurant, a piece of culinary paradise enclosed in glass.

On the walls hang trophies of stuffed deer heads Opapa and Uncle Geza have killed on hunting excursions. Deer that haven't made it on the wall end up hanging on hook in Janči's attic, food for winter. Skinned by Martin first, they are then pickled by Mamička using a sharp knife which punches holes into the raw flesh that are filled with garlic cloves.

Lacking refrigeration, the restaurant has its own complex system for this basic need. To learn about this, Janči was taken on an educational expedition last winter with Opapa and Uncle Geza to a huge cave in the mountain behind Baračka. Sneakily, burly Uncle Geza, with dark hair and a thin moustache in his majestic forest green suede coat surrounded by a collar of thick fur, tucked a piece of chocolate wrapped in silver foil into Janči's coat pocket, a treat to keep his mind off the cold. Just looking at Uncle Geza's jacket made him feel warm despite the core-chilling weather, but the chocolate didn't hurt. His attention was also diverted to the men they hired with horses and sleighs.

Laboriously, the men cut blocks of ice from the lake with their saws, steadily moving back and forth until a block almost three feet high was achieved. Sleighs drawn by horses were then manually loaded with all the ice and moved into the cave where they were covered with sawdust shavings. Embedded in the mountain was the front of the cave which was sealed off to prevent hot air from entering. Janči watched in awe as these men had superhuman physical strength to get such a job done. Now he knows where the restaurant's ice storage and supply is, one that lasts until the following winter when the restaurant will close, and this intensive ritual repeated.

Tourists visiting the restaurant always have an aura of relaxation surrounding them, one that locals can't bask in during this busy season from May to October when the population of Trenčianské Teplice triples from its normal four thousand.

Economic vitality of this town revolves around catering to tourists with food, entertainment, accommodation, and most importantly, spas. A desire to experience their relaxing and healing properties ignites a migration of tourists flocking to this small town in hopes that their arthritis and other medical ailments will be cured with the miracles these spas are sworn to work. Only one reason is good enough for visitors to depart the tranquil oasis of hydrotherapy and hot mud massages and that is to savor in the unfalteringly delicious food at Baračka.

In the corner sits a middle-aged couple. A red summer dress elegantly sits on the woman. Every strand of her shoulder length auburn hair is in place. Curly hair would normally look more unruly. Bright red lipstick and rouge on her cheeks overpower her striking features. Across from her is who Janči believes to be her husband, the famous Austrian writer, Roda Roda, Opapa's good friend. Distinguished salt- and pepper-colored hair fills his head. His cultivated appearance made complete with a white blazer, pale blue shirt underneath, and khaki dress pants. Two large plates sit in front of them. Gingerly, the woman is eating cabbage soup with smoked ham, probably cursing the fact that it wouldn't be ladylike to eat it faster. Manners are not on her companion's mind as the beef in sour cream sauce is rapidly being devoured. Mouthful number two is already going to his lips before the first one is even swallowed. The beer next to his plate is a fixture found on most tables at Baračka. Barrels of beer are rolled down a shaft from the main floor into the basement. When ordered, the barrel opens and the pressure of the gas pushes the beer up to the bar.

Momentarily, they excuse their company beside them and make their way to the dance floor, the transformation flawless. One moment, the man is rapaciously eating his lunch, and the next, he is an elegant ballroom dancer. Equally lithe on the dance floor is his partner. Closing their eyes and feeling the music penetrate their feet, they move their bodies in tune with each other. Leading at the precise moments, she follows expertly. Their half-eaten meal is waiting to be finished, slowly getting cold as the irresistible dance continues. Whispering something in her ear, they glide back to their table to resume their feast.

Bread dumplings are the perfect combination of firm and soft, the *kolbasy*[17] is fried to perfection, melting in your mouth, and the schnitzel has flawless crispy breading with just the right amount of tenderized veal cutlet inside. Portions are huge but never enough. A few seats

---

[17] *Kolbasy* is home-smoked sausage.

behind Janči, a woman exclaims, "I can't eat all that," as a large serving of steaming goulash is brought to the table. Little does she know that size can be deceiving but taste cannot. Plates always come back to the kitchen, licked clean, and so will hers. Overstuffing yourself here is a rite of passage, one everyone effortlessly concedes to. And then of course, there's the always-anticipated dessert. No matter how full you are, there is always be room for groundnut cake, the pieces of walnut and layers of fresh cream beguiling the eyes and causing the mouth to salivate.

A wet tongue licking Janči's leg interrupts his gazing. He looks down to find the expected culprit. Their slobbery Saint Bernard, Bernie, that lives up here has found their table and has nestled against his leg. Both Janči's hands reach down and give his huge head a friendly shake, the folds of skin jiggling from side to side as if in slow motion, and the drool spraying in different directions, defying the force of gravity. Bernie stands up taking Janči's pat as an instigation to play. His shagginess and mammoth size are overpowering, about twice the size of Marta, but with his harmless passive nature, he has never intimidated her.

Alena, their favorite waitress, already knows what to bring them; so Janči grabs Marta, and they run outside with Bernie, eagerly bounding behind them, happy to have company he can play with. Ferociously, his tail wags, and his tongue doesn't seem to fit back in his mouth. Drool constantly flows out of his mouth, creating a slobbery mess. Although he is excited to see them, Bernie always looks sad with his drooping eyes and perpetual frown.

"Janči, put me on," Marta asks, so he lifts her onto Bernie's back. Immediately, Bernie begins walking like a horse with a trained rider instead of a clumsy Saint Bernard.

"Go, go," Marta yells. Bernie obliges, picking up the pace. When her ride is over, Janči eagerly gets on, pretending he's a cowboy trying to catch his invisible enemy, although Bernie leaps in any direction he pleases, oblivious to where the enemy lies. Ten of the small black dachshunds that live at Baračka try to keep up with their short legs but fall far behind.

In the distance, Alena is beckoning them back, their hot chocolate ready. Without missing a beat, Janči slows Bernie down. Marta is already walking toward the restaurant, not wanting to waste time waiting for Janči. She is seated at the table by the time he arrives, indulging in her first sip. Janči picks up his hot chocolate between his two hands, prepared specially by the chef for him, and gazes into the cup of smooth melted dark chocolate mixed with thick cream. He takes the cup to his lips and lets the chocolate pour into his mouth. Rich flavor and creamy texture overwhelm his taste buds. He tries relishing each sip, but within an instant, the empty bottom of the cup is all he sees. Not satisfied with just one cup, he looks at Marta who is not even halfway through hers. She immediately pulls her drink close to her, defending it from his unquenchable sweet tooth. Jealously, he watches as she takes her time, dramatically reveling in every sip with a pleasing sigh and smacking her lips.

Alena brings over a plate of freshly baked layered butter cookies filled with raspberry jam and sprinkled with chopped walnuts. "Here, have some of these. They just finished baking." Swiftly Janči takes two. Once finished, he clutches Marta's arm.

"Let's go outside. I don't want to miss the band."

She agrees after stuffing a cookie in her mouth, and they settle under a tree. Patiently, they wait as the band begins setting up. Instruments are laying on the ground, waiting for their turn to come alive, Janči being able to name all of them from Opapa's lessons. There's the zither made of single piece of poplar with metal pegs driven into one end to hold the steel strings while tuning pegs are screwed to the other end. A piece of horn is used to pluck the string. Beside it is the cimbalom, recognizable by its trapezoidal shape. It has four legs, a pedal, and is slightly smaller than Janči's desk at school. The sound box portion of it is made of pine, the wrest plank of maple wood, and the metal strings are played on with long carved sticks the size of a ruler. The curved tips can remain bare or wrapped in cotton for a different sound as they are now. This instrument has an ease of showing off each players own incredible technique. Janči's favorite, the accordion, is the last instrument on the ground. He admires it longingly, knowing the fun he would have pushing all those buttons, compressing it in, and pulling it back out like a fan, wishing he could pick it up and play, but smart enough to know, he would topple over at the weight of it in his arms.

The first chords are played on the cimbál. Soon, the rest of the players join in, each forming a part of the musical composition. Once the band finishes playing their third song, Janči and Marta go search for Mamička to let her know they're ready to go home.

At only five years old, Janči feels more grown up than ever before. Today is his first day of school. Barely sleeping a wink the night before, he is already awake and dressing in the brown pants and white shirt Mamička laid out for him the night before. A brown leather backpack filled with books, pencils, chalk, and other tools wait at the bottom of the stairs beside his loafers. Unwilling to part with his bag or any of its contents, he bears the burden of the heavy bag over his shoulders while Mamička walks beside him.

They leave their house on the west side of the valley and head toward his school on the east adjacent to the woods. A small creek runs in front of them which they cross to reach the schoolhouse. Inside the classroom are fifteen wooden desks, each fitted with its own inkwell, lined in long military style rows of five. He finds one in the middle. White walls remain bare, except for the lone black chalkboard and the emblem of the Czechoslovak Republic. A handful of kids are already seated, each of them bigger than Janči. He indifferently notices he's the smallest. Out the window, Mamička is still waving at him. Janči waves back and motions that it's time for her to leave. Finally ready to let go, she gives one last wave, turns, and leaves her son to fend for himself. Relieved, Janči pulls out his notebook and a pencil, ready to start. He carefully writes his name and date on the top of the page like Mamička taught him on all those cold winter afternoons.

December 14, 1935—the front headlines of Slovák read "Tomas Garrigue Masaryk Resigns." Opapa intently reads the story about the first president of independent Czechoslovakia, a much loved and respected leader. He will be succeeded by the leader of the Czechoslovak Independence Movement, Edvard Beneš, who will continue on with the legacy of democracy.

Feeling a pair of eyes over his shoulder, he turns in his chair and sees Janči intrigued by the picture of Masaryk.

"Do you want me to explain who this is?" Janči nods, already curious about topics well beyond his age and now even keener to learn since he's started school. Opapa smiles remembering the simple conversations they used to have about nature and geography, and how they are slowly progressing into ones typically reserved for adults. He pulls Janči into his lap and begins the explanation of the political situation and their president, pointing to the picture in the newspaper. He speaks in the simplest of terms to his grandson who is almost six years old.

Darkness has fallen over Trenčianské Teplice, invading the city with its ominous presence. Cables run from one house to the other across the streets. Suspended from them are triangular-shaped black steel shells enclosing the lights in glass to keep the birds out. With the light wind, the fixtures squeakily fly back and forth, illuminating a path for the way home. Cars hurriedly drive past, splashing periodic light across the black canvas of the sky. Streets are still full with people walking along, some at a quick pace trying to escape the dark, others strolling despite it.

Glancing at his pocket watch, the pin lever movement shows it is four in the afternoon. Home is Janči's destination, and like animals, hibernating inside seems like the most reasonable thing to do without the daylight that enables him to spend endless hours playing outside with his friends. Around here, the sun works in strange ways, always setting extremely early during their long winters, like on a distant planet. Being situated between two mountains that rise against the sun causes impenetrable blackness, making the nights even longer. Only an hour ago, Janči was able to bask in the sunset, its resplendent beauty flaming in the sky with brilliant hues of orange and gold, making any hardened skeptic believe they have experienced something spiritual.

With the snow being too deep to tread with boots alone, Janči takes cross-country skis to and from school. His maple wooden skis, painted red under the foot, skim over the smooth white surface, unencumbered by the snow's cold and depth. On the weekend, he'll propose a ski outing with Apu and invite Ali along.

Knowing how quickly two young children get bored, especially without a television, Mamička always finds creative ways to entertain them, both by being resourceful and using her skill in the arts. Painting, crafts, music, and even wood carving are among the activities she teaches Janči and Marta.

When Janči walks in, he finds Marta sitting at the piano clinking away on a few keys. Mamička has just finished a piano lesson with her, probably planning a time she can coerce Janči onto the bench and spread his fingers across the sheer white keys, hoping her musical passion will enter his body. To Mamička's dismay, the piano never ignites a passion within him, but he does pick up and learn to play the accordion and guitar on his own as he gets older.

On the dining room table, Mamička has set up an arts and crafts station. Balls of yarn, knitting cable needles, threads, and sewing needles have been moved aside, the practicality of learning to mend socks with double stitches or creating colorful quilts patterns to be continued on another day. Instead, paint, paintbrushes, and pencils are all neatly laid out. Beside those tools is an assortment of paper and scraps of colorful fabric—silk, canvas, and cotton. Homemade adhesive has been put in a small bowl which is also on the table. Janči made it with Mamička the day before by mixing vinegar and milk resulting in repugnant sticky clumps. Mamička could open up her own art store with the amount of supplies she has.

"Janči, I brought something I thought you'd like." From a bag hidden on the floor beside the table, she pulls out stencils of different types of airplanes, her round, peaceful face glowing with animation.

"Thanks, Mamička," he says, examining the stencils for a Wright Flyer and Zlín plane. Grabbing a piece of paper, he begins outlining the first one. Marta has already glued a handful of pink fabric on her paper, wasting no time. Happily, she adds more and more decoration from the piles on the table until her entire sheet is filled and evolved into something completely abstract.

"That's beautiful, Marta," Mamička praises, coming closer to look at her design. Marta proudly beams. No lines constrain them. Painting outside of them is totally accepted. Mamička leans in and begins mixing some paints together, demonstrating the new colors that can be created with a little speculative thought. Compelled to be the pioneer of a new paint color, Marta joins in, adding blue to yellow and getting a new shade of green.

Feverishly, Janči cuts out his stenciled drawings which still need to be decorated with the right emblems and colors. He tries to drag on his project, not wanting to face the inevitable. Avoiding any eye contact with Mamička, Janči remains quiet, snipping and gluing, without drawing attention to himself, vainly hoping Mamička will forget about the exam he should be studying for. Knowing his devious tricks all too well, Mamička tells her inconspicuous son to wrap up soon because studying is next on his agenda.

That evening, once Janči's eyes are too tired to keep studying, he grabs a blanket and two pillows from the couch in the living room and calls Marta. The tall American cast iron and steel stove in their house has been filled with coal, the glowing orange embers visible through the glass doors, heating both their parent's bedroom and the family room for the next twenty-four hours. There is a minute opening in the wall in their parent's bedroom where Janči and Marta get comfortable on the floor with their books and blankets. Janči reads to Marta from an illustrated children's book filled with words he has learned at school. A throbbing headache interrupts him momentarily, one that Janči always gets when lying on the floor here. Without a fan connecting the stove to the outside, the gas emitted from the coal remains contained within the walls of the house and leaches into his head. Even so, he refuses to budge.

―⁂―

Sounds from the keys of a piano rouse Janči from his sleep, his usual wake up call. Turning over, he sees it is seven o'clock. Dread creeps into his body, debilitating every ounce of confidence he had built up studying last night. Mamička is expectantly waiting for him downstairs, not giving him the extra time to muse over his situation. Programmed to his routine, he gets out of bed, puts on his morning gear, and struggles downstairs to the living room, where Marta is already stretching and Mamička is tuning the dials on the dark brown polished wood radio, looking for the right station. Finally, it lands on an energetic beat that bursts through the round speaker and emanates throughout the room.

"Good morning, everyone. Welcome to our morning exercise," a cheerful female voice chirps. *Too cheerful*, Janči thinks, for this early in the morning. And so it begins. Stretching this way, bending that way, running on the spot, breathing in and out. All windows in the house are open a crack to let in the fresh air for them while they exercise. Fifteen minutes later, the workout session is finished, and Janči knows his second one is fast approaching.

On his own, he makes the ten-minute walk to school, finally proving he's old enough to do it. He crosses the electric car bridge, above the rapidly flowing river. Tracks are inlaid on top for trolleys to make their steady route into and out of the city. Trees line both sides of the riverbank, their leaves gently rustling in the breeze. High above, the honey-colored Catholic Church has its crucifix floating in the sky and its spires grasping at the heavens.

Reaching the end of the bridge on the other side of the river, his feet lead him in their trained direction. Freely opening the gate leading down a narrow passage, he walks through the familiar backyard and winds up outside the bakery. He pulls open the gleaming brass door handle, bells ringing above, marking his entrance. He is no stranger here at his best friend's bakery, a common thread linking them in their mutual understanding of the sweet tooth curse.

Before school began, Ali and Janči's friendship had already sprouted. Janči, in the market for casual unpaid work to keep him occupied, approached the owner of Altman's General Store one day. Having frequented it with Apu on their many walks together, Janči was familiar with the owner. Inside, traditional mini-pendant lights shone down on the simple wood floor piled high with shelves full of jars of pickled garlic, peppers, and eggplant. Jams and marmalades of all flavors and colors filled another entire shelving section. Milk was in the back in the icebox.

"Excuse me, sir, but I was wondering if you might need some help here?"

Looking down at him, Mr. Altman recognized this boy as the son of Maria and Dezider Teschner, a couple he had known for several years. Seeing the eagerness in his face, Mr. Altman knew there was always something that could be done around the store.

"Actually, you're in luck. Follow me." He led Janči outside. "Ali, Janči is here to help you pump gas. Make sure you show him how it's done." With an encouraging pat on the back, Mr. Altman headed back into the door to continue stocking the bags of golden potatoes.

Immediately, Ali took Janči over the pumps, glad to have company his age outside. "This container here is full—it has five liters of gas in it. To get the gas into this cylinder, first, you have to pump it from underground. Once the cylinder is filled, you can then release the gas from it over here to fill the car." Janči digested the simple instructions and began practicing on the next car that drove in. Without a drop spilled, he was able to fill up the car. Within minutes, their friendship grew even more when Janči learned of the bakery Ali's family owned through a narrow passage behind the general store.

Daily visits here on the way to school have become part of Janči's routine. Inside the bakery, freshly baked breads are being dumped into the metal gridded bins, the smell is heavenly.

"Good morning, Janči," Ali's mom welcomes him, with short brown hair resting on her shoulders, happiness sparkling in her brown eyes, and a pleasant smile revealing rows of perfect white teeth. Immediately, she places a bright red apple along with a *pogach*[18] in his hand. Having worked at the bakery during the cold winter months, Janči has learned that baking bread with potato helps maintain its freshness.

"Ali," she yells, "Janči's here." Ali's compact physique appears, pushing a stray strand of chocolate colored hair out of his intense dark brown, deep set eyes flecked with yellow that becomes more prominent as he walks past the window with sunshine sieving through.

"Okay, Mom, we're going now."

"Not without this" placing Ali's portion of rye bread in his hands. Content she has fed them well, they are free to leave.

Devouring their breakfast, the two friends walk in silence, the school growing in size as they near it until the gravel crunching beneath their feet marks educational territory. Dropping their backpacks against the wall, they head over to the yard. Thirty children with canvas shoes strapped on their feet, begin running laps around the school at the command of Mrs. Nemecová. By the time they're done, Janči feels faint of breath and is worried the oxygen he needs for his brain is traveling elsewhere in his body. A series of stretching follows, bringing Janči's heartbeat back to normal.

He heads to class and takes a seat at his desk, hands behind his back maintaining an erect posture, waiting for the recalcitrant stragglers to arrive. Mrs. Nemecová already stands in position. Her heart-shaped face is held in a stern expression, her crinkly blue eyes piercing the students, and her thin blonde hair hanging limply on her shoulders. She is eager to test them on all their classes from geography to etiquette to arithmetic.

---

[18]   *Pogach* is a slice of dark rye bread with kimmel and salt.

Twenty-five questions of all sorts and subjects fill the chalkboard. Taking a deep breath, he puts his pencil to paper for the ease of erasing mistakes and begins writing. Formulas and short answers fill page after page. Question twenty terminates his writing streak. What is the currency used in Poland? Angst, seeing a moment of weakness creeps into his body and causes his palms to start sweating. He flips through information reserves in his brain like a library catalogue to see if he can find the answers, but his mind continues to feel like the page—blank. How he wishes he could insert a coin in the clock to buy him more time. Skipping over question twenty, he manages to find answers to the remaining questions. With five minutes left, he goes back to that looming question, figuring it's better to put something down than nothing.

Twelve o'clock strikes and all pencils go down. Within a week, the exams will be graded and handed back with their report cards. The excruciating torment of writing exams is undergone three times a year and report cards are distributed twice a year.

Ali is waiting for him in the schoolyard afterward, ready to walk home together. "Well, it's over, so we don't need to worry about it anymore." And with that piece of wisdom, they completely forget about their stressful school experience and head over to Ali's for their afternoon snack. Seeing them approach the bakery, Ali's mom sets in motion the preparation of the boys' rye flat bread. As soon as they walk through the door, she places a scrambled egg on top with a dash of salt. Hungrily, they sit at the table and happily eat their food.

"Janči, don't forget to take your bread home. It baked overnight and is done," Mrs. Altman reminds him. Fingering the nametag he received for the five-pound loaf of bread, he remembers lugging the dough Mamička prepared to the bakery yesterday.

"How did your exam go today," Mamička questions as Janči walks through the door, giving her the baked bread.

"I think okay. Some of the questions were hard."

"I'm sure you did your best. That's all that matters."

Janči's not sure if those last words of moral support will make him feel better or worse if he gets a bad grade.

A week later, Mrs. Nemecová haughtily walks around the class distributing their exams. Fate is being handed out as each package of paper is given over to its rightful owner. Parents are also required to sign them, confirming their knowledge of their child's aptitude. Mulling over the possibility of forging Apu's signature if need be, Janči realizes his biggest challenge is in its complexity, and his handwriting is too basic; his dexterity not advanced enough to get the pen to move in those awkward strokes, fanning out in all directions with no rhyme or reason to them. Apu's signature bears no resemblance to his name. Based on the futility of his idea and the disastrous consequences if he was discovered, he abandons it.

Mrs. Nemecová approaches his desk like a slithering snake ready to attack with its venomous bite. In her grasp are the sheets of paper that represent his future. They are put face down on his desk, giving him the time he needs to build up the courage to turn them over. Inhaling with a deep breath, Janči hesitantly flips over the pages. Staring back at him is the big letter, piercing his eyes with its finality. He questions what he should think about this mark.

Taking Ali's advice from the week before, Janči's doesn't focus on his marks once school is over. Rather, he directs that energy into playing hide-and-seek at the train station of the electric tramway with Ali, Eli, and Marta. Stealing into the unlocked warehouse at the train station, the large boxes and cases of merchandise sprawl all over the floor create the optimal conditions for their game, a wonderland of hiding places.

Covering his eyes and leaning against a wall, Janči counts down from twenty, hearing three pairs of feet scurrying about. With three seconds left, there is silence all around. Dust is still settling on the floor, proving the existence of human life only moments ago. Scanning the large area, Janči strategically begins looking in the most obvious places. Behind and in between crates and in boxes large enough to hold his friends. His ear perks up to a small cough from around the corner—one that is cut short in fear of being found. Following the sound, Janči winds up in front of Marta who guiltily looks up at him, knowing her uncontrollable cough gave her away. Reaching out his hand, Janči helps up his sister.

"One down, two to go," he yells, warning the others of his success so early on in the game. A vibration echoes around them as a train rumbles into the station. Janči looks at Marta for help on finding Ali and Eli. She just shrugs her shoulders, not willing to give her friends up. Knowing he can't convince her, he investigates the area. Behind an empty barrel sits Eli, patiently waiting to be discovered and not appearing disappointed that she has been.

"I'm starting to get a little hungry," Eli says.

"We can go back to my house. Mamička will make us something to eat," Janči proposes. "But first, I have to find Ali."

Eli's eyes travel in the direction of a large concrete column. Janči follows her gaze and acknowledges her silent clue. He creeps over, making sure not to step on anything that might generate unnecessary noise and alert Ali of his presence.

"Gotcha," Janči yells grabbing Ali's shoulders from behind. Completely startled, Ali jumps up, and seeing it's his friend, instantaneously tries to regain his composure by smoothing out his shorts and tugging his shirt down. "I scared you!" Janči roars, hysterically laughing at Ali's reaction.

"No, you didn't," he emphatically denies.

"Sure, I didn't. Anyways, we're going to my house to get some food." Glad to be off the topic of his scare, Ali readily agrees.

Moving into the forest, they gather as many raspberries and blueberries as they can in their hands, staining them with a blend of red and blue. Hungrily, they toss them into their mouths, the seeds from the raspberries getting stuck in their teeth.

From the open window, Mamička's voice yells out to them as they approach the house, "Jančika, come have your sandwich." Seeing the troupe with him, she quickly ducks inside to prepare more bread with goose liver before they walk into the house.

Goose liver is stored in abundance in their house in large jars filled with the unappetizing thick pinkish brown spread. Having grown up eating it, Janči has acquired a taste for this delicacy, even with its slight gamey flavor. But he'll never get used to having it spread on this chest by Mamička when he has a cough or cold. She swears it is a cure for such ailments.

Set on an easel in the kitchen is Mamička's current oil painting. The canvas displays a lively scene of Hlavné námestie[19] in Trenčín. Colorful Renaissance-style houses and shops line the irregular Square. People are milling about, browsing inside stores or sitting with coffee, finding shade under the trees fringing the Square, making anyone want to climb inside the painting and experience the carefree afternoon. Charcoal sketches on the canvas show the remainder of the piece that hasn't been painted yet. Set aside on the kitchen table rest several hardwood-handled paintbrushes with tips of varying shapes—round, flat, filbert, fan, mop, angle—each serving its own artistic purpose, either for detail work, good coverage, or blending broad areas. A fan-shaped palette rests beside them, filled with paint of all colors.

---

[19] *Hlavné námestie* means Main Square.

After Janči's friends have left, he decides to get it over with and hands Mamička his exam. She looks up with a smile on her face. "Honey, you did so well. Apu will be so proud too."

When Apu comes home for the weekend, he signs it at once with his favorite jade-and-black-colored Montblanc fountain pen, the smooth and glossy body moving up and down to the rhythm of his name, the light from the window reflecting off the gleaming flat cap. Examining his signature again, Janči feels relieved he didn't have to copy it. The route of the large scribble is too disorderly he wouldn't even know where to begin. Forging it would've been much harder than getting a B.

SCHNITZEL SANDWICH, 1936

GETTING THE SUNDAY blues has never afflicted Janči, merely for the fact that it's his favorite day of the week. Outside his window, the sun is brilliantly shining. Larger clouds linger in the distance, trying to appear menacing but only holding an empty threat. Wisps of smaller clouds looking like cotton balls gently being pulled apart are serenely floating in the air, not intruding on the warmth of the sun.

Apu has finished writing the speech for the priest's Sunday sermon and has gone to deliver it. With his knowledge of Latin—one the priest can read, but not write—Apu, the linguistics master in six other languages—Hungarian, German, Czech, Slovak, Italian, and English—is a sought out man. Priests are not the only ones converging to stake a claim in Apu's speech writing gift. People from all political and corporate positions manage to hear about Apu and track him down.

Jožka is getting their things ready, considering it's a quarter to ten, and Apu should be back shortly. Soon, the park will start filling up, so they have to get there to claim their usual spot. Today, all of them are going together, but usually, it's just Jožka with the children.

Janči finds Jožka in the kitchen, wrapping up their lunch, the last piece of parchment paper covering what is in her hands before he can catch a glimpse of it, leaving him in suspense about the lunch menu.

"Janči, I'm just about ready, and I packed a special treat for you," she tells him while inconspicuously placing something in his hands. Opening his palm, he finds a chocolate covered prune. Before any evidence remains of his secret treat, he devours it and throws away the wrapping.

Jožka has always treated Janči as if he were a younger brother, occasionally taking him with her when she goes home to visit her parents in Nemšová. Janči looks forward to these trips—an adventure for him because two trains are required to get there, one of them is a motor train.

Together, the five of them set off on their daytime journey. Jožka carries the brown wicker picnic basket brimming with food that has seen countless picnics. Under her arm, Mamička is holding a red and white checkered blanket—the epitome of picnics. Apu has Marta and Janči on either side of him, clasping their hands inside his soft and smooth ones, accustomed to paperwork rather than manual labor.

Upon arrival, they instinctively head over to their regular spot—an area filled with picnic tables. They take great care in making sure not to step on the grass after getting fined a few months ago when Mamička had nicely dressed Marta and Janči for their walk with Jožka to the park. Mr. Doubrava, the photographer at Baračka, saw them and wanted to take pictures and send them to Mamička. As soon as he finished, the park warden fined Jožka two crowns because they stepped on the grass. He pointed to signs stating not to step on the grass, "or else it will never grow," he said.

Wooden benches surround the park, but they always opt for the table which is more accommodating of their sizeable lunch spread. Hanging in the air is the smell of freshly manicured grass. One on either side, Jožka and Janči unfold the blanket, parachuting it out with a soft landing on the table. Mamička and Jožka then begin to unpack the basket, systematically setting things up in the order they are to be eaten. Bottles of fruit juice and bowls of cucumber salad come out first, followed by large sandwiches that Janči's mouth will barely fit around.

In the distance are the chess tables filled with legendary players and a game always in progress. Situated to the right of them is the band shell. Light classical music spills out from it into the park. All the musicians on stage are engrossed in the melody they are constructing, oblivious to their fans. Violins, flutes, and a piano converge into one harmonious blend, resembling Vivaldi's *Summer*. Following the path of music, Janči walks over to the conductor who is not surprised to see him. Wearing a sharp black Callaway style tuxedo complete with tailcoats and bow tie, he offers a quick nod to acknowledge Janči's presence and then shifts his attention back to the band he is dexterously leading. Ensuring not to disturb him, Janči stands on his left side and begin conducting the musicians himself. Mimicking the conductor's movements is tricky, so Janči resorts to improvising his own version of conductions, resembling a frantic call for help, naively believing the band is taking its cues from him. Crescendos and dips put him on a roller coaster ride of music.

Out of the corner of his eye, he sees Marta taking a bite of a sandwich. His stint as a conductor ends as there are more important things to be doing right now. Getting comfortable at the table, he swiftly grabs a schnitzel sandwich topped with lettuce and tomatoes from the basket. Hot peppers sit to the side, saved for Apu's appetite for spicy food. Another container holds the baby dill pickles that make this feast almost complete. Slices of dense black forest cake with juicy cherries and real cream interspersed throughout mark the last and most important element of this lunchtime meal.

Janči carefully implements his plan of attack on the large sandwich in his hands. He has to determine the best way to bite into the kaiser without the middle coming out all over him. It's a mathematical equation of getting the exact combination of schnitzel and bun in each bite. No one wants to be left with all bread and no meat toward the end of the sandwich, so it must remain proportional at all times.

Two lakes serenely sit on the perimeter of the park. One is fifty feet above the other, and all the swans congregate there, there long necks overseeing the action in the park. Gracefully, they swim through the tranquil blue water creating small ripples, ruining the perfect reflection of the oak and birch trees in the water.

From afar, splashes of various shades of moving green fill the road. It's hard to distinguish the individual elements of this green composition. Up close one is shocked and amazed to see thousands of frogs and toads coming through the road and steadily making their way to the lower lake from the upper one, an army on a mission. Every June, they fill the streets, making it virtually impossible to get around them, several people frantically try to avoid them, acrobatically stepping and sliding all over the place.

In a mellow state, lazing in the sun after eating such a big meal, they soon begin feeling sluggish and decide it's time to start moving around again, easing their heavy lunch into digestion. Behind the band shell in the lower part of the park is a grand Victorian building, the Kursalon, which houses a café, library, dining room, large theatre, and concert hall, the cultural and social core of the town. Uncle Palko manages the café and dining room where breakfast and lunch is served. Apu spends time there with his friends for afternoon espressos and usually extends an invite for Janči to join him. Today, they all head over for an afternoon cap, knowing they will just end up sitting down again, but the walk there validates the visit.

A hundred tables fill the hardwood floor, leaving enough room for dancing in the middle. Straight away, Janči heads over to his favorite part of the restaurant. Peering in, he presses his face against the glass, hoping it will disintegrate, eliminating the blockade between him and the enclosed desserts, like jewels that need to be protected from ravenous bandits. An array of mouth-watering baked goods fills the display. Poppy seed and walnut rolls, cakes almost a foot high, something ready to fulfill any craving—chocolate, vanilla, coffee, or nut. "You can look all you want, Janči, but you just finished the largest piece of cake we had.

That's enough sweets for you today," Apu says, coming over to inspect the delicacies, almost as tempted as Janči to get something. Reluctantly, Janči goes back to their table and gets a raspberry soda to mollify him while the adults contentedly sip their espressos and cappuccinos.

Thinking about the walk back home, Janči asks Apu a question he always wondered but never knew the answer to.

"How come you never drive?"

"Well," Apu begins, repositioning himself in the chair, getting comfortable for his storytelling, "this is actually a funny story. I wanted to visit Babka, so I asked to borrow Opapa's car to drive to Beluša. I had never really driven before, and we didn't need a license to drive at that time. I took the car anyway thinking I'd be fine.

"The road to Beluša goes through a mountainous narrow road from Teplice. In the middle of the mountain, a cart with oxen that had long horns approached the car. I thought I could pass, but I didn't calculate the width of the road properly.

"I was driving on the left side so I was on the edge of the road. I didn't want to slip or skid down the ravine. I came too close to the cart and one of the oxen's horns caught the passenger's door and scratched it. And when it came to the end of the car, the horn broke off. I stopped the car and was very upset at what happened. The farmer was even more upset and made me pay for the damage to his oxen.

"When I finally got to Beluša they were all wondering why I was so late. They loved my explanation so much they forgave the damage I did to the car. That's the first and last time I drove."

They all laugh uncontrollably at his story and are grateful to walk home rather than be driven by Apu in a car.

The tranquility of the forest permeates each cell in Janči's body. A home in the middle of these trees, a place that will be his own private sanctuary, hidden from the outside world is an idea he's been toying with for months now. He decides it's finally time to implement it. This house of his won't be too extravagant, just enough room to relax in. Maybe he'll allow a few honored guests to visit from time to time.

Only a few meters beyond the backyard is the forest where Janči finds stones that are sturdy enough to form the foundation of his house. With a tight grip on the wooden handle of his shovel, he digs up the ground with the metal head, one scoop at a time. The soft earth allows him to move at a relatively fast pace. He just needs a small amount of depth, a few inches, for him to build the floor.

Once an area of one meter by two meters has been dug up, all the dirt shoveled to the side in a pile, Janči covers it with leaves and branches that he gathered around the forest. Pine needles have always triggered a pleasant nostalgia from the years of outings in the forest with Apu and Opapa. Piling the floor with them and creating a carpet of prickly green, he deeply inhales their intoxicating fragrance.

With the floor intact, he begins taking out the soil that has accumulated between the large rocks, which are to be his walls about one meter high. Scraping the shovel between the gaps, he manages to extrapolate most of the soil, replacing it with more leaves and branches. Although his home doesn't have a roof, he is ecstatic with four walls and a floor.

Filled with satisfaction, Janči stands in the middle and looks around at his finished masterpiece. Four sturdy walls made of sticks tactically latticed together incredibly stand alone on top of the forest floor in a perfect rectangular-shaped structure. An opening in one side where stones are not positioned allows for visitors to easily move inside and outside. It's a doorway without a door. Janči gallops home, eager to interrupt his family from their activities and take them on a spontaneous excursion into the forest.

A warm afternoon settles on the city inviting people to bask in the sunlight.

"Janči, let's go outside and play," Marta says. He instantly agrees, not needing much convincing. Taking her hand, they walk along their path, the grass on their route beginning to wear down.

"Let's get some berries first," Janči suggests, changing direction and moving them toward the bushels of strawberries and raspberries growing wildly in the forest. They each carefully pick the berries off, not wanting to bruise them. Raspberries prove to be the trickiest to pull off from their beds until you get the hang of it. Their incessant snacking depletes their collection of berries only a few minutes into their walk. With nothing occupying his hands anymore, Janči hoists Marta up on his back for a piggyback ride. As he climbs up the faces of stark rock formations freckled with rare types of flowers, Marta's eyes dart around absorbing the atmosphere, enraptured at the scenery from her vantage point above the ground. Birds are singing overhead in the trees, and there is a distant chirp of crickets. Breathing in the natural beauty, the cool air caresses her face as Janči traipses through the woods. Taking on the role of explorers, the duo pretend they are discovering a new land. Being her tour guide, Janči points out things Apu and Opapa always show him on their outings.

"These are beech trees," he says, pointing up. "See how large the leaves are?"

Marta looks up at the leaves creating a shaded canopy, fascinated by her unprompted tutorial. Sensing her interest, Janči thinks of more facts to teach her.

"If you're quiet, we might see a red deer."

"Really?" she asks intrigued.

"Yup. And did you know that they have really strong neck muscles to hold up those big pointy antlers on their heads."

"Hmmm," Marta muses now on high alert for the animal.

Finally, tired of carrying her, Janči puts her down and stealthily sneaks around the base of a large pine tree, ducking at the influx of pine needles aimed for his head. No longer able to see him, Marta guesses where he is based on the trundling sounds of his footsteps and crackle of branches. He emerges with a branch large and soft enough to use for carving. Inspecting it, Janči mulls over the choices on what to carve, having recently completed a plane and ship. The wood speaks to him, showing him that the shape of a sheep already exists in it deep within the wood, and it is Janči who needs to let it out.

Taking out his pocketknife in his right hand, a tool every boy owns, he pulls open the firm carbon steel blade from the dark blue fish shaped handle. Once his mind enters a meditative state for this task, he begins whittling away at the wood in his left hand. The quiet aids his contemplation of the imaginary lines only his eyes can see, based on a shape his mind has invoked. Pared shavings fly off the wood, needless pieces in this new masterpiece.

"Marta, find me another branch like this," he tells her, hoping to find another workable branch as good as the one he already found.

"No," she adamantly shakes her head.

"Why not?"

"I don't want to."

Angered that she won't listen to him, Janči unkindly threatens her for no good reason.

"I'm going to leave you here if you don't do it."

Marta shrugs her shoulders with indifference, making his ultimatum useless. Out of spite, Janči begins to walk away from her. Every few steps, he stops and turns back, his feet only allowing him to go so far, and then their guilty conscience echoes in his mind. He then hides behind a bush to see how his sister will react to his disappearance.

Marta plops herself down on the ground and amuses herself, not paying attention to her brother's abandonment. She digs holes, and once getting bored of that, picks up a branch filled with pine needles that has a clear semblance to a broom, and sweeps together pinecones, cleaning the forest floor. Meticulous as if it were her own home, she continues until pleased with the final result. Although afraid of being left by herself like this, she doesn't want to give her brother the satisfaction of knowing. Convincing herself she can handle this situation, she focuses on her sweeping rather than the vast emptiness around her. She searches out the plentiful yellow crocuses blooming in the meadows and valleys, picking a few to decorate her neatly swept area.

Thinking Marta is probably getting scared, Janči comes out of his hiding places and goes to retrieve her. As he approaches, her blue eyes look up at him filled with a silent anger. Janči tenderly picks her up and puts her up on his back again, making up for his earlier lack of sensitively. Her clutch around him is firmer than before, and they continue to explore the secret land unfolding in front of them.

After long evaluation, with his firm grip on the rook held high above the chessboard, Janči carefully lowers it without putting it down, not wanting to lock himself into an erroneous choice. He looks around at his possible new position to see if he can uncover any potential enemies lurking around. Confident he is making a strategic move, he places his rook beside Opapa's horse. Opapa blithely grins, examining the board, either meaning he's about to beat his grandson, or Janči has put him in a tricky position.

Above the mantle, the ticking of the clock exacerbates the stress Janči is feeling watching Opapa mull over his next move. With a swift reach, one Janči barely has time to digest, Opapa's smooth voice gleefully rings out "checkmate."

Taken aback that he made such a blunder in his carefully thought-out plan, Janči looks down at the discouraging board. After a moment, it's staring right back at him. Moving his rook left his King vulnerable to attack from a discrete angle that he didn't notice. He throws his hands up in exasperation.

"I can't believe I missed that!"

"Don't worry. You'll get me next time."

"You bet I will. Let's play another game," he quickly suggests.

"I think we've sat long enough. Let's go for a walk instead, and we can play again later." Janči quickly agrees, always looking forward to these walks that have become rituals for them, stolen moments of time the two of them share together.

The duo head out, Janči dressed in casual khaki shorts and plain white T-shirt, unconcerned about appearance while Opapa walks out in style, wearing a white three-piece suit. Smartly underneath sits a navy blue shirt with the collar overlapping the lapels of his suit. Without the blue and red striped tie carrying a flawless French dimple, his outfit would not be complete. At sixty, he looks more distinguished than any forty year old.

"Which way do you want to go?" he asks.

"To the park."

"Ah," he says with a smile creeping on his face, "you really can't get enough, can you?" Janči shakes his head knowing Opapa would catch on to his ulterior motive. Easily, Opapa gives in to his grandson's request. Unhurried, they walk through the uncongested town streets side by side. Narrow lanes jut out onto main roads, each winding their way through a maze of small cafes and parks, always with an unoccupied bench or seat, inviting passersby to enjoy the scenes of a living city and feel its quiet vibe. A multitude of shops offer the convenience of a hedonistic adventure, best taken advantage of when slowly walking through the streets.

"Did you know Trenčianské Teplice is located at the foot of the Western Carpathian Mountains," Opapa begins his geographical lesson. He points out the various tree groves that lend to Teplice's natural beauty, making sure Janči learns to appreciate them.

After eyeing the trees, Janči looks up at the large Castle Teplice, built during the Renaissance, displaying elements of Baroque and neoclassical styling, bold massing, a contrast between light walls and a dark roof, and immense lighting created by numerous arch windows plastered on the façade.

Opapa follows his gaze and reports back with more insight. "All over are these castles where very wealthy people used to live. If you go into the courtyard of this one, you can see the foundation of the medieval monastery. There are also hot thermal springs one and a half meters below the ground, said to have healing properties. The round opening is decorated in beautiful tiles with Slovak ornaments. A lady wearing a colorful Slovak country dress serves the healing water to guests bringing their own mugs."

"Can we go in there sometime?"

"Sure."

Inevitably, they stop in at their favorite ice cream parlor. One long counter stretches across the small space with several red chairs lined up behind it. Walls are painted a bright yellow, giving the place a colorful and airy feel, instigating the craving for ice cream even further. Without hesitation Janči orders a combination of his two favorite flavors—chocolate and vanilla from an animated teenage boy wearing a white apron and matching white cap resembling that of a sailor.

As they walk along in silence, Janči notices Opapa's eyebrow furrowing, a physical nuance he recognizes all too well as a sign of deep, troubled thought.

"Janči, I think we should talk about some of things that have been happening around here lately. I'm sure you've noticed them or heard things, and you probably have some questions."

A curtain of insecurity *has* been hanging around his family, one that Janči has mildly sensed, even though things still appear relatively the same. People are still going about their regular lives, buying whatever they want. Development is on the rise, and the political landscape seems stable, at least from the little he knows; but there is still some lingering doubt about things he hears on the radio. Opapa believes the optics of an ordinary civilian life are deceiving, something not right underneath it all. Never one to keep information from Janči, he is ready to share some of his thoughts with his grandson, although filtered to make sense to a boy of his age. Relieved to let the floodgates open with Opapa's prompting, Janči begins his innocent questioning.

"Well, when you and Apu are listening to the radio, I hear about this Hitler man, and kids at my school are starting to talk about him too, and how great he is and all the good things he will do for our country."

Carefully choosing his next words in this volatile conversation, like a package stamped with the words "handle with care," Opapa continues, "He's a politician, a greedy one, who always wants more."

BECAUSE OF A FISHBONE

"More what?"

"More land. More power. One person should never have too much power." He pauses, trying to think of the best way to phrase the next part of his sentence. "He's also not doing nice things to Jewish people in Germany."

"Like what?" Janči asks, filled with curiosity and fear.

"Well, he's taking over businesses Jewish people own. He's firing Jewish workers and managers from all sorts of companies. He's not allowing Jewish lawyers to practice law anymore. He's not allowing Jewish doctors to treat non-Jewish people."

Not knowing how to react to such news, Janči remains quiet. They don't live in Germany, he thinks, but they are Jewish. He doesn't know what that means for his family anymore.

"But he's in Germany, so we'll be okay here, right?"

"I hope so, Janči," Opapa offers, not wanting to insist everything will be fine and also not wanting to expose his true intuition of where things are headed.

"What are we supposed to do?"

"All you need to do is keep enjoying each day to the fullest."

"But I already do that."

"I know," Opapa wistfully says.

Janči's superficial thoughts along this walk that included ice cream and chess have changed into intense, deep-seeded wonderings about what he has just been told. Something threatening is brewing in the air around them. That much he can comprehend solely from the look Opapa gave him at the end of their discussion. He's never seen such gravity in his face as if trying to telepathically articulate an unspeakable warning. But a warning for what? That is the question that now haunts him, and Opapa either truly doesn't know the answer, or he's hiding it from Janči in an attempt to protect him from something.

"Oh, Janči, you're in luck," Opapa exclaims, interrupting Janči's thoughts and moving them elsewhere. Chess tables are set off to one side of the park, fairly close to the band shell, the bulk of them filled with men deep in concentration, whether they are playing or merely spectators. Janči recognizes a lot of them as regulars from their restaurant, especially Mr. Pavel Slaný, an extroverted, wiry man with congenial eyes who always gives him lemon candies that are perpetually stored in his pocket for the times they meet.

A large crowd has formed around one particular table, swarming the game, suffocating the players who have become celebrities for the moment. Even with all those men who normally prattle away like old women, it is deathly silent.

Opapa and Janči fall in place behind the crowd. Squeezing among them, Janči pokes his head through the mass of bodies, catching a glimpse of the action but a second too late. Checkmate is declared with no other viable options for the loser. Janči empathizes, reliving his fateful move this morning.

"Are you ready to beat me today?" a robust man with a cigar dangling from his mouth asks. His pudgy face outfitted with spectacles that look too small in proportion to the rest of this body. His name is Ondrej Šrobár, the Minister of the Interior. Opapa looks up and grins at his old chess friend. "I will try," always up for the challenge.

Pieces are rapidly put in place on the brown and cream-colored squares. With a new game to watch, the men resume their positions, focusing on each move and pondering the potential moves that may come next—believing in their own minds that they all know the most strategic one.

Opapa's pawn takes its first leap over two squares, leaving a path for his Queen on another move. Janči knows this line of attack, having fallen victim to it several times before. Half of him wants to warn Mr. Šrobár, but the other half wants to see Opapa win. Following the etiquette of the game, his mouth is kept shut. Mr. Šrobár sees through the plot and cunningly wipes out Opapa's Queen before it can be of any use to him. With his most powerful piece gone, it doesn't take long for Mr. Šrobár to finish him off, showing no mercy while piling Opapa's pieces on his side of the table.

"Good game," Opapa offers shaking his hand.

"Now you know what it feels like to lose."

"Well, you can't win every game."

Expectantly, Janči waits to see if he will be invited to play a game as he is at times, but the crowd has dispersed for an afternoon break. He'll have to wait for another day when he can be part of this elite chess club.

Lining Park Teplice are benches seeking refuge in the shade of the chestnut trees above. Benches here have a life of their own, beckoning you over to treat yourself to a peaceful moment away from the heat, putting your life on hold long enough to soak up the atmosphere of this town.

Fishnet cotton yarn bags are filled with fresh produce from the markets and are propped in hands carrying them; mothers leisurely push carriages along the sidewalk that hold little babies blissfully babbling in their own dialect. Store owners take a break outside, breathing in the fresh air while couples stroll along holding hands, lost in their own world of lovers; workers on motorbikes and cars loudly speed by, excited at the prospect of going home to their families.

Opapa walks over to the kiosk beside them to buy his daily newspapers. Each day, without exception, he reads at least two papers, one in Slovak and the other in German, from front to back. Beside the bench they sit on, children's squeals of delight fill the air, lodging a smile on people passing by who begin to reminisce about their long-gone childhood. The sandbox has been converted to a factory with several pairs of little hands working away, digging with a surprising amount of effort and making mountains come to fruition. Opapa peers over his newspaper to make sure Janči's staying out of trouble. Seeing that he is, he smiles and disappears behind the black and white lines describing the news of the day.

Chestnuts are falling from the trees around Janči, creating a hazard to any innocent head that intrudes on their descent. Pretending he's mining and each one is a nugget of gold, he begins collecting them, plucking them one by one off the grass. A rush of excitement fills him every time his eye locates one, like finding a lucky charm. Opening a few for a nibble, his fingers immediately turn brown, but he eagerly continues his triumphant search until his hands are full.

"Those are a lot of chestnuts," Opapa exclaims.

Water shoots up several feet high from a fountain in front of the Grand Hotel just across from the castle. Surprised at its lack of warning, Janči jumps up causing the chestnuts to fall out of his hand and scatter on the ground. More intrigued by the fountain, Janči disregards his lost chestnuts and joins everyone watching the water shoot up and fall back down with the force of gravity into an unsettled pool of colored water caused by the colored lights lodged in the side walls of the fountain.

When the show is over, Janči anticipates their last stop at one of the two local dairy stores on their way home. Entering the store, cold air catches him off guard for a moment, but he immediately adjusts, his skin no longer feeling the chill. Rather, his eyes have taken over his sensory nerves, sending a signal to his mouth to begin watering and his stomach to begin growling. Row upon row is a plethora of cheeses packed into the quaint store. Havarti, goat's cheese, bryndza, gouda, edam, parenica, emmental, beer cheese, and hermelin—all overwhelm his nostrils with their pungent scent. Other milk products are also available, but it's only the cheeses that get Janči's attention. At the cash register, a liter of milk and two hundred grams of parmesan are placed down, enough cheese for Opapa and Apu to nibble on with a full bodied glass of red wine tonight.

Back at home, Marta is playing with her dolls in the living room, carefree and oblivious to the harsh realities of the grown up world, Janči has been initiated into today with a simple conversation. Opapa showers Marta with hugs and kisses and then retreats to his room for a brief nap before dinner.

Sitting on the floor beside her, Janči examines the intricate dollhouse Marta is playing with. Picking up a tiny doll wearing a little red dress, he gently places it in a miniscule bed. Inside this dwelling, the miniature furniture seems too small for adult hands to have painted and crafted; however, the perfection of the complex details proves otherwise.

Outside, the adult world needs to be kept very separate from Marta, and playing these innocent games with her is Janči's noble attempt at doing so.

Days are getting longer, and the echoes of children's boisterous laughter bounces off the light still suspended in the mild air, indicating with a wide-sweeping gesture that summer is approaching. Change is apparent not only in the weather but in moods of everyone who all seem legitimately happier. With this transition of seasons, Apu decides it's finally time for Janči to join Boy Scouts.

"Janči, I'm going to sign you up for Junior Boy Scouts this summer while we're in Trenčín. It's very important for you to do this because you need to keep increasing your practical skill set. It will always come in useful," Apu announces, waiting for possible rejection, but no convincing is required to get Janči excited about this idea. Learning to build fires and hike through the forest are his exact ideas of how to best spend his summer.

Janči's family takes off to their summer home in Trenčín, a yellow stucco two-story duplex. Uncle Robert has his law office on the main floor along with the superintendent's residence while Janči's family lives on the second floor. Two small apartments in the back close to the railroad and the river are rented out to other residents. This is where Janči spends most of the summer before visiting Babka in Beluša with his cousin Ivor.

Apu is just as excited as Janči about starting Boy Scouts. He walks with Janči to the first meeting at the Public Community Hall close to the park. On their way, Apu keeps looking over at his son, smiling and remembering his own Boy Scout days.

"You're going to have so much fun doing this. I know I did when I was your age."

"I'm sure I will. I'm really excited about it."

In a large room for the parents, chairs are pushed up against the wall for them to rest while their sons are inducted to this time-honored movement.

Twenty boys, ranging from six to seventeen years old, are milling about, chattering away with friends. Some of the faces look familiar to Janči—students from school. Upon hearing their leaders ask them to sit in a circle, they immediately scamper off to take a seat. Crossing his legs, Janči's not left with much room on either side of the dense circle, his knees bumping into the boys beside him.

"Good afternoon, everyone. Thanks for joining us on what is the beginning of a very exciting journey for each and everyone one of you. Let me begin by telling you that Scouts will strengthen your character, citizenship, and personal fitness. You will measure yourself against the values written out in the Scout Law and continually try to improve. The goals and expectations are high, but they will shape you as you work to achieve them.

"As you may well know, our activities take place outdoors to allow you to share responsibilities and learn to live with one another. The skills and activities we practice at troop meetings will show their significance once applied outdoors. You will gain an appreciation for the beauty of the environment by working in it.

"We will challenge you and put obstacles in your way, all of which can be overcome at your own individual pace. Each achievement will be rewarded.

"We, your scout leaders, will be role models for you. We will listen, encourage, and take an interest in your lives. All our planned activities will allow you to progress toward your goals. You will learn, understand, and practice leadership skills. Your uniforms will become your identity," they say, holding up a khaki collared shirt with two front button-flap pockets and shoulder epaulets, olive green shorts, socks, and twill cap with a red front panel and the Scout emblem.

"Wearing the uniform is an action that shows your commitment to Scouts. It demonstrates your participation in a brotherhood of youth who believe in the same ideals. It is also very practical for the activities you will undertake and provides a way to showcase your achievements through badges that will be sewn on."

The boys learn of the first set of Tenderfoot Tests they will be expected to pass. These range from reciting the Scout Law and Promise, salutes, signs, tying knots, and whipping a rope. Once they have passed those, they will then face second-class tests consisting of first aid, signaling, fire lighting, compass, cooking, axemanship, and pioneering. Badges are awarded after successful completion of these. First-class tests are then the final series of examinations where badges are at long last approved. Second-class tests are repeated in this round but at more of an advanced level, and the new ones are added, which include swimming, estimation, mapping, and journey. Proficiency badges can be achieved in boatman, camper, carpenter, explorer, surveyor, forester, air mechanic, metalworker, and more. Lists are churned out to the scouts, and although not exhaustive, they already wind up Janči with a thrill. He's ready to conquer the wilderness already.

The boys learn the Scout Law—words they are expected to live by.

A scout speaks the truth.

A scout can be trusted and is loyal.

A scout is useful to society and helps others.

A scout is a friend to all people of goodwill and a brother to all scouts.

A scout is courteous.

A scout protects nature and valuable human products.

A scout obeys his parents, superiors, and Scout leaders.

A scout is of cheerful mind.

A scout is thrifty.

A scout is pure in thoughts, words, and deeds.

All boys stand tall, their right hands raised level with their shoulders, palms to the front, thumb resting on the nail of the little finger and the other three fingers upright, pointing upward—the scout's salute and secret sign. With confidence, they intensely recite the promise that must be taken, their rite of passage before entering the world of a scout.

> On my honor, I promise that I will do my best: to serve the highest Truth and Love faithfully at all times, to fulfill my own duties and to observe the Scout laws, to be prepared to help my country and my neighbors with all my soul and body.

Upon uttering the last words, clinching his commitment to this movement, a sense of pride and goose bumps engulf Janči.

Based on their age, they are split into junior and senior sections. Each troop averages eighteen scouts with one leader assigned to them. The troops then subdivide into smaller patrols of six scouts to engage in the outdoor activities in which Trenčín's mild climate will be of great advantage. Hiking trails in the Povarsky Inovec region of Trenčín, and canoeing in the waters of the Váh River are in their near future, but they begin by practicing in the smaller breakout rooms down the hall.

It doesn't take long before all the scouts in Janči's group end up trusting him the most in getting them where they need to go. Developing a keen sense of direction, Janči takes his group along scenic ridge trails buried deep in the forest, through head-high scrub, downhill through densely forested areas, and edges overlooking limestone gorges, using simple tricks to figure out where they are, like the bark of a tree or different types of plant growth. Building fires comes too easily to him, detecting the driest and strongest wood for this purpose while others drag back branches that wouldn't cause a spark. He seeks out the best location to camp at night under shelter provided by the hefty trees and in close proximity to a water source. He directs them how to hammer tent poles into the ground to erect a sturdy tent. His hands transmit the passion he has for the outdoors into the practicality of passing all his tenderfoot exams.

Janči wants to bring his closest friends from Boy Scouts to Conditoria Weil to relish in the cakes and ice cream he has grown up with. The only impasse he faces is that he has six friends, and he is worried that would be an imposition on Uncle Miki. Another plot is designed in his head to accommodate all his friends and not upset his uncle.

Janči sneaks through the back kitchen door with one of his friends, and they sit in a booth, indulging in vanilla ice cream on top of *Rigó Janči*—a cube-shaped cake filled with a thick layer of rich chocolate cream filling accented with a hint of dark rum which sits between two layers of chocolate sponge cake. A dark chocolate glaze drenches the top of the cake. In need of a second dessert, they order *palacinky*[20] stuffed with strawberry jam and walnuts and a side order of *kifli*, small crescent-shaped pastries.

Once fully gorged on sweets, his friend leaves through the same back door they slinked in and another one craftily steals in and sits in the booth with Janči, picking up the fork dangling off the plate of *palacinky* and continues where his friend left off. Wearing the same uniforms, Janči is sure the hard-working staff will not pick up on the fact that they are all different people.

A week later, when visiting again, Uncle Miki pulls Janči aside in the pastry shop. "Jančika, you don't think I know you're bringing all your friends in? You don't have to sneak them in. Bring them through the front door. They are all welcome."

"I was worried it would be too many people."

"When has it ever been too many people?" he asks. Janči smiles knowing the answer.

---

[20] *Palacinky* are crepes.

VANILLA COOKIES, SUMMER 1937

FROM HIS DESK, Janči drags the chair across the carpeted floor of his bedroom, leaving trail marks of his route. On the top shelf in his closet, one out of his reach even on tiptoes, he spots the worn out black leather suitcase that travels forty kilometers with him to Beluša. Positioning the chair directly under it, he climbs up and firmly grabs the handles with both his hands. "Watch out, Ivor. It's coming down." With his warning, his cousin Ivor moves his tall lanky body safely out of the way. Janči swings the luggage off the top shelf, and it lands with minimal impact on the floor. Ivor's packed suitcase already sits in the corner of the bedroom, filled with their necessities—toys, books, and clothes.

Items that are waiting to be packed in Janči's suitcase are piled in the middle of the floor, more than enough for their one-month stay. Janči begins sorting through his pile, plucking out the clothes, the first necessity that must go with him. On top, in whatever space is leftover, come the books and toys.

"One more sleep," Ivor reminds him excitedly.

"I know. It's not soon enough."

Ivor and Janči are up earlier than everyone else the next morning, barely able to contain themselves. To speed up the process, they roll their bags down the hall and set them by the front door. Lazily, the apartment rouses from its slumber, coming to life after drifting into unconsciousness for the night. Coming out of the bedroom and expecting to be the first one, Apu laughs seeing them anxiously sitting on the couch. "Your train doesn't leave for another two hours."

"We know, Apu, but we couldn't sleep. We're too excited."

"Well, let's get you some breakfast, and we'll leave right after that. I wouldn't want you two to go crazy waiting here." They nod in agreement and wait for Marta and Mamička, so they can eat breakfast together. As quickly as Mamička fries up the eggs and puts them on their plates, they disappear.

"Honey, I think you better take them soon," she happily cautions. Finishing his last bite and taking his last sip of coffee, Apu walks them to take the tram station.

Incessant chatter and giggles fill the air, the two boys energized about going on a train. Disappearing behind the steel ticket dispenser on the wall, Apu gives the information to the cashier sitting there. Two tickets are pulled out of drawerlike compartments and stamped with the date. Apu returns with two cardboard tickets budding from his hand, each one printed with their destination and the price.

"These will get you right to Beluša, even though you have to change trains in Trenčianské Teplá."

"We know. We've done this plenty of times with you."

"Yes, but this is the first time on your own. Just be very careful." Taking both suitcases, Apu helps them get on board.

"Be safe and have fun."

"We will."

Hurriedly, they each give him a hug and kiss and scuttle off to get their seats, each promising to take turns at the window seat.

Inching its way along like a worm, the electric train begins rolling forward on the tracks, not taking long to gain full speed. On the platform stands Apu, still waving. They wave back, but within minutes, Apu is no longer visible. Janči turns over and looks at Ivor who already has a book in his hands. For the most part, the two stare out the window to pass the time, absorbed in their thoughts about this expedition.

Trenčianské Teplá is announced, their transfer point to Beluša. They nervously look up at their bulky suitcases bulging off the luggage rack. Sensing their trepidation in taking them down, a man offers to help. Swiftly, he takes them right down to the undersized platform where people of all ages and sizes are milling about. Reunions are occurring almost everywhere you look—arms thrown around each other, kisses given, and helping hands lent with heavy luggage.

The conductor of their next train, a mild mannered man with stark white hair against the traditional navy blue conductor's cap, wearing a navy suit with red piping, sees the two boys and approaches them. Dangling at his hip is the gold chain of his pocket watch, an essential tool in keeping the trains on schedule. In his hand, he carries a petroleum lamp emitting an intense red light. By swinging it in one direction, he signals that the train is ready to go. Swinging it in the other direction becomes a signal for the engineer. Across his shoulder sits a black leather pouch, his personal cash case for selling and collecting additional tickets on board. A ticket punch is also in his possession, one that makes a distinctively shaped hole in the ticket which allows him to easily determine who has a cancelled ticket.

"Okay, boys. Let's see where you're going, so we can make sure to put you on the right train." Janči hands over his ticket. "Ah! Beluša. It's this train right here," he says, pointing to the raven-black steam locomotive idling on the tracks.

"Thank you, sir," Janči says, retrieving his ticket.

The two climb aboard the train, the conductor following with their suitcases. Relieved that this part of the expedition went smoothly, they sit back and wait for the grand finale. Picking up speed, the locomotive huffs and puffs along, pursued by a plume of steam and smoke. On the platform, anyone in a white shirt is now covered with black specks, the coal marking its territory.

Rousing Janči from his sleep, the conductor's jovial voice booms, announcing they're in Beluša. The train station is about two kilometers from Babka's home. To get to her house, they will have to take a horse-drawn buggy.

Precariously, their suitcases perch above in the luggage compartment. To avoid any unnecessary accidents, they ask a man walking by to help them bring them down. He does so with ease, and once the train comes to a final stop, he even takes them to the platform for the boys. Thankful to be helped again by a stranger, they scamper down the stairs and leap over the gap between the train and platform. Safely in Beluša, they look over to Babka's waiting spot beside the glass-enclosed ticket counter underneath the large clock on the bench. She's not there.

"Maybe she went to the bathroom," Ivor offers.

"Or maybe she's running late." Figuring it's one of those possibilities, they drag their suitcases to the occupied bench and use their luggage as alternate seating to watch the action going on. Ten minutes go by.

"Wait here, Ivor. I'm going to look around for her."

Janči scours the entire area, hearing the clicking of hooves in the distance against the dirt road. He looks over to see a white horse galloping on the road, heading away from the train station drawing a dark open carriage resting on four large spoke wheels. Four people sit in the carriage, lined with plush red velour, two on one side and opposite them the other pair. Sitting on a perch is the coachman, a local farmer wearing brown trousers held up with black suspenders and a grimy white shirt that has seen many fields. Urging himself to stop getting distracted, Janči keeps up with his search but doesn't see Babka anywhere. Ivor looks up when he returns, concern lining his face.

"She's not here. What do we do?" he asks.

"Let's wait a little while longer, and if she's still not here, we'll go to her house. I know how to get there."

"Should we call home and let them know."

"Not yet. I don't want them to worry about us."

Agreeing with his idea, Ivor sits back and continues to take in the people moving about the station, certain his cousin has the situation under control.

Two pairs of eyes continually inspect the area, springing up each time a plump and huggable woman wearing a kerchief walks by, but it's never Babka. Impatience converts to panic. What if something happened to her? This is extremely uncharacteristic of her. Glaringly, the hands on the clock show that half an hour has passed. Janči finally decides to stop wasting time at the station and go to Babka's house. Maybe they will find answers there. Schlepping their heavy suitcases to the entrance, they look for a coachman. A few are loitering outside, socializing with each other. Janči tells Babka's address to the first coach in line. He nods and puts their luggage up. Immediately, he lights a cigarette after just stubbing one out and rapidly leaves by whipping the horse into a trot.

Farmhouses roll past. Farmers in coveralls are seen working with cows and horses over vast fields. Sharp-bladed metal hoes move the soil around plants to haul out destructive weeds, and others are bending over picking root vegetables from the earth, bunches of carrots filling baskets beside them. Turning on to the familiar wide street lined with fruit trees, they safely arrive at Babka's house. Having to pay the coachman a flat fare, Janči pulls out the money Apu gave him. He was hoping to use it on candy, but he knows Babka will treat them anyways. The coachman gets their luggage and sets them in front of the two-story house on the sidewalk. The buggy quickly pulls away, leaving the two boys standing alone.

Babka used to have a spacious old farmhouse with a small creek running beside it. It was filled with chickens, geese, a big vegetable garden, and a portly German Shepherd. Fruit bushes and trees allowed the boys to pick gooseberries, black and red currants, walnuts, apples, and pears, climbing up on an unsteady small ladder, storing their produce and nuts in straw baskets on the ground.

When they were with their parents, Janči and Ivor would visit their ninety-eight-year-old great-grandmother, Babka's mom, Netti Gartenberg. Completely deformed from arthritis, her fingers were crippled, bent like branches of a tree, each digit unable to fully extend, its joints seemingly fused in a permanent crooked shape. "Jančika, could you bring me a cup of water?" she would ask, her body almost as bad shape as her fingers. Unable to properly hold the glass, Janči would help her drink it, tipping the glass at the right angle for her to get just the right amount of water without choking on it. Missing teeth, Janči remembers how slowly she would chew bread, each bite expending all her energy. Janči would never be sure if she'd be able to swallow, but with a loud gulp, her muscles would contract pushing the masticated food down her throat.

The two boys would also spend hours selecting items from the brightly packaged candies and chocolates that filled the huge barrels in the general store Babka also owned. Village women would come here to sort through shelves of different colored cotton and linens.

Before Ivor was born, Uncle Lajko and his wife used to work there, and once they decided to move to Trenčín to open up a successful deli, Babka knew she couldn't handle the business on her own at that age. Selling it was the only viable option which she did three years ago along with the farmhouse. Now their visits are made to the large three-bedroom, two-story house she rents, also surrounded by a small peaceful creek and bountiful orchard.

Lifting the brass doorknocker, Janči bangs it against the wooden door. No answer replies, not even the slightest shuffle inside the house can be heard. Trying the door, they find it's locked. He searches for a way to get in the house, but the front windows are sealed. Walking around the side of the house, he notices the basement window open a crack. Bending down, he pulls at it and finds that it easily moves left, leaving just enough room for him to squeeze through.

"Ivor, I'm going to crawl through here, and then I can go upstairs and open the front door for us. Wait there for me."

Before Ivor goes to his commanded post, he watches Janči ungraciously squirm his way through the slight opening, jiggling around his body parts to make them fit. The basement sits untouched from how it was during their last visit—a plush beige carpet flattened and disintegrating in color having suffered years of trampling, a velvety brown couch with an orange throw over it, a short coffee table used more as a foot rest than anything else, a green glass flower lamp shade roosting on a gold light stand, and a painting of snowcapped mountains are among the items ornamentally furnishing the room that Janči and Ivor rarely come down to.

Up in the kitchen, Janči sees it hasn't changed a bit either. The wooden stove sits in the corner, different-sized cast iron plates waiting to heat contents of a pot or warm slices of bread that are then smeared with garlic and butter. Wood logs are piled on one side, the oven on the other, surrounded by fire bricks where the baking occurs. Beside it is the waist high wooden icebox. It is never full of food because Babka, like most people, does her grocery shopping daily and stores a lot of nonperishable food in the cool basement.

Across the room is the chimney, emitting smoke into the sky above the house. Italian tiles of yellow, brown, and blue design cover the floors underneath the small pinewood table for four. A large pinewood counter is her workstation where she prepares the food, peeling and chopping vegetables, and cutting meat. Pots and pans are stored in the pantry, a separate room, creating less clutter in the kitchen.

Loud banging on the door breaks him from his observations, and he dashes to open the door for Ivor. They drag their suitcases inside and leave them in the front hall. Immediately, they head to the kitchen feeling like a *nash*[21] of some sort.

Acting as accomplices, they begin opening cupboards in hopes of finding something that will satisfy their hunger. On instinct, Janči opens the oven and sees a silver cookie sheet full of their favorite vanilla cookies. He pulls the large cookie sheet out, still warm and covered with close to fifty cookies, and places it on the table. Happy to have something to alleviate their cravings, they waste no time in eating. The cookies melt away in the confines of their mouths, the sweetness disintegrating, no chewing required. Powdered sugar remains around their lips that they casually wipe off with the back of their hands. Putting away the contents of the entire tray in their stomachs, they both feel reprehensibly full. Deviously, Janči puts the empty sheet back in the oven, concealing any evidence of their gluttony. Janči and Ivor push their chairs away from the table and stretch out their legs, rewarding themselves with repose after their marathon of eating. Lessening their worry about Babka's whereabouts is the fullness of their stomachs.

Suddenly, an extremely frazzled and petite Babka appears before them in the doorframe. Even in her tense state, her brown eyes still dance as she sees her grandchildren. As expected, a black kerchief tied under her chin covers her coarse white hair. She is simply clad in a black wool frock with black stockings and sensible flat black shoes, unconcerned about making a fashion statement.

"Where were you?" she worriedly asks, "and how did you get in?"

"Through the basement window. And we were at the train station waiting for *you*," Janči lightheartedly says.

---

[21] *Nash* means "snack" in Yiddish.

"I was looking all over for you. I didn't know what happened. I was so scared I was ready to call your parents. What time did your train get in?"

"One o'clock."

"Oh," she says, realizing the problem. "I thought it was at two. I went and did some shopping first. I'm sorry, but I see you managed to get here without my help," she says with her usual big smile forming. "Are you hungry? Because I made something special for you."

Janči and Ivor pass knowing glances and start laughing as Babka opens the oven door and discovers the empty cookie sheet. She turns around.

"You *hunszuts*.[22] Now I have to bake more cookies," she says, laughing while already tying the red apron around her waist.

Waking up to the bright light filtering through the sheer white curtains, Janči creeps over and begins shaking Ivor who is still soundly asleep, the freshly made bed from the night before now rumpled and creased.

"It's time to get up, Ivor." Janči coaxes. Mumbling nonsense, Ivor turns away from Janči's irksome hands.

"We have to go play." Janči tries enticing him. Hearing the magic word, Ivor flies out of bed without the drowsiness that was infecting him seconds earlier and makes it downstairs in a flash.

"Good morning, sweethearts," Babka genially greets the boys, signaling them to sit at the table while she stands over the cast iron plate where mouthwatering French toast is directly frying. Hot water for tea is ready in the enamel container that sits on one of the rings. Thick

---

[22] *Hunszuts* means "tricksters" in Hungarian.

golden honey has been placed on the table for the bread to be dipped in, complete with a wooden honey dipper. Their mouths expend a lot of energy manipulating the substantial pieces of bread swathed in the sweet honey. Every last morsel careens down their esophagus. Eager at roaming around Beluša, they kiss Babka goodbye and rush out the door.

Knee deep in grass, they find themselves amid sprawling fields rimmed by the creek, where they venture later to play with frogs and toads, prodding them with sticks to see them jump. Queen Anne's lace flowers spread across the meadow with their unmistakable flat white petals. Hidden inside are several of black *Janko vyskoč*[23] bugs. Janči delicately lifts one off the petal, not wanting to disturb it or have it jump away. Maneuvering its body, Janči is able to place it in his secret matchbox that he snuck out of Babka's house for this specific purpose. A few more need to be captured to keep each other company. He gathers more, becoming skilled at the process, and loads them in his special hiding place.

Behind the clouds, the sun is lowering as if a puppeteer were handling it on a fragile string, signaling for them to head back. Janči puts the matchbox in his pant pocket, needing to put it out of sight or else he'll never get it by Babka.

"Dinner will be ready in a few minutes. Go wash up."

They trudge upstairs to wash their hands from the grime they've been in and change out of their grass stained clothing, signs of exploration. Janči also knows he has to find a decent hiding place for his box of bugs. If Babka ever saw them in the house, he'd be thrown out with them.

"Janči, Ivor," Babka calls walking up the stairs, "it's time for dinner." Wildly looking around the room, Janči carelessly hides the matchbox

---

[23] *Janko vyskoč* are small bugs, slightly larger than ants, which jump up when you touch them.

under Ivor's bed cover before she comes in, reminding himself to retrieve it after dinner, but on a full stomach of schnitzel and mashed potatoes, Janči's mind is elsewhere.

As night falls, they each climb into bed, sporting their pajamas dotted with cars, and go to sleep, anxious for a new day to begin. An agonizing howling noise from Ivor's side of the room wakes Janči up in the middle of the night.

"Something is biting me," he screams madly, diving out of bed. *The matchbox*, Janči thinks, having completely forgotten about it.

Babka comes running in still tying her pink robe around her nightdress, hearing all the uproar, her hair wildly standing up in awkward angles and pillow creases still visible on her face. Bravely, she sweeps the covers aside in a grand gesture and sees the *Janko vyskočs* crawling all over the bed. Narrowing her list of criminals, she casts a disapproving glance toward Janči, knowing he is the only one that could be responsible for this prank.

"Janči, get them out of his bed right now and then go back to sleep." Leaving him to solve this problem, Janči begins plucking the bugs up one by one as their legs flail in the air, and deposits them back in the matchbox.

"Are you trying to kill me?" Ivor accuses his cousin while Janči scuttles after the bugs that jump out of his grasp.

"Ivor, I'm so sorry," unable to contain his laughter. "I completely forgot I hid them there." Catching the last one, he informs Ivor that they can go back to bed now. Ivor steadfastly shakes his head insisting they switch beds for the night. Janči obliges, knowing he will not win this battle.

Their flawless summer holidays have come to an end. School has taken over the luxury of free time, drilling more numbers and facts into their heads. The weather is changing, the sky is becoming grayer, warning that cold air will surge through shortly.

At home, Opapa is reading the newspaper, outlining the tragic death of Masaryk on September 14, 1937. In the house and even on the streets, the subdued tone suggests that many people are affected by the news. Having learned what a good man Masaryk was, Janči is able to understand why and feels a part of the sadness everyone is experiencing.

To see what is happening outside, he ventures out on his wood-bottomed, steel-piped scooter with big heavy rubber wheels that Apu recently bought him from Prague. It has become his typical mode of transport when going to the park with Jožka and a big source of envy among his friends who all wait in line to have their chance at a ride.

Briskly, he wears down the sole of his right shoe, constantly hitting the pavement to propel him forward. Looking around, he notices people are quieter than usual, and there isn't as much activity going on. A hill confronts him, and expending all his energy, he pushes himself up, then he effortlessly coasts down, a welcome relief from the strenuous exercise upward. Wind blows his hair into disarray, and Janči goes back to being a child, unconcerned about politics for the moment.

"Tomorrow, you will be dressing up in the new suit I bought," Mamička gloats, ecstatic at the prospect of seeing her son in his new ensemble that she carefully selected at Mr. Fried's store.

It is never a full day of class when celebrating Independence Day which makes the dress-up part more tolerable for Janči. He is left to put on a crisply ironed white shirt and short white pants with creases in all the right places. A white jacket is the finishing embellishment to his outfit. Bending down on her knees with buffers, Mamička shines his brand new black and white shoes, getting rid of the invisible scuff marks she sees, making them so shiny that her reflection stares back at her. Licking her finger, she wipes the leftover breakfast from corner of Janči's mouth. He cringes at this motherly assault. She then proceeds to flatten the untamed cowlick at the back of his head which disobediently pops back up until water finally mattes it in place.

"See how beautiful you look." Janči looks at his reflection in the mirror and admits that Mamička did a good job primping him this morning.

In the yard, the students cluster around and listen to the importance of that day, marking Czechoslovakia's restored independence from Austria-Hungary with the fall of the Habsburg Monarchy on October 28, 1918. Explanations are waged about the war and how Czechoslovakia gained its independence after President Masaryk fought for it.

At twelve o'clock, they are free to leave, like animals released from captivity into the wild. They disperse, not wasting any extra time at school. Jubilantly, Janči grabs his light brown leather backpack—another recent purchase by Mamička—swings it over his shoulder, and heads home, looking forward to the fireworks display tonight.

Approaching the creek, Janči sees the spot he normally clears with a standing long jump, a personal short cut of his instead of walking all the way around to the bridge. Knowing today isn't the day to risk jumping, his conscience still isn't strong enough to ward his legs away from the edge of the creek. Steadying himself, he swings his arms back and forth, pumping momentum into his body. On takeoff, the smooth soles of his new shoes give way, not providing the same firm grip he's used to. Gravity pulls him down with an unforgiving splash into the frigid water. Realizing the impact the fall is having on his new clothes, he jumps out right away as if a fire has been ignited under him, trying to salvage any of the remaining unsoiled material. Looking down, he sees it is a futile attempt. Everything is already dripping, soaked to the fibers of the fabric. To make matters worse, the shallowness of the creek has also slicked mud upon his suit.

Climbing out, he appears like a creature from a horror movie. Trudging home in that state is very uncomfortable, the clothes adding five pounds weighing him down. Sloshing noises rise from his shoes, where a puddle has formed, and his socks absorb the water, making his toes turn into prunes. Behind him, a trail of water follows him as he continually drips.

As Janči approaches their house, Jožka sees him and races to get him before the family sees him. "Why do I have a feeling this wasn't an accident? I don't even want to know right now. We have to get you out of these clothes," she scolds, pulling him into the house, undressing him right away in the front hall.

Mamička walks in hearing them and gapes at his appearance, not the well-dressed boy he was when he left the house.

"What did you do? You ruined your expensive new clothes! How did this happen?" Grimacing in pain as if her own clothes were damaged.

"I tried jumping across the creek."

His white shirt, leather shoes with white and black are all smeared in an unpleasant brown muck. The clothes are carried to the laundry room upstairs on the second floor, like an inmate waiting for its death. After the rigorous washing, the clothes make their way up to the attic. Opaque glass shingles allow light to come through that dry the clothes. A faint brown mark remains on the shirt, but luckily, that's the only proof to remind Janči of his unsuccessful jump.

Days are getting shorter, and the inescapable chill heavily hangs in the December air. Snow has covered the mountains, creating a white sheet balanced on high peaks. Snowflakes fall, the delicate and fine details of each unique crystal form remaining invisible to the blind eye. Too cold on this day to go outside, Janči finds other ways to keep himself occupied.

He converts a small space in the basement into his own lab, eager to begin his own scientific experimentation. A table is reserved for his bottles, jars, tubes, and a ship that sits in a large bowl of water, Janči's first trial item. At the bottom of the ship is a boiler filled with water. Janči adds a dry white alcohol tablet to it and lights it. A fire builds, warming up the water, which in turn forms steam that propels the boat forward. After the successful operation of his steam ship, his mind rambles to other tests or jobs he can perform.

Deciding Marta needs another dollhouse, he makes it his next mission to build one. Wood carvings of miniscule furniture outfit the interior. Functional electric lights are wired in, allowing her to turn them on for her dolls. Hidden away in the basement, Janči doesn't disclose anything about the dollhouse to his sister until it's all finished, presenting it to her weeks later with a grand unveiling.

With that project over, Janči begins thinking about why money always needs to be spent buying ink for his fountain pen. His next exercise is to make ink using blackberries by distilling the juice. First, he will have to cook the berries in a pot. Only once they are soft will he use the rounded back of a wooden spoon to crush the berries, collecting the juice in a bowl. Although a small amount would be enough, Janči has collected plenty of berries that will need mashing. Vinegar and salt are waiting on the table, ready to be added to the berry juice once it's ready; the vinegar helping the ink retain its color, and the salt to prevent it from molding.

In a dish, he places four dry alcohol tablets. He lights them and a flame shoots up, heating the berries. While the berries simmer, Janči starts distilling water. A loud clang and hot liquid spurting everywhere disrupts him. The lid of the pot has flown off due to the mounting pressure inside. Blackberry morsels have exploded and land all over his face and shirt, covering everything in the vicinity with a dark mess. Mamička runs downstairs and cries at the sight of it.

After exhausting his scientific and carpentry projects, Janči and his family frequent the spa resorts in need of warmth during the bitter winter months. Sometimes, Eli and her mom also join them. A profusion of mineral hot springs is nestled in a valley among rolling hills. Zelená žaba is their favorite, situated in an old stone quarry. When the snow is too heavy, it is impossible to get up with a car, walking being the only unappealing alternative as the road leading up to the pool is exceptionally steep. The three-story Bauhaus-style complex hidden in the woods boasts two swimming pools, one of them for children, where the water is always cold and green because there is no filtration system; two restaurants; rides for kids, like a merry-go-round; a boating alley; and the main feature—a thirty-three-meter thermal pool cut in a rock. Designer Bohuslav Fuchs recently built all of this.

Lying covered up to his neck in hot-spring water, Janči looks up watching the snowflakes fall from the sky, their cold temperature landing on his uncovered scalp and melting away upon contact, initiating a tingling effect that rushes down his body right to the tips of his toes. These outdoor pools are fed by hot mineral springs that are found across the Carpathian mountain region. Relaxing, Janči looks out into the unobstructed panorama of the pine-forested mountains, which is made murky by the steam clouds levitating out of the water.

In the warmer weather, Mamička would lie in a lounge chair, sunning herself. Next to her would sit the picnic basket that accompanies them on most outings, abounding with scrambled eggs on rye bread, Janči's favorite, and *alma rétes*[24] for an unhurried afternoon picnic on the grass.

During the winter months, their picnics are taken indoors to the two-story restaurant and café that greets patrons with cauldrons of home-cooked meals. Sizeable balconies off the restaurant offer fantastic views of the flowing meadows below, allowing people to relish in both the ambiance and gastronomy.

Worn out from a full day of gluttony, they go home to recover, Janči making his daily pit stop at the Jewish farmer for milk. He waits as the large dairy cows are milked, their pink udders, painfully full and heavy. Expert fingers clamp on and activate a light stream of milk that fills the two-liter enamel can, which narrows toward the top protected by a lid. Janči takes the handle of the full can, paying Mr. Martin, and heads back home. Instead of carrying the can properly, Janči removes the lid and swings it around a full three hundred and sixty degrees, in awe of how the milk never spills out, the centrifugal forces keeping it in as if glued to the side of the can.

A hub of activity fills the sidewalk as he sidesteps men bringing blocks of ice and ice picks to residents for their icebox. Beside him, a chute opens and coal gets poured in, flowing down into the basements of houses to heat their stoves.

"Make sure you don't spill that," their next-door neighbor, Mr. Uhlar, lightly yells to Janči, seeing him swinging the can around. "Your mom wouldn't be very happy."

"Don't worry, Mr. Uhlar, I'm a pro at this," giving the can an extra strong swing to substantiate his skill.

Being Friday afternoon, Apu comes home shortly after Janči, carrying a large object in his arms. Stepping closer, Janči sees it is a beautiful

---

[24] *Alma rétes* means "apple strudel" in Hungarian.

toboggan, another souvenir from his travels. It is made from bentwood and has steel rails on the bottom. Four people can comfortably fit on it, which works well for him and his friends. Without wasting time, Janči calls up Ali and twins, Milan and Miran who are identical to a tee, from their dirty blond hair to the fact that when one has to go to the washroom, so does the other.

Steep slopes are their main criteria when selecting hills. Today, their usual hill is filled with children bundled up in brightly colored snowsuits, leaving only their faces exposed as they race down the incline. The troupe decides to find another hill that's not as busy where they can ride in comfort from the top of the hill all the way down to the valley below without the worry of hitting a child. Hills, valleys, and mountains surround Trenčianské Teplice, so they are never a shortage of choices. They find a suitable one and begin the trek with the toboggan to the top, each one taking turns pulling it.

Close to the top, Milan proclaims he wants to steer it down the hill. For this, he must sit in the back and steer by digging his heels in the snow. Janči agrees, not wanting to appear overly protective of his new toy. Instead of his usual position in the back, Janči ends up sitting in the front. It's the first time Milan is steering a toboggan of this sort, making Janči nervous. The other two pile in between them, adding extra weight. All their hands and legs begin pushing in unison to get a fast start. Imprints of their limbs are left in the hard packed snow. Beginning slowly at first, the toboggan needs only seconds to get them at full speed. Howling sounds of the wind blow past Janči's face; his eyes tearing from its intensity. Trees race by in a blur. Janči's adrenalin pumps harder as the toboggan goes faster. Side to side, the toboggan guides itself out of control, not taking any cues from the amateur boy steering in the back.

"To the right," Janči screams, knowing how risky a reckless toboggan is. Janči hears boots grinding in the snow behind him, but instead of getting them on a straight course, they lurch further to the left. A Silver Fir in front of Janči is getting dangerously close with each passing second. He tries digging in his own heels to slow them down or change direction, but his efforts are futile. Nothing will stop them at this speed. Completely exposed to the threat of the tree, they continue heading toward it. Instinctively, he buries his head into his knees and uses his arms as additional protection. Silently, he says a prayer to anyone willing to listen. He doesn't want to die like this.

The impact of the crash interrupts his pleas. His body is thrown over the sled like a rag doll into the rough bark of the tree. His head snaps against the tree trunk. Pain surges through, although he can't tell exactly where because it feels like it's everywhere. What he cringes at most is the awful crack he hears his nose make and the feeling of it moving to the side, out of its normal position on a face. Scared to even touch it, Janči dreads it's broken. Still conscious and seemingly okay except for the crooked nose and blood trickling out of it, his friends just laugh. Not finding the situation humorous or impressed by their reaction, Janči angrily takes his toboggan, ignoring their protests, and walks home, blood dripping onto the snow, leaving a bright red stain on the sheer white background.

"What happened?" Mamička shrieks seeing his bloodied face.

"I think I broke my nose. I'll be fine." Looking down at his toboggan, Janči expects a tangled mess of wood and steel. Pleasantly surprised, he sees the toboggan survived the accident, too.

GONE FISHING, 1938

THE SEVEN OF spades is calculatingly placed on top of the pile. Janči stares at the reviled card, forcing him to pass, unable to put down an eight as none sits in his hand. Directly across from him, Janči can't escape the sly grin on Marta's face who knows she has her brother exactly where she wants him. Only two cards are left in her confident hand. Unless luck is on Janči's side, the outcome of the game is already determined. She tactically plays her eight which finally allows Janči to release his nine without much comfort. At the end of this round, Marta has gotten rid of all her cards first, winning.

Unexpectedly, cold air bursts through the front door along with Apu, slicing through the warmth pent up in the house. Apu's cheeks are windburned red, but even in his freezing state, he is smiling.

"Apuka," Marta springs up dropping her cards and latches on to his leg with the fervor of a leech. He bends down to pick her up for a proper hug, lifting her effortlessly.

"What are you doing home today? It's only Thursday," Janči asks surprised by Apu's appearance since he recently started working at Hoffmann-La Roche in Basel, Switzerland.

"Oh, I decided to come home early, so I could spend more time with my lovely family. I also brought something with me that I thought the two of you would like sooner rather than later."

Hearing the familiar voice, Mamička emerges from the kitchen, her face lighting up at seeing her husband. Before a word is spoken between them, she goes over to give him his anticipated welcoming kiss.

"What a treat to have you home early. Get comfortable, and then we'll have some soup." He gives her a kiss on the cheek in appreciation.

"First, I want all of you to stay right here and close your eyes." They all do as they're told, not questioning the unusual instructions. Apu steps outside, a blast of frigid air let into the house again, and he returns a moment later. "Okay, you can open them now."

Jánči opens his eyes and sees a small black and brown ball of hair, just a little bigger than the palm of Apu's hands. It begins lifting his head presenting itself, a fox terrier puppy. Barely visible with the hair falling over them, his eyes momentarily poke out revealing their existence. They shriek excitedly and run over.

Unsure of how to react to strangers showering him with attention, the puppy begins shaking. Before either of them can lay a hand on him, Apu warns them to be very gentle. Tentatively, they pet him, hoping the shaking will cease. Through his fine hair, it is easy to feel the skin and bones that lie underneath. Jánči scratches under his chin and behind his ears, the puppy responding by tilting his head up asking for more, swiftly accustomed to his new owners.

"How do we get him to stop shaking?" Marta wonders.

"He just has to get used to us and the house. He probably misses his mom, so you have to take good care of him."

"We will," they assuredly reply, eagerly accepting this responsibility.

"Now, more importantly, what are you going to name him?" Marta and Jánči quizzically look at each other. The last time naming was involved in their family was when Marta was born, and Jánči didn't have any say in that. They need to think carefully about such a big decision. Nothing frilly or typical would make Jánči happy. It has to be an original name, something meaningful. Then the most obvious choice hits him.

"I know! Gypsy."

"I like that," Marta counters.

"So do I," Mamička chimes in.

"Then it's agreed. Welcome Gypsy Teschner to the family."

Gypsy instantly becomes another member of the family, although Janči selfishly spends most time with him after growing attached to his steadfast personality. Everywhere Janči goes, Gypsy usually tags along, listening to all his stories and playing with him. At home, all of Janči's attention falls on Gypsy. After dinner, Gypsy always crawls into Janči's lap and contently sits while his owner strokes his head and tells him about the lessons he learned at school and the games he played in the forest with his friends. Attentively, Gypsy listens, responding by licking Janči's face. He then takes a deep breath as if bearing a huge weight on his tiny shoulders and lets it out, relieving imaginary stress while settling further into Janči.

Each day Janči comes home from school, Gypsy is eagerly waiting by the door to greet him. He can sense Janči's moods, giving extra affection if he appears upset about something. Only a month has passed and Janči doesn't even remember what it was like not having Gypsy around. Although having the closest bond with Janči, Gypsy offers enough love and affection to the entire family that they all feel the same way about him. Apu talks to him and asks for a kiss when he thinks no one is watching. Mamička, Jožka, and Marta aren't as covert, plucking him up any moment they can to nuzzle their faces into him.

"Let's take him out," Janči suggests to Marta one afternoon, who immediately runs to the closet for their gear. As they begin putting on their shoes, Gypsy knows they're going somewhere and stands excitedly beside them. Bringing out the basketlike muzzle and black leather leash from the closet, Gypsy begins eagerly running around Janči in circles, knowing he gets to be part of their outing but making it difficult to put his leash on.

Outside, Janči lets him loose in the forest, free from his muzzle, where he bounds around, a tiny speck in the tall grass, easily getting lost. His little legs won't take him far, alleviating any concerns about losing him. He does wander off to explore and mark his territory but never out of their sight. Still, they diligently watch.

Playing catch with Gypsy is difficult because most branches they find are too big for him to carry. He tries to lift one in his mouth, but he can barely get his teeth to make a firm grip around it. It just wobbles until he can't hold any longer and drops it. Janči finds a smaller twig Gypsy can actually fetch and return back to them. He throws it, but not too far for Gypsy's little legs. He races through the snow, returns and drops the twig in front of them, anxiously looking up, waiting for another throw. Marta picks it up and throws it a much shorter distance but one that is still a journey for Gypsy. Endlessly, he runs back and forth until all his energy is spent. Janči picks him up and starts walking home. Clearing the trees, their house warmly stands across the road. Behind them, twilight has fallen over the forest.

Homework is at the forefront of Janči's thoughts, fermenting in his mind as he walks home with Ali. The sting of Mr. Dubček's ruler forcefully hitting his buttocks right on target causes his walk to be slightly lopsided.

Unable to find the stick he would normally use to beat children who he claimed were rowdy, Mr. Dubček's resorted to the ruler sitting on his desk. This isn't the first thrashing Janči has endured under the cruel hands of his teacher. Several, if not all of the other Jewish students have bared the red welted skin that turns into hideous purple bruises, the soreness lasting long after the initial strike, making the act of sitting in a classroom chair almost unbearable afterward.

Assignments in geography, reading in history, and twenty questions in math have been given with a due date of tomorrow, not leaving much time for him to procrastinate as incomplete homework would automatically render another beating, one that he aptly wants to avoid, given the current state of his raw skin.

Upon entering his house, he instructs himself to promptly begin his work, starting by learning the capital cities of states in America. Only afterward will he reward himself with time to work on his new jigsaw puzzle of a cowboy on a large white stallion. In the front hall, he almost trips over luggage that surprisingly isn't theirs. Bulging out the sides, the black leather bags with color fading to gray where it's been worn out resembles the suitcase Janči uses when going to Beluša, with as much crammed in as possible. No trips have been planned to his knowledge, and visitors weren't expected. Confused, he goes further in the house in search of answers.

In the living room, rigidly sitting on the walnut couch is a family he's never seen before. A lankly boy slightly younger than him with the clearest skin stares back with gloomy eyes that are overpowered by a soothing face and docile demeanor. His mother is slightly plump with cheeks that have a natural rose blush. Sincerity emanates from his father, a thin beard framing his lean face, straight white teeth exposed through his numerous smiles. Intently, he speaks in German with Apu, Janči understanding most of it but trying to piece together unfamiliar words in order to make sense of what is going on. One unusual word stands out among the rest that he's never heard before, tweaking his interest, and he commits it to memory for later when he can ask Apu about it: *Anschluss*.[25]

---

[25] *Anschluss* is the annexation of Austria into Greater Germany by the Nazi regime.

Apu looks up and sees Janči. "Janči, come here."

He walks over, diffident of the situation.

"Please meet the Meyers. This is Dietmar, Hilde, and Erich," motioning to the young boy. "They will be staying with us for a while. They came all the way from Austria." Seeing all the questions floating in his eyes, Apu continues. "Austria is not a very safe place right now for Jewish people, so we have to help them. They will be safer here."

"Okay." Janči nods. "I'm Janči," he says, personally introducing himself to the Meyers. Focusing on Erich, he continues, "You'll have fun living here. We play lots of games in the forest right behind the house. You'll get to meet all my friends. They're very nice." Erich smiles, relaxing more in this house full of strangers.

Jožka is in the kitchen helping Mamička with dinner. Pots are cooking all four iron rings of the stove.

"Janči, could you help set the table, please? Don't forget to set an extra three places. The Meyer family will be staying in Omama's old room. That way, we'll all have some privacy."

"How long will they stay with us?"

"I don't know."

Looking out the window, Janči sees a small black DKW parked in the laneway adjacent to their backyard. It must be the family's car all the way from Austria. It couldn't possibly have fit a fraction of their belongings, forcing them to leave most things behind. Thinking of his own belongings, Janči wouldn't be able to decide what to part with, everything too important for him to desert.

"And Erich will be going to the same school as you."

Janči takes his homework to the living room, wanting to be around his family instead of alone in his bedroom. Steadfastly, he completes it and then just sits there, staring into space, thinking about all the unexpected events of the day.

"Janči," Apu says, looking up from his book. "Is everything all right?" Janči shrugs, unsure. "Come here," Apu waves him to the bed. "I know this is all very confusing for you, with the Meyers staying with us now, but like I mentioned, it's what we can do to help."

"Things are really that bad that they had to leave their home?"

"Sadly, yes. The German Nazis have taken over Austria, and so the Meyers were worried about their safety and left home. Fortunately, things are better here, and that's why they came here." Janči nods, sympathetic to their situation, glad they are able to help them. Trying to move the conversation on a lighter note, Apu asks, "Did you know Dietmar is an engineer? He used to work in a factory manufacturing Minerva radios in Vienna. I bet he'll be able to teach you a lot about radios."

"That would be fun. I like Erich. He seems nice, just a little quiet."

"I'm sure he just needs time to open up. Leaving everything behind from him wasn't easy. He still needs time to get used to his new surroundings."

"I'll help him. I'll bring him out to play with my friends and show him how to make wood carvings."

"That would be very kind of you. And he would appreciate it." Pausing for a moment, Apu looks at Mamička who gives an imperceptible nod of encouragement. "I have some big news for you," Apu says, turning back to Janči. "I was going to tell you and Marta tomorrow, but since you're both here, I'll tell you now. Hoffmann-La Roche is sending all of us to Palestine early next spring. They've offered me a new job there."

"Why so far?" Janči asks startled at this unexpected update.

"We can't stay here anymore. Even though things are still okay, Trenčianské Teplice is not the place it used to be. It's only going to get worse, and I don't want to put us in such danger like the Meyers had to face, especially if we have a way out. There will be a good job for me there. I will be overseeing the building of a new pharmaceutical factory.

It's a great opportunity for me." Seeing Janči's fretted expression, he continues on, trying to convince him this is an ideal circumstance. "All our furniture and belongings will be shipped by sea to Palestine. Hoffmann-La Roche has already arranged our tickets and British visas. We will leave around the end of February or beginning of March. That should give us enough time to prepare."

"Okay," Janči says, unsure how he really feels about all this. "I think I should go to bed now." With a goodnight kiss from both his parents, Janči goes upstairs, puts on his pajamas, and crawls into bed, stunned, trying to digest the news that won't go down, not meant for the human body. His home, friends, and the only life he's ever known will be gone in only a few months. Now he can truly empathize with the Meyer family. Dubious about moving to Palestine because it is full of the unknown, Janči also knows Apu wouldn't make them move if it wasn't in their best interest.

It doesn't take long before Janči gets used to living with the Meyers. In a house so big with separate living quarters, getting accustomed to the new guests is easy, especially now that Marta and him have a new playmate in Erich. Upstairs in the house also lives a Czech family, not refugees, but lodgers renting a room helping to supplement Apu's income.

On afternoons that Janči is around the house, Dietmar begins teaching him about the inner workings of radios, using the Philips as a reference point. He starts with the basics—a radio is a simple circuit containing valves. He shows the capacitors and resistors, tuner scale, the mixer and the radio frequency amplifier stage, and finally, the audio amplifier. Peering through the rectangular cutout between the tuning scale and Philips insignia, Janči sees the moving capacitor part that acts as a tuning meter. Half the time, Janči is unsure of what he is looking at or the definitions of the words Dietmar uses, but Dietmar welcomes all his questions and provides as much clarification as necessary until Janči understands.

Friday's, Hilde makes plump dumplings and leaves them on stairs to cool. The temptation the previous week was almost too much to bear, and this week, Janči gives in, sneaking his hand into the large metal pot and taking a dumpling. He shoves it into his mouth before anyone catches him, but the dumpling is still too hot to eat and begins burning his mouth. He starts juggling it around in his mouth, blowing out the steaming air, too late to spit it all out. Hilde walks by to check on her pot and sees Janči. "What are you doing?" she lightheartedly asks. Unable to answer with his full mouth, she laughs. "I see you like my dumplings. Next time, wait till they cool down before you eat them," she says, teasingly giving him a playful slap on the wrist.

With the impending move to Palestine, English lessons for Janči and Marta are imperative. On the other side of the river Váh, a Jewish English teacher welcomes the two new students. The four kilometer round-trip is an hour's walk in each direction, two or three times per week. The private lessons will be valuable, helping them make friends and understand teachers better once in Palestine. Both siblings find it to be a strange language with letters showing up in the most peculiar places, and to make things even more difficult, some aren't even pronounced, like the "gh" at the end of *through* or *cough*. Then there are same-sounding words with different meanings and spellings, *see* and *sea*; *to, two,* and *too*; *there* and *their*. It's all very confusing, but they struggle through it, determined to be proficient, if not fluent, by the time they move.

In the summer months, with the nicer weather, the commute to their English lessons isn't as wearisome. Practicing their conjugations on their way home, Janči quizzes Marta in preparation for their tutorial.

"Conjugate the verb 'to be.'"

"I am. You are. She or he is. We are." She stops midsentence. Janči follows her stare to the wall of a local tailor.

"Janči, look what they did," she distressingly exclaims. *Zid je nas nepriatel*[26] is prominently displayed for everyone to see. A cartoon drawing below in black illustrates the words, depicting the stereotypical features of a Jew, a nose disproportionately large for his face, a balding head, and bushy eyebrows. Although she may not be able to read and understand the abusive words, she can deduce that the illustration is not comical. More Jewish store properties are defaced with slanderous graffiti, something they can't ignore each time they venture outside.

"You, Jewish pig, may your hands rot off!" "Do not buy from Jews." Bile rises up in Janči's stomach, the humiliation of it making his cheeks burn red with anger and his heart burn crimson with hate, disturbed that it is all in plain view for Marta to see.

Off of the main curved road Svobody, butted between other Buildings, stands the classicist Magistrát města Teplice.[27] A forest green triangular-domed clock tower transpires from the top, ornamented with a wind vane pointing in an easterly direction. Sloping downward over the fourth level is a burnt red roof, juxtaposed over butter-colored outer walls that are embellished with several windows on all three levels.

---

[26] *Zid je nas nepriatel* means "the Jew is our enemy."

[27] Magistrát města Teplice is Teplice's Town Hall.

Walking through the grand foyer, Janči veers to the right and approaches a door where indiscriminate letters signal his entrance into a world of books, all at his fingertips. Today, he'll take out three books for his trip to Babka's in a couple of days. Since he and Ivor will be there for eight weeks, he can't risk the chance of running out of reading material.

Pushing the door open, Janči is met with the familiar smell of paper pages and the written word that have been exhaustively read by countless eyes, all taking up space in the stuffy apartment-sized library brimming with books on dark wooden shelves. The librarian, with her black hair up in a bun and glasses balanced on her nose, is checking out books for some younger children who can barely see above the counter. A stack of picture books are piled high in front of her, and she neatly writes each book title and due date on the borrower's card as well as the library's record.

Janči goes to his section of the library where shelves are lined with books on cowboys, science fiction, and American Indians. It is almost like sorting through Apu's library at home, except the books there are leather bound and deal with politics and science. He pulls down a few books by Jules Verne, *A Journey to the Centre of the Earth* and *The Adventures of Captain Hatteras*. He then goes to search for some by Karl May.

"Are you boys almost ready?" Uncle Lajko calls from downstairs.

"We're coming." Learning from their struggles in the past due to overpacked suitcases, the boys have opted to pack lighter this time around.

Going through the repeated motions, they get driven to the train station much earlier than necessary, their zealousness not giving Uncle Lajko much other choice. They playfully roll their eyes while Uncle Lajko talks to the conductor because they are fully capable of making it to Beluša without any special assistance.

"Don't forget to transfer trains in Trenčianské Teplá," Uncle Lajko reminds them.

"We know, we know," they assure him, brushing off his concern. Once the train emerges in the station, the two boys climb on, not wasting a single second. Janči sits back in his seat, envisioning the days ahead while the locomotive slithers through the small towns of Czechoslovakia. Fishing expeditions will be the highlight on their agenda this summer.

Arriving in Beluša, Babka is punctually waiting at the station for them in their agreed upon spot, having carefully checked the time their train got in over and over, paranoid at the thought of leaving them stranded again. After dumping their luggage and eating vanilla cookies, they head into town to buy necessary fishing supplies. Stocking up, they fill tackle boxes with floaters, sinks, hooks, and plump brown worms for bait that won't stop squirming. Long, thin, and flexible cane fly fishing rods were already been packed when they left Teplice. Two rivers flow by Babka's house, making fishing too irresistible. One is the wide Váh, and the other is a smaller, lesser-known one that runs behind the orchard of the house.

Each day, they venture out, hoping their luck at catching something big like a pike or perch will materialize. Three weeks into their trip, and their catches have been nonexistent or meager minnows. All they have caught are heatstroke, bad sunburns, and aching arms from holding the rods all day, dampening their optimism. The basket of food Babka packs each morning filled with juice, fruit, jam sandwiches, and walnut cookies barely lasts them till lunch, their boredom from the lack of fishing action translating into incessant eating to pass time.

"Okay, Ivor, today is the day we'll catch a huge carp,"

Janči says, trying to motivate him with this possibility. They head out in their black swimming trunks, carrying their fishing gear like protective armor, and make their way through the tranquil trails masked by trees they've come to know so well. Rarely do they encounter people on their walk, the length of the trail spanning kilometers.

Janči sets his tackle box down and begins attaching the worms to their hooks, Ivor, too squeamish to do it properly. Whenever he tries, the fish take off with the bait and leave their rods empty. Even after numerous lessons, he can't bring himself to trace the sharp hook through a random part of the meaty worm while it continues wriggling in his hand. Ivor swears he can hear it pleading to stop the torture being inflicted on it, and so Janči is left with the job.

Along the edge of the river, they find a spot that provides them with sunlight and trees close by for shade. Instead of a weighted lure, their fly rods use the weight of the fly line for casting. Casting their rods in, they settle back into their standard positions and wait.

"Oh, I think something bit," Ivor elatedly says, feeling a tug on his line. Janči jumps up and helps reel the line in. Bringing it closer for inspection, it is easy to see that no fish is attached, and the bait is gone, proving, yet again, how smart these fish are. "Let's try for something this time," Janči flippantly says, dropping the line for Ivor to cast back out in the river. With no sign of any movement in the water, Janči sets his fishing rod aside, ready for a break.

"Are you hungry?" he indifferently asks Ivor, wanting to prompt the ceremonial opening of their food basket. Ivor feverishly nods, hearing growling noises stemming from his stomach. Setting their rods aside with the carp still dangling, untroubled, they plunge into the basket, retrieving apricot jam sandwiches on rye bread and washing it down with apple juice.

Reenergized, they pick up their rods again, focused on catching something worth all this time and effort. Two more hours go by before another jerk is felt at the other end of the rod. Ivor shoots up at the strong pull.

"Janči, help me. It feels like something big." Janči rushes over and works with Ivor to steadily reel the line in without compromising what might be waiting on the other end. Swaying from side to side is a large silvery carp with barbels on either side of its upper jaw. Measuring about forty centimeters long and weighing a few hefty kilos, they have won top prize for their fishing expedition.

"We should probably start packing up and heading back. We did well today," Janči says.

"We did! And I think Babka made her chicken soup for us today with *csiga*[28] noodles." Gathering their belongings and leaving the carp mounted on the rod, the weight of the fish bending it forward, they make their way back to Babka's along the river, their energy desiccated by the sun and fish. Advancing toward the two boys are ten gentile Slovak boys from the village whom Janči recognizes. Normally, this would be no cause for concern, but Janči's gut reaction to the menacing eyes reveals that this group isn't going to be friendly. "Ivor, I don't think this is good," Janči warns his cousin.

"What should we do?" he asks, the fright in his voice unmistakable.

"If we try to run, they'll just catch us. Just keep walking right by them, and don't look at them. Hopefully, they won't bother us."

Straightening up, trying to give himself extra inches of height and confidence, Janči continues walking alongside his cousin, not making eye contact with any of the group ahead. Ivor desperately tries to appear assertive, but the trepidation in his step minimizes the effect. He looks

---

[28] *Csiga* is pronounced CHI-GA and are small noodles for soup.

MONICA KOCSMAROS

down at the ground, his eyes skirting from left to right, but never straight ahead. As the group of boys get closer, their size grows exponentially, and the ten-year age difference between them and their potential targets become apparent. Beady eyes with a glint of corrupt waywardness glower down at Janči and Ivor, the bodies of this gang adopting an offensive stance. If their intention is to hurt, they undoubtedly will.

Between them the gap closes, siphoning off any chance of fleeing. Their footsteps on the dirt path get louder. Janči worries they can sense his fear, like a pack of rabid dogs. In one hand, Janči holds his fishing rod and in the other, he grips the tackle box so hard his knuckles are turning white.

"Where are you two going?" one of them with greasy hair and a blemished complexion authoritatively asks.

"Home," Janči simply states.

"I don't think you're going home just yet." He casts a glance with his steely eyes over at his friends and grins. They nod in perverse approval.

"What's that you're carrying?" he asks eyeing the fishing rods, and the carp dangling off the rod.

"We just went fishing," Janči tells him, trying to keep his voice from shaking.

"Give me the fish you caught."

"No."

His stare bears into Janči at the unwarranted answer. Trembling beside him, Ivor doesn't dare make a peep or any impetuous moves.

"Now I don't know about you, guys," he says to his friends, "but I don't know if these are true-blooded gentiles."

"Well, there's only one way to find out," one of his friend's sneers. The callous reality of what they're talking about sinks in as Janči follows their gaze between his legs.

"Run," Janči screams, dropping everything he's carrying. Their attempt at escape only gets them a few paces before several pairs of hands are grabbing Janči and Ivor from behind and throwing them down. With a thud, Janči sees Ivor's thin body hitting the ground a few feet away. Kicking, screaming, and wriggling around, Janči does anything in his illusory power to stop this from happening. Ivor, whose swimming trunks are already down at his ankles, has relinquished a fight even before he began. As much as Janči tries resisting, he's no match for the impervious hands that are pinning down his legs and arms, while the others gratuitously peel down his trunks, brazenly exposing what they are looking for, confirming their suspicions.

Crippled by a hopelessness and vulnerability unlike any other he's ever felt, Janči doesn't have the heart or strength to retaliate. All that seems possible is numbly waiting for it all to be over, temporarily removing himself from this space mentally and emotionally, and then afterward, he can unreservedly let out the tears that are filling his eyes. Once the brutes decide to leave, he can then start assembling the damaged fragments of himself that are being torn off.

"I knew it," the leader sneers. "Dirty Jews," another contemptuously spits. "Don't you know Jews aren't allowed to be fishing here. You're making our home filthy."

A sharp pain hits Janči's stomach, moving to his head and legs. The sensation of ten fists and feet taking their aggression out on his body is agonizing. Putting his hands up to shield his face, he curls his knees into his chest, completely helpless, succumbing to the attack. Ivor's screams of pain and the dull sound of shoes kicking his stomach, crashing into his ribs, pierce Janči's ears, each blow feeling like it's being inflicted on him and not on his cousin. Janči tries to think of a peaceful place—the meadows in the Tatras instead of the searing pain that has enveloped his entire body. The metallic taste of blood enters his mouth, his face violently shoved into the dirt, destroying his serene mental image. An eternity passes before they decide they've had enough, having taken out all their aggression on two bodies that now lay limp below them. To add to the humiliation of their victims, the group takes possession of Janči and Ivor's belongings, fishing rods, tackle boxes, and worst of all, their swimming trunks.

"Get out of here, you stinking Jews." Seeing they are in no condition to move festers them even more. "Get out of here, dirty Jews," they yell louder as if the volume of their words will instantaneously yank the two boys off the ground. Beaten, naked, and shamed, Janči tries getting up, but there is too much pain shooting out across every limb. Slowly, he gathers the strength he needs to make it up, the drive coming from not wanting to suffer another beating.

Ivor lies crumpled in the grass, quietly sobbing like a baby. Janči gingerly helps him up, careful not to hurt him even more. He clings on to Janči for dear life. With his arms wrapped around Janči for support, the two of them limp along the banks of the creek toward Babka's home two kilometers away. There are no words that need to be spoken as the humiliated and raging thoughts swim in their heads, never to drown, and sounds of twisted laughter echo behind them.

Horse drawn wagons rattle by above, ignorant of the state Janči and Ivor are in, going about their daily lives while two naked Jewish boys have been disgraced beyond repair. Another small creek meandering through the middle of the village offers a new route home, one that might spare them additional embarrassment of being seen. Preceding Ivor, Janči takes that creek, walking while crouched down, hiding from the people on the road beside them. Inexplicably, they make it back to Babka's, not paying attention to anyone who may have seen them. At the sight of her door, Janči is inundated with relief and breaks down crying.

"What happened to you," Babka cries seeing her grandsons walking through the kitchen door, bruised, bloodied, and naked. She rushes over and cups their faces in her two hands. Ivor begins to cry again, leaving Janči to explain. Before he can, she continues outraged, "Who did this to you?"

"It's okay, Babka. We'll be okay." Although Janči can hardly convince himself of that, unsure if he'll ever be the same again.

"Oh, my precious *gyerekek*."[29] She examines the children from head to toe and starts her grandmotherly work. Freely, Janči lets her, feeling safe in her hands. Using a cloth, she soothingly wipes the blood and dirt from their faces. Using rubbing alcohol, she cleans the wounds and kills any infection that may fester before she wraps them in bandages. Ice from icebox is retrieved and enfolded in another cloth to prevent the swelling of their bruised eyes and cut lips.

That night, Uncle Lajko and Apu make the insistent decision that Babka leave her home and come live with one of them. Ever since Uncle Lajko moved to Trenčín, they have always wanted her to move closer, but she shrugged off their request, resolute about staying in her familiar village. After much pestering, Babka agrees to move in with Janči's family, considering that at the age of sixty-four, if she doesn't do it now, she never will.

Two days after the incident, Janči and Ivor go home, not in the mood to continue their stay and be reminded of what happened to them. Janči's childhood memories of his summer escapades with Ivor in Beluša have now been tarnished, someone throwing a can of black paint over them. Internally, Janči struggles with the anger and bitterness being fueled like wildfire, not wanting to have the best days of his life overshadowed by

---

[29] *Gyerekek* means "children" in Hungarian.

this incident. He vows to do his best in keeping the good memories at the forefront of his mind and making all others fade into the background.

Babka is left to finish packing her belongings for her own move. Most of the furniture she's owned for a lifetime will have to be sold. Reminiscing on times of the past, she goes through her albums while packing them in boxes, memories she wishes she could recapture in the present day. Anything that doesn't need to go with her to Teplice will remain behind. Everything with sentimental value makes it into the several boxes and bags, items she is unable to part with and doesn't believe she should.

On her last day, she takes a look around at the home she made for herself and her family. She wanted to leave on her own terms, but instead, the decision has ultimately been made by a group of boys she will never know. Walking into the kitchen, she smiles at the recollection of her grandsons mischievously eating all the cookies she baked for them. Their bountiful laughter will never be heard between these walls again.

On September 30, 1938, Germany, Great Britain, France and Italy sign the Munich agreement. The western Czechoslovakian territory, the Sudetenland, has been turned over to Germany. This was a result of complaints by the German speaking population living in the region that the Czech majority mistreated them. This treaty is seen by the signing countries as a peaceful means to conciliate Hitler's greed for land. The Czech army is eliminated without a fight, and its arms and ammunitions taken into possession by the German army.

On the radio, Janči hears Chamberlain boasting "peace in our time" has been achieved. Obviously, Chamberlain didn't foresee that this appeasement by Western powers would lead to the outbreak of the Second World War only one year later.

Home has transformed into a large, comfortable prison cell with full amenities, minus the added luxury of outdoor recreation time. "It's too dangerous," Mamička tells them. Daily errands like grocery shopping are becoming riskier. The Green Frog and the library are distant memories. Like dust particles, secrets, conspiracies, and hidden agendas hover around them, giving Trenčianské Teplice a mask of orderly and justified conduct while hidden underneath is the complete uncertainty about their lives and future. Janči has been warned not to say anything against the new regime outside, keeping all comments within their four walls.

Refusing to put a halt to life and becoming a prisoner in his own home, Janči ventures on to the front porch, carrying a small piece of wood, testing the obtrusive boundaries imposed on his physical space. Through the overcast sky, the diluted rays of the fall sun do enough to invigorate him. Pulling out his pocket knife, he automatically starts shaping a train carving.

Footsteps approach him as he begins forming the wheels, the sound getting louder as the feet get closer. Looking up, Janči sees a familiar face that he doesn't want to. Klaus, a stocky older boy with blond hair always falling into his eyes, an aquiline nose, and thin lips perpetually curved into a scowl. The son of German parents is staring down at him. Janči is convinced Klaus's only objective in life is to torment him, probably something his father, Mr. Sommer, taught him. Mr. Sommer is a watchmaker who used to fix Apu's watches, but as soon as Slovakia turned fascist, he became a member of the Nazi Party. The children born of this group are a small minority in Trenčianské Teplice, and even so are particularly nasty. When living together with them in the same little town, there's nowhere to hide. One option for Janči is to run away, but where to? Because he's already home, and isn't home supposed to be the safest place? Hijacked by physiological changes, Janči's heart pounds rapidly, and his breathing becomes shallower. He can't think clearly as if a thick fog has settled over his thoughts.

"You are a dirty, stinking Jew. You don't belong here," Klaus yells so loud the vulgar words seep through the walls of the houses lining the entire street. The words, thrown like daggers, only pierce Janči's skin leaving a surface wound. Janči keeps looking at him, not letting his eyes waver, unsure how to react, but knowing he doesn't want to give in.

Inside, preparing a sandwich, Apu hears the resounding words laced with hatred. His body leaps through the kitchen window and chases Klaus down the street. Janči loses sight of them as they round the corner. A moment later Apu is walking back, fruitless in his valiant effort. Head hanging, he's disappointed. He was unable to protect his son and avenge his perpetrator. With his long, lanky legs, Klaus was too fast for him and got away. Janči's sure that's not the last he'll see of Klaus or the last that he'll hear those vicious words.

Almost a year has passed and the Meyer family is still living with them. No other options have presented themselves that are safer than the Teschner house. At the beginning, it was awkward sharing personal effects and space with strangers, but they have grown close to them and inherited a good new friend, each one empathetic to the other's circumstances.

The faint smell of smoke wakes Janči. He climbs out of bed and clambers down to his parent's bedroom, sleep still in his eyes. Apu is not in the room, and Mamička is looking out the window.

"What's going on?" he asks hoarsely rubbing his eyes. "I smell smoke."

"There's been an accident."

Janči runs over to Mamička observing the scene outside. The small black car, the one that had carried a family of three and whatever belongings they could fit, a car that was driving them to safety over treacherous land, sits in their backyard burned to the ground, the charred mess of steel remains, the skeleton of the car. Hilde and Erich huddle together outside, taciturnly watching, while Dietmar, Apu, and Opapa pace around the car.

"I want to go outside."

"No, Janči. Stay here," Mamička firmly tells him, and he knows with that tone not to argue.

Apu comes inside, the smell of smoke adhering to him. "Apu, what's going on? How did the car catch fire?"

"The car was parked on a slight angle so the gas started leaking out." Not understanding how that could cause the fire, Janči probes further.

"But what made it catch fire?"

Drawing in a deep breath, Apu begins. "Someone threw a match at the car," he candidly tells them, knowing it won't do any good to withhold this pertinent information from them. "We found the matches and some cigarettes beside the car."

"Oh," Janči nods gravely in understanding. "They did it to hurt the Meyers, didn't they?"

Hearing those words, Apu realizes the speed at which his son has been forced to mature in the past few years. "Yes. Whoever did it knew that they were hiding her."

"Because they're Jewish?"

Apu soberly nods, and Janči doesn't need to ask any more questions.

The suitcases Janči almost stumbled over close to a year ago are back at the front door. A driver pulls up outside, letting them know it's time to face reality and leave this house they've come to call home.

"Dežko, I can't properly express the amount of gratitude and appreciation we have toward your unlimited generosity. I don't know where we'd be today if it wasn't for you taking us in."

"You would have done the same thing for us."

Sadness revolves around their departure and can be felt through all the tight hugs, solemn goodbyes, and tears that are shed. Janči and his family stand on the porch, watching the two suitcases get packed into the taxi, and the Meyers slide into the back of it. Their meager waves and disconsolate faces, uncertain of what they will find at their next destination, become imprinted in Janči's memory. Then they are gone, and Janči never sees or hears from Erich again.

BECAUSE OF A FISHBONE, DECEMBER 1938

SIX OF THEM sit around the table on Friday evening for dinner, chattering on with the smell of food wafting into the dining room. Opapa just walked through the door in his black wool winter coat, having walked home in the cold from synagogue. He takes a seat at the table, unconcerned that the Shabbat traditions are not followed in the house. However, each week, Opapa does attend schul for prayer services and then sits down to eat with his family afterward. He will also be at synagogue tomorrow morning after opening Baračka, never imposing upon his family to attend, as he knows these are very personal decisions that only an individual can make for himself.

Snow lightly falls outside their window, creating a white layer on everything, almost making Janči forget that grass ever existed. Snowflakes gently land on the tree branches, delicately piling up, one on top of the other, creating a whimsical winter wonderland serenely undisturbed like a picture postcard. Although it looks cold sitting on the inside looking out, the temperature outside is quite pleasant. It's one of those mild winter days where you can play outside forever, the sky dimly lit from the reflection of the snow, carrying an orange tinge.

Janči intently waits for the plate of challah to reach him, always eager to demolish his favorite part of the meal. He takes the end piece, the softness of the dough melting in his mouth. Mamička and Babka start carrying out plates of piping hot matzah ball soup. The matzah balls, just like Mamička's dumplings, are the perfect consistency—not too hard and not too mushy. Babka carries out a medley of lightly steamed vegetables—carrots, cauliflower, and peas are bulging around the sides of the glass dish with a serrated diamond pattern at the bottom. White rice speckled with chopped parsley is in her other hand. Mamička carries out the main dish—lake carp—which they eat at least once a week. Straight from baking in the oven, the carp is drizzled with rich garlic butter sauce and a slight splash of lemon. On the side, cucumber salad has made it on to the table sprinkled with extra paprika. As the food is being passed around like an assembly line, Janči heaps everything onto his plate until there is no more room.

"Apu," Janči begins between mouthfuls, "I finished another carving. I have to show it to you later."

"I can't wait to see it." After quickly chewing and swallowing the food in his mouth, Apu's expression becomes even more spirited but mixed with a tinge of seriousness. "I should tell you all that everything for our move has been finalized. Our belongings have been put on the boat which should get to Palestine before we arrive there. Once we're there, I will begin in my new position immediately. This new facility I'll be managing is actually very quite interesting. We will be extracting the medicinal properties out of herbs. Hoffmann-La Roche has arranged a house for us, which is close to a school for the two of you," Apu explains, looking over to Marta and Janči, "and also to my work. It will be very nice being able to see you two every day. It will be easy to get used to a new life there, I promise. It may take a bit of time, but it will definitely happen."

Apu begins clearing his throat, each attempt becoming louder and more aggravated. Trying to heave up something from deep within his stomach, Mamička rushes over and instinctively begins hitting his back.

"Micka, something's not right. We need to go to the hospital," he manages to expel between coughing fits. Marta frantically stares at him, eyes wide at the vulnerable state he's in. "Apuka," she cries, adding extra stress to the already nerve-racking situation. Babka quickly scoops her up, moving her away from Apu. Opapa runs outside to wave down a taxi. They all pile in, squeezing into every square inch of seating. The twelve-kilometer distance between Trenčianské Teplice and Trenčín takes a nail-biting twenty minutes to drive with Apu not getting any better and no one being able to help him ease the coughing. Mamička incessantly talks to him, ensuring he remains fully conscious, although his breathing begins sounding forced, not enough air is getting into his lungs with each breath.

With the taxi still rolling to a stop, they begin jumping out and running to the door of the three-story hospital. Rushing through, they are met with a burst of air clinging with disinfectant, so sterile it's almost repellent. A severe looking nun, a nurse in a stiff white apron which looks like it's been starched one too many times, and a hat under which a mane of auburn hair is pulled back into a tight chignon, asks what the trouble is, oblivious or purposefully just choosing to ignore Apu's horrible coughing.

"We were just having dinner, and he started coughing like this. It hasn't stopped for almost an hour, and he can't breathe properly anymore. Please help him," Anu hysterically explains to the nurse.

"Calm down. I'm going to take him in, so a doctor can check him. In the meantime, you and your family wait here and there will be some paperwork for you to fill out," she apathetically tells them.

All five of them are cast into the waiting area, evasive of any knowledge on Apu's condition that they are worriedly seeking. Ignorant to what is going on behind the closed doors makes the passing seconds more overwrought than any Janči ever experienced. All he wants to do is go in there, hold Apuka's hand, and tell him he'll be okay. No family is there to be by his side, only the unemotional doctors, working like robots on him, seeing him as just another patient, a piece of flesh to be poked and prodded, not someone's apu.

Uncertainty hangs above them, a menacing cloud with no sign of passing, not allowing any rays of light to peek through to help ease their angst. Waiting is all they can do—the only power they have been granted enclosed within the four walls of this building. Under Janči, the gray chair squeaks as he changes position, nothing being comfortable, interrupting everyone in their thoughts for a second. Then the sound is gone, and they are pushed back under, drowning in distress. White barren walls stare back at him, gleaming tiled floors reflecting in the pendant lights hanging above, the bulbs enclosed in milk glass. Gurneys loll in the hallway against the walls, waiting for a severe injury that would merit their use.

A young surgeon finally transpires through the door that flaps behind him, an air of self-importance following his muscular body. He heads in the direction of Janči's family. A brief sense of relief comes over him knowing the surgeon has news about Apu.

"We have found that his lung has been punctured by what looks like a fishbone. It is quite serious. He will require numerous surgeries over an extended period of time and an extensive recovery period. We can't predict when he will fully recover, but we're confident he will."

Cries of happiness erupt, hearing the sought after words that Apu will be okay, not registering what came before—the numerous surgeries. Examining Apu's file, the surgeon informs them that he is the one scheduled to perform the initial surgery.

"Teschner, that's a Jewish name, isn't it?" His words are spiked with contempt and the obvious insinuation that his services will not be free. The noble profession of helping others is tainted with hypocrisy, his concern for the well-being of a human carrying certain stipulations. Staring at him coldly, knowing the impossibility of switching surgeons, and not having a friend in the nurses who are all nuns, Mamička pulls him aside and offers him the dollar bills he is soliciting in return for his work. Another option would be for them to take Apu to the Jewish hospital in Bratislava, a hundred and thirty kilometers away, but unfortunately, time is running out, and the first surgery needs to happen right away. Janči is now forced to put hope into a surgeon who doesn't care if Apu lives or dies.

They all inhabit their temporary home, the chairs even more unappealing now, knowing the amount of time they will have to spend in them while the surgery takes place. Janči falls into an erratic sleep, trying to make the time pass by faster. Each time he opens his eyes and looks at the clock hanging on the wall opposite him, the black hands barely having moved. No estimations on how long they'll be waiting here were given. Really, they should just be satisfied that Apu is getting the operation he requires and not being left to die.

The next set of news delivered to them is that the surgery was successful, but Apu still can't leave the hospital. His lungs aren't strong enough to survive without the assistance of hospital machines and nurses. More surgeries are also scheduled in the coming weeks.

—⚟—

Each day after school, Janči and Marta visit Apu, Mamička greeting them from her regular post in the hospital room. Although he is fully awake and coherent, all the tubes running everywhere pumping oxygen or some type of liquid unsettle his children, but he eases their fear by explaining what each apparatus does, switching their fear into curiosity and amazement. The two of them sit on either side of his bed and rhyme off what their day was like at school. Daily visits become a newly-adopted ritual they look forward to; however, with each passing day, the date of March fifteenth looms closer, producing a foreboding unease. It is their deadline to escape Slovakia before they can't anymore. Rapidly, the situation is getting worse, and they don't see an end in sight for Apu's committal to the hospital. Every day, they ask the doctors "how much longer" and are met with "it will still be a while."

Days turn into long drawn out months, and finally, at the end of February, Apu is able to come back home. Relieved, they begin gathering their things until a phone call shatters that plan. Although the fish bone has been extracted, the unsympathetic surgeon tells them that it will still take him three months out of the hospital to fully recover from the damage it caused to his lungs. Their fate is now sealed, stamped with wax that's not even dry—all of this because of a fishbone. Who would ever have thought that what they ate for dinner could alter the entire course of their lives like this.

Without Apu working, the steady income he used to bring in is dwindling. All of them are now extremely aware of how their Slovak korunas are spent. An extra income source becomes taking in more boarders. There is no scarcity of families and individuals looking for even an ounce of hope in surviving the war. Apu is able to offer them a bit of that hope, or perhaps just delaying the inevitable for a little while longer. Apu welcomes them all, more out of kindness than a need for money. Parents with young children, middle-aged couples, singles unable to bring their families with them, each one of them comes with heart-wrenching stories of all they were forced to leave behind and an uncertainty of their future.

Sitting around the radio in the evenings, the inhabitants of the house hear news of Germans abusing Czech tanks. Any semblance of a structured country has been utterly lost as Hitler's evil Nazi force leaves a trail of destruction behind everywhere it goes, invading the western Czech provinces of Moravia and Bohemia with no resistance, allowing him to declare the area to be a German Protectorate under the rule of the Germans. A puppet government is set up in the new Slovak Republic,

Slovakia finally getting the independence they've been demanding, and strategically, it's the German heroes that bequeath it to them. Almost immediately, anti-Jewish laws are enacted.

Janči and his family live on the side of the new Slovak Republic. Unable to leave at this point, Slovakia will remain their permanent home; immigrating to Palestine is a dream of the past. Their belongings are out at sea somewhere, lost to them, just like their hope.

THE WRONG WAY, MARCH 1939

A STROKE OF genius hits Janči in the middle of the night, finding its way into one of his dreams. Jerking with impatience, he can barely wait until the morning light comes through his window, telling him he can now go to the train station. Running out the front door with coins jingling in his pocket, he looks right, and seeing no cars approaching, crosses the street. An aggressive horn honks and someone slams on the brakes too hard, making a deep turquoise two-door Opel Olympia grind to a halt, only one foot short of hitting Janči. A disgruntled man with eyes bulging out of their sockets and foam forming at the corners of this mouth yells at Janči while simultaneous hand gestures try to articulate something foul. Janči then remembers—he looked the wrong way. Cars are now coming from the opposite direction, traffic having shifted from the left side to right overnight—the way it is in Germany. With a quick apologetic wave, Janči finishes crossing the street, this time, ensuring no cars are coming from the other direction.

Safely on the other side, he retrieves the coins in his pocket and carefully studies the new quarter the Slovak Republic has introduced. Placing it up against the old *hallier*,[30] they are a perfect match. With the new currency of coins already in use, the old *hallier's* are worthless, and Janči has an abundance of them left over.

Taking the streetcar to the tram station, he rushes off toward his anticipated landmark, the bright red candy machine. He pulls out two old *halliers* from his pocket. Although the sign informs him that the

---

[30] *Hallier* is the old Czechoslovakian ten-cent coin.

machine accepts the new Slovak quarter, he places the first old *hallier* into the narrow slot, the coin fitting in perfectly and dropping down into the receptacle with a clang. His finger moves across the buttons, deciding between the Stollwercks, caramel bonbons, and chocolate-covered candies. Stopping on the Stollwerck, his finger pushes the button. Silence ensues as the machine decides whether it wants to dispense the candy in exchange for a useless *hallier*. A rumble of noise sounds within, and a loud plunk signals that the candy has dropped into the tray at the bottom. Through the flapping glass window, Janči quickly retrieves it, feeling almost like a criminal, but the thrill was too exciting to stop. He inserts his second *hallier* and gets the same result. Elated at this most useful discovery, he runs home to show Marta and Ivor what his genius thinking has accomplished.

"I'll take you and show you."

They both look at each other, a bit nervous about the expedition but concede to coming along—partway.

"I don't want to go further," Marta says once they reach the bridge before the station.

"Yeah, I don't think I want to either," Ivor agrees.

The two of them leave Janči to do the dirty work with their money. Three coins clang down the dark receptacle of the machine. Triumphant, he returns to the bridge with three more candy bars.

A couple of days later, Janči craves candy again. He heads over to the tram station on his way home from school and puts in the first coin. Strangely, nothing happens, just the regular hum of the machine. *Maybe the machine is broken*, he thinks, trying another coin. Still nothing. Stupefied, he stands there trying to figure out what happened. The weight of a hand on his back suddenly disrupts his contemplation.

"Jančiko, what are you doing?"

Janči freezes in his tracks. Slowly, he turns around to face his unforgiving accuser, but instead, is met by the familiar face of the station manager, Mr. Komar, the father of Janči's good friend, Anička.

"I'm buying candies from the machine," Janči stammers.

"Yes, I see you're buying candies. But what I would like to know is what kind of money are you using to buy these candies?"

Muted, his rambling apologies can't find a way to his mouth. Shaking badly, he knows he can be severely punished for this. Janči's bladder, scared into shock, involuntarily releases itself, a warm stream of liquid running down his leg in plain view of Mr. Komar.

"Do you know what?" Mr. Komar asks, but doesn't wait for a reply. "I like you, and you are a good friend of Anička's, so I am not going to do anything to you. But you have to pay me back all the *halliers* you used with Slovak quarters. I can't use the *halliers* anymore, and I have to bring this money to my boss. Bring it to me by the end of next week, and we'll forget about this, just don't ever do it again," he says with a stern look.

According to Mr. Komar's calculations, Janči owes two and a half crowns all together. Babka is the only person he can trust with his secret and who can help him get the money. Without an immediate lecture, she walks to her room, Janči following her up the stairs. A window faces out to the river and beyond that, the train tracks. A quiet man from Bratislava is renting out one of the other rooms down the hall. Half of the bottom floor remains occupied by refugees flowing in from Austria, Germany, and Hungary.

Babka fishes into her worn out, cracking leather amethyst change purse and takes out the coins, a strict look on her face.

"Here, Janči. You go and pay back the station manager. We won't tell Apu about this and get him all upset. I assume you will know better than to do something like this again." Earnestly, Janči nods his head, and with the money in hand, he goes to pay off his debt earlier than anticipated.

—⚏—

Apu still requires that his dressings be changed on a regular basis, and Mamička is always there to make sure it's done, skillfully removing them and gently applying new ones. The glow in Apu's face is starting to return and lighthearted banter comes out of his mouth rather than concentrating on their unpromising future. Optimism becomes his own crutch to keep going even though it takes him almost a year to fully regain all his strength. In May, when the spring weather rolls around bringing the smell of mud and chirping of birds, Apu moves into a lounge chair in the yard on the lawn, tired of the musty air indoors, the sun tanning him to a perfect golden brown. He is entertained by Babka who expertly plucks a chicken she killed moments ago, exposing the bumpy skin underneath. She proficiently tends to the animals, which provide them with a supply of food while money is low, having done it when she owned her own farm.

In no physical condition to go back to work in Switzerland, Apu finds a job closer to home within another pharmaceutical company, Schnöbling, working as a chemist doing research. Based out of Prague, he still holds a work permit allowing him to travel from Slovakia to the Czech Protectorat. Every week, he comes home with the express train for a few days, and Janči waits for him at the station to welcome him home.

—⚏—

Drums start banging outside, a steady rhythm with one second between each beat, signaling an announcement for citizens. Janči scrambles out the front door, leaving his carving of a freight ship in the backyard. A thick red strap fastens the large drum around the stout body of the messenger. Doorways along the street are thrown open, filled with people curiously peering outside, waiting for the announcement to be made. Janči's ears perk up as the middle-aged town crier lets everyone know that on Wednesday, at the Market Square, new rules for Jews will be declared. Making a mental note of this date, Janči steals a glance back at the house, seeing his parents standing in the doorway, indifferent to the news.

When Wednesday rolls around, Janči leaves home while his parents remain behind, uninterested in publicly hearing the new rules. Arriving at the wide boulevard, its girth lined with trees and benches leading to the main square, he hears a loud voice projecting through the din of the crowd, trying to quiet the incessant chattering below. Hundreds of people have already gathered there, mostly Jews with a few gentiles scattered among them. Straining to see through the throng of bodies, Janči makes his way toward the stage, moving forward in the crowd to get a better view. A German officer wearing a dark green combat tunic and a fascist Slovak army lieutenant in his black uniform, stand on a makeshift podium of blue milk crates which somehow diminishes their legitimacy.

Deliberately removing his gloves, the officer clears his throat, preparing the harsh words in his mouth. Although the majority of the crowd understands the language, the Slovak lieutenant acts as a translator. Janči shrinks into the background, not wanting to call attention to himself, and intently listens, his mind reeling at the new laws he and his family must abide by or else face severe consequences.

"All assets Jews possess must be registered." *Does that mean all of Mamička's figurines*, Janči wonders.

"Jews can no longer run a business. All their business will be taken over by the Aryan Trustees who will supervise their management, sale, or 'aryanization.'"

What about *Baračka* and the pastry shop? How can those be handed over to strangers? Turning back, he catches the second half of a sentence.

"Carry with them a yellow star stating "JEW." No Jew can be on the street without this star. If they are caught without one, they will be punished."

A slight roar comes from part of the crowd while the rest remain dumbfounded, staring straight ahead, devoid of any emotion. One man holding his son's hand, has his jaw set in a hard line, his eyes stone cold, mentally trying to heave daggers at these men on the crates. Others continue to cry out in protest at this desecration of human rights.

Once the soliloquy is over, the crowd disperses, most unable to digest what they heard. A long list of anti-Jewish decrees, identical to those in effect in Germany, are now to be implemented here—designed to destroy the economic viability of the Jewish population.

Jančí walks home, perturbed, mistrusting everything and everyone around him. He tells his parents where he was and what he heard. They nod knowingly, already having been informed.

"Jančí, we just keep living the way we have been. A few obstacles are now in our way, but nothing we can't overcome."

Reassured and easily convinced of Apu's advice, Jančí tries to forget what he heard this morning and calls Eli over to play with Marta and him on this warm June day. Having an old friend around offers him the reassurance he desperately needs.

Wooden hula hoops become their source of entertainment. Each of them carries a stick to push the spinning hoops in front of them. Their speed turns from a walk into a run as they try to keep up with the hoops, daring not to lose them which would mean losing the game. Jančí's hoop has other plans in mind as it veers toward the river forty meters below them. It carts off the road and down the length of the steep hill. In his panicked state, without thinking, Janči runs after it down the embankment of the river. His body loses control traveling at such a high velocity, going down twenty meters, then thirty. From above, he doesn't remember the ravine being this steep when he started chasing the wheel. The last ten meters down to the river is filled with jagged rocks and sharp sticks. Nothing within reach can act as a brake mechanism. Unavoidably, he falls into the river. Thinking fast, he tries to break the fall with his arm, and immediately, excruciating pain shoots through, like thousands of knives stabbing him. Looking down, blood has covered his entire mangled arm. Oddly, the sight of it does not sicken Janči. His eyes absorb the unnatural form his hand has taken; the pain is just white noise in the background.

"Janči! Are you okay?" Eli cries down to him. Peering over the road, she and Marta helplessly watch, unable to safely make it down the steep hill themselves to help him.

"I'm okay!" he yells up to them to ease their concern. "I think I just hurt my arm."

Awkwardly, Janči gets up with his functioning hand. Each muscle in his legs contract and expand with every step while he manages to make the exhausting climb back up, clutching at rocks and cliff edges on his ascent to keep him moving along. His left hand is becoming scratched and scraped with all the grabbing and pulling, but it still does not compare to the state of the other one. Dangling limply, his right arm is still streaming with fresh blood, leaving a trail of his accident behind him. Marta madly cries at the top, not quelled by Janči's appearance. When her eyes reach his arm, the cries get louder and more out of control.

"Janči, your arm! We have to get home!"

"It's okay. I'll be fine. But we can start heading back."

Dreading the fair walk they have, his legs are beginning to feel like two pieces of lead walking through an ocean. Passing the tram tracks that run along the river, Janči watches as a streetcar runs off the rails. They still have halfway to go to get home, but he stops and curiously watches as workers lift the streetcar and put it back on the tracks.

"Stop watching. We need to get home," Marta bawls, tugging at his shirt. "Don't you see that you're bleeding?"

Seeing the worry consuming her, which he doesn't want to amplify, he continues his languid walk. An eternity later, their house comes into view.

"Janči's hurt. Janči's hurt!" Marta screams at the top of her lungs to anyone listening in the house. Apu is at work, so it is Opapa who comes to see what all the commotion is about.

"What are you screaming about?" he asks walking out of the kitchen. Spotting Janči's arm, it registers very quickly that he had another one of his incidents. "What happened to you?" he asks running over.

"We were playing and . . ." before Janči can finish his explanation, Mamička rushes downstairs followed by Babka, responding to the frenzied cries of her daughter.

"Janči! What did you do?" Her face becomes ashen, and her eyes start focusing in and out. Swaying slightly, Opapa glides behind to break her fall if she faints. Managing to recover from the sight of Janči's bloodied arm, she moves in closer to view the damage. All three of them cluster around, clucking at his mishap, and completely in shock at what his arm has become.

"I'm okay," Janči says, brushing off their concern. "I just fell," which seems like the simplest explanation to give.

"It must have been quite a fall. We need to get you to a doctor right away to check you out," Opapa says.

Large russet leather chairs and sofas are arranged in the waiting room of Dr. Bogner, a friend of Apu's. Janči and Opapa sink into one, waiting for the local doctor to summon them inside an examination room. Moments later, Dr. Bogner calls them in and scrutinizes Janči's injured arm, peering at it from all directions while Janči recounts the incident that got him there. Janči is placed in front of a seven-foot-tall machine that is held in place with tracking along the ceiling and wall. Dr. Bogner, who dons a lead apron, although one isn't given to Janči, places a film behind his patient. A loud noise erupts from the machine as it begins taking x-rays of the crushed hand.

"I cannot help you too much," Dr. Bogner says, examining the x-rays. "The bone has come right through the flesh. That is why there is an excessive amount of blood. You have to go to a hospital for this."

Mamička's next option is to call Uncle Lajko. She explains what happened, and within half an hour, he is at their front door, ready to take his nephew to the hospital in Bratislava on the express train. At the first hospital they arrive at, Doctor Lanik, an orthopedic surgeon, dissects Janči's arm from all angles, dubiously tutting while he does. The x-ray he takes confirms his hypothesis.

"Well, the only option we have is to amputate his arm." Janči prays he didn't hear that word correctly. Life would be over if he lost one of his arms. How would he make his wood carvings or carry Marta around or write at school? Uncle Lajko steps in, not satisfied with that option.

"Are you sure that is all you can do to help my nephew?"

The doctor insistently nods. "Yes. His arm is broken in six places. There is no way it will recover, and it will never function properly again," he indifferently informs them.

"No way. I cannot let you do that. My brother is not here, and what would he think when he comes home from work and his son is without an arm?"

"Well, here is a prescription for painkillers in the meantime."

Exasperated, Uncle Lajko hurriedly grabs the prescription and Janči, directing him out of the room and straight out of the hospital. "Amputate your arm! Is he crazy? We'll find a doctor who knows how to deal with this properly."

They spend the night in the elegant Hotel Carlton in a spacious classic-styled guest room where Janči can at least endure his pain in comfort. Endless searing pain forces him to take a couple painkillers, knocking him out minutes later.

The next morning, they head over to the Jewish hospital that Uncle Lajko heard about. More smells of disinfectants strike them upon entering. Janči goes from boy to guinea pig, with more x-rays taken of his arm. Dr. Neuman, the surgeon on duty, studies the x-ray and is amazed at what he sees.

"If your bone had shifted two millimeters more during its break, you would require an amputation, but that fraction of a quantity has made the difference in us being able to keep your arm intact. This is incredible. I've never seen anything like it in all my years." A wide smile stretches across Uncle Lajko's face and a cry of relief resounds from his lips, but it's hard to whose is louder—his or Janči's.

Stretching Janči's arm is the first step in this long healing process even before a cast comes on. To ease his suffering, he is inoculated with different vials of medication. He is placed in a special chair and then tied down. Gadgets and lights jut out of the chair, and six doctors surround him, each one holding his body down in various places. Three doctors take his right hand and pull it as much as they can for two hours, which is necessary as his bone has split on an angle, protruding from his skin instead of lying neatly underneath it, making it two inches shorter than his other one.

Dr. Neuman draws a picture of a conceptual device, the first one of its kind. It is made from wires, and inside the wire, there is a tension bolt with a nut. It will be attached to Janči's side, supporting his arm. When the doctors are satisfied that they can't stretch his arm any more with their own force, they place it in the new machine that has been promptly constructed. In an L shape, Janči's arm cannot instinctively retract, ensuring the proper healing process takes place. If the machine was straight, his arm would go back to the decimated state it was just in.

Every day, for six long and agonizing months back home, Dr. Bogner will have to monitor Janči's healing and tighten the tension bolt which will gradually stretch his arm until the bones aren't parallel to each other, a process Janči will quickly learn feels like torture, the pain utterly unbearable. The hope is that his muscles will be strong enough to pull together back over the bone.

"Your arm will be saved, but I don't know how it will affect you. As long as you don't have any damaged nerves, you should be fine."

Janči learns to do everything with his left hand, Mamička teaching him to eat, write, and dress himself to the best of his ability. He can still bend the fingers on his right hand, but it's still of no functional use to him. He doesn't go to school as regularly because it is too difficult. Someone always has to open the door for him, and he is placed at a separate desk where he sits alone as if in quarantine, far enough to prevent anyone from hitting his arm mistakenly. He switches beds with Apu, sleeping beside Mamička because his bed is too narrow to accommodate the machine. Janči sleeps on his back with his arm stretched out to the side.

To help the healing process, Janči is given calcium and cod liver oil. The pale-yellow, thin, oily liquid in the bottle with its fishy taste is hard to swallow, let alone keep down, but Janči is not given a choice in the matter. Holding his breath each time, he swigs back the oil and downs it in one gulp, the stomach-turning aftertaste lingering in his mouth.

A week into having this contraption as an extension of his body, going everywhere he does, Janči begins getting antsy, only being able to sit for a few minutes before the need to get up and do something overwhelms him. Laughter resounds from the backyard causing Janči to go out and investigate. He sees Marta playing with her two new friends, Eva and Babitza, Hungarian refugees that came to their house with their mother. Crouching behind trees and receding behind bushes, the three girls play an endless game of hide-and-seek. Janči seats himself on the sawhorse and unable to participate, his only alternative is to watch. Unconcerned with his stability on the sawhorse, he lets his legs freely dangle below. Mamička spots him through the kitchen window.

"Be careful, Janči. Don't fall off." He acknowledges her admonishment with a noncommittal wave and resumes watching the girls play, jealous at the freedom of their limbs. Adjusting his bulky apparatus, he feels his weight shift unevenly, the balance slipping out from underneath him, and he topples backward, contraption and all. A screaming Mamička runs out of the kitchen into the backyard toward him. Half an hour later, he's back at the familiar doctor's office. Dr. Bogner is displeased at having to take more x-rays. Luckily, no further damage was done. Jožka has now been promoted to act as his personal bodyguard, keeping an eye on him. She will open doors for him, help him eat, and go to and from school with him. Now he has two new appendages.

Bored, he single handedly invents a clamp from a few pieces of wood. In order for it to work as it should, Janči sits on it, then inserts a piece of soft wood, able to finally start carving again with his sharp pocketknife, this time using his left hand that has to get used to the contours of the knife and the way it slices through the wood.

After six arduous months, the time finally comes to get his arm out of this inconveniently wretched pain-inflicting machine. His body is in terrible shape since the machine has been bandaged to it for so long. As soon as his arm comes out, he feels that it's dead, useless, and limp. He can barely move it. All his sense of mobility is gone.

Janči is commanded to use physiotherapy equipment in the spas and to start lifting weights. The first task he is instructed to do is to cut wood with an axe. He looks at Apu, and Uncle Lajko is startled at the egregiousness of their request. Apu and Uncle Lajko take him out to the backyard with Opapa following, an awful initiation stunt, and give him the axe with a dense wood handle. Gripping it in his left hand, he is scared to put any of that weight into his right. Patiently, they wait, standing around as if waiting for a bus while Janči builds up his courage. Finally, he transfers some of the weight to his right hand, the grip noticeably weaker, feeling like he will drop it at any moment. Gradually, he shifts more weight. He shakes his head in defiance, tears stinging his eyes.

"I can't do it," he pleads.

"You have to. We'll all be here as long as it takes you," Apu tells him.

An hour later, tired from the monotonous passing of time, Janči swings the axe around, and the blade breaks down on the wood. Agonizing pain shoots through his muscles, which have drastically atrophied.

Eva, Babitza, and their mother continue onward with their uncertain journey, leaving the Teschners' house as they can't seek refuge there forever. Replacing them is a tall Slovak Jewish teacher, Jozef Mittleman, who is joined by his pregnant wife. The young couple, with a pleasant and nonintrusive disposition, stay for a few months in Opapa's bedroom. Opapa moves to the main floor, where the rest of the family is. Janči already moved down there a few months ago to make room upstairs for the boarders and refugees. Luckily, there is a self-contained kitchen upstairs that the guests are able to use for their cooking without disrupting the Teschners downstairs.

The education system morphs into a cultlike nationalist curriculum where teachers preach about Slovak history, Slovak heroes, and the Slovak people who fought for the Slovakian language. Students learn more about Hitler, and they celebrate his birthday on April 20 along with all German holidays like the fiftieth birthday parade where Berlin is ornamented with flags and floral displays by its citizens and throngs of Germans congratulate their leader, proudly thrusting their hands out in front of them. Around Janči, even the hands of students are vehemently doing the same, demonstrating their allegiance to the Germans. Luckily, summer is approaching, and Janči can escape from all this.

Happy to be done with school, Janči is ecstatic about being in Trenčín for part of the summer and starting Boy Scouts again. Today is his first meeting of the year. Bursting through the front door after spending time playing outside, with a quick hello to Mamička and Apu, he runs to his room. Getting undressed, he eagerly looks at his uniform hanging in the closet as if on display in a museum. He takes the khaki shirt and olive green shorts in his hands and delights in the fact that in a few hours, it will finally be against his skin, letting people know he is a Scout. All his clothes are stripped off and haphazardly strewn about. Delicately, he lays out the uniform on his bed, momentarily admiring it. He puts his arms through each sleeve of the shirt, pulls up the shorts, hikes up the socks and laces up his shoes with a strong knot. Looking in the mirror, he feels the uniform emanate a sense of power through his body with a pulse of its own. Hurrying out to the living room, keen to get to the meeting, Janči is met with a heartbroken look from his parents. He is told simply that Boy Scouts are no longer operating. They have been disbanded to allow room for the Hlinka Youth Movement, recruiting only non-Jewish youth. Under his feet, the ground is slowly slipping away, and Janči is losing control over aspects of his life he once looked forward to. He hangs his head in utter defeat, knowing there is nothing more to do or say, and goes back to his room to undress.

At the end of summer, school is also removed from Janči's daily schedule. Home tutoring becomes the only alternative available to Marta and Janči, and Mamička adopts the role of school teacher. Disheartened at being denied a right to an education and at not being able to see his friends each day anymore at school, Janči puts his favorite games like hide-and-seek at the back of his mind. Maybe he can still find a way to play with Eli after school. His worst fear is that she will begin regarding his religion as an infectious disease, not wanting to contract it. To his relief, she remains his loyal friend and still plays with him and Ali, just as outraged that they can't attend school anymore. But their play time is short lived, not by choice, but because Eli's parents are concerned about her safety.

Grappling with losing his non-Jewish playmate, a sense of turmoil and feeling uprooted from a stable life makes each day harder to cope with. The simplicity of life, the days of freely going anywhere, the unassuming walks with Opapa and Apu, are all found in the past tense now, and the future is starved of optimism. All he wants is another carefree Sunday picnic with the family where their only concern is what to pack for lunch.

Thinking about what his life is becoming, a wave of fury swells inside him, and unable to contain it, Janči runs out into the backyard screaming a deep guttural cry that momentarily releases his frustration, pain, and anger—all emotions converging as one. All his fond memories of everything he misses dearly play themselves like a movie reel in perfect detail in his head.

Mamička comes running outside with harsh look on her face.

"Janči, stop that right now. Do you know how dangerous it is for bring that kind of attention to our house? We can't talk about these things outside."

The scream lodges itself back in his throat, and the invisible muzzle is back on his mouth. The agitated thoughts don't stop, and now they have nowhere to go, bottling themselves back up inside his head. Mamička goes back inside dragging Janči with her.

Shortly after the home-tutoring begins, Apu learns of a Jewish school in Trenčín that Janči is able to attend the following year. Excited at this prospect, Apu enrolls Janči even before discussing it with him. Hearing this news, Janči's spirits lift, and he daydreams about being back in a classroom with a blackboard and other children his age.

In October, the first deportations of Czech Jews to concentration camps in Poland begin. Only three years later, seventy-five percent of Czechoslovakian Jews are deported, most of them killed at Auschwitz.

ŽID, 1940

JOŽKA HAS TO leave. Jews aren't allowed to employ workers anymore. Janči is distraught at this news, feeling like he's losing an older sister. Standing at the front door, Jožka says her tearful goodbyes to everyone. She has been part of this family for so many years it feels like her own. Once it is Janči's turn, he feverishly hugs her, and she discreetly puts something in his hand. Without looking, he already knows it's a chocolate covered prune.

"Promise you'll still visit," he imperatively tells her.

"You know I'll do whatever I can," she softly replies, knowing she probably won't ever see the Teschner family again. She picks up her suitcases, waves one last time, and then turns around heading toward the train station, not wanting to draw out this sorrowful ordeal longer than necessary. Her heart can't take it.

Each radio in every Jewish household is recalled, having to undergo a surgical procedure where a hole is drilled in the tuner button and a piece of lead plumb cabling is put through, causing the tuner to remain in one static position, only playing news from one station in Fascist Slovakia—Tiso Bratislava. Accessing news from Budapest or Vienna is no longer permitted on their Phillips radio. Being nosy, Janči opens the back of the radio to examine the reworkings. Using his hand, he manually turn the capacitor to any station he wants—BBC in London, others in Zürich or Malmö Sweden, even the sweet sounds of Beethoven's Fifth before the

BBC news. An extra state-approved radio is kept in their house as a ruse that needs to be dusted off once in a while to maintain the appearance of use.

Apu and Opapa burst through the door each day, each wearing an immaculate suit, anxiously having waited for this time to share a new joke mainly about the Germans, with the family.

"Shall we go on the nut today?"[31] Opapa asks, expectantly waiting for the laughter once the punch line of the joke is figured out. Giddy with amusement, they manage to keep their spirits up when everything else is collapsing around them.

Walking to buy groceries with Mamička, Janči presses his face against the invisible chain link fence, peering longingly through to the other side where children carelessly splash about the water, throwing colored balls in the air, shrieking as they chase one another through the shallow end. Grudgingly, he turns around to leave, kicking a rock standing in his way.

Back at home, the conversation between Opapa and Apu defaults to politics as it always does, especially during these unstable times. Opapa carefully relays new developments he's learned of—no detail escaping his mind—to Apu who is home from work. With each fact comes Opapa's carefully constructed and logical opinion. Janči catches traces of their conversation over the sounds of the radio playing in the living room.

"The Germans are continuing to rearm."

"This doesn't look good for us," Opapa seriously comments. "The situation isn't getting better and it won't. Germany has gained too much of a hold."

"We'll just have to wait and see. There's not much else we can do at this point." Yielding to the quandary they have been unwillingly thrown into, like pigs in a slaughterhouse. Janči puts his hands over his ears,

---

[31] *On the nut*, literally translated in Hungarian, means "radio."

creating a wall for the words to bounce off and land on the floor, not making any impact on his life.

—⚏—

Outside, the winter hills are summoning Janči and Ali to go tobogganing. They each stuff the last bite of their egg sandwiches into their mouths, swiftly bundle up in their hefty snow gear, and hurry out of Janči's house. Waddling more than walking, the padding of the snowsuit impedes their full range motion. Powdery snow outside creates the perfect tobogganing conditions for them today.

"This time, I'm going to beat you," Ali says to Janči confidently.

"We'll see about that. You never beat, me so what makes you think today will be different?"

"I've found a new way to steer my sled. I can go faster now."

Janči smiles at his friend's determination. "Okay, Ali, whatever you say."

As he begins mounting the hill, Janči feels something hard hit the back of his head. Ready to retaliate against Ali, he turns around, but instead, sees a group of six German kids who derive pleasure from harassing him. Another snowball hits him in the chest with added force, winding him for a second—the snow too easy to compact into weapons. Ali also gets pelted with these missiles. One after another, they are thrown with no intermission, pummeling the two of them, leaving no chance for them to make their own revengeful snowballs. Rather than continue to suffer the humiliation, they run, something they've grown used to, not letting the toboggans out of their grips even though the weight and awkward shape of them doesn't help their hasty getaway. Eventually, the snowballs fall short of hitting them because of the distance they have gained from their perpetrators. Exhausted, they fall into the snow, trying to catch their breath. High hopes of having a fun day tobogganing have been crushed. Glumly, they walk back to Janči's house, lean their toboggans against the wall in the doorway, get out of their winter gear, and sit in the kitchen staring out the window. All they see are the snow-covered hills waiting for more children to come and play on them. It won't be them today.

Four Hlinka militia guards clad in black Fascist uniforms complete with a double red cross inside a white circle on a blue armband are disrespectfully yelling at Ali's mother inside her bakery. "This bakery and your general store are now property of the Slovak Republik. You are no longer authorized to run any type of business in this city. However, you are still to work here under our supervision.

"How can you do that? We own these businesses!" Mrs. Altman protests.

The ringleader, wearing a gold wedding band, grotesquely sneers at her, contorting his already-unsightly features. The puglike nose and wrinkles on his face age him well beyond his years. His steel blue eyes, void of emotion, do not seem to have the capability of looking lovingly at a wife, yet he has one. The snarled lips, spitting such harsh words, couldn't possibly speak kindly to a child, and yet he probably has a few.

"Not anymore."

Throwing the papers at her, he takes one last triumphant look around at his new property and leaves with his entourage in tow.

Ali's father walks toward the bakery, his arms filled with paper bags containing flour, sugar, and the butter needed to bake shortbread cookies that are in high demand. He is anxious to get started on them before more orders are placed. The bell rings as he opens the door to the bakery, unaware of the fact that it's not his anymore.

The next day, the same insolent guards return. They audaciously take a seat at the front of the bakery, outstretch their legs, and watch all the work that is being done by Ali's family. Demands for pastries and coffees frequently flee their mouths causing Ali's mom or dad to stop what they're doing and attend to the superfluous needs of their new bosses. With the constant shuffle back and forth and dealing with the critiques of not cleaning thoroughly enough or not kneading the dough properly, productivity decreases with fewer baked goods lining the shelves. Customer service falters with not enough time to properly attend to them. High profits the business once used to enjoy dwindle, and the guards can't figure out why. Blame lands on the Altmans for not working hard enough.

Loud knocking stirs Janči from his sleep. Rubbing the sleep from his eyes, it takes a moment to realize he's not dreaming as the knocking gets raucous and more persistent on the front door as if substantiating its reality. The arms on the alarm clock show that it's two in the morning. *Who would be knocking at this time?* he wonders.

Momentarily disoriented, Janči remembers he is sleeping in a bedroom downstairs on the main floor room because his room has been given to a Jewish couple who escaped Hungary and needed a place to stay. Janči creeps out of his room and sees Marta peeking out of his parent's bedroom. The two of them tiptoe down the hall behind their parents who are already close to the front door, getting extremely nervous, each step inciting fear. Janči wonders if Apu should even open the door, but if whoever's on the other side wants to get in, they will.

A group of five men stand in their doorway. Hlinka Guards wearing long black leather coats cinched together with a black belt. Around the arm is the signature blue band bearing the double cross. Black pants are stuffed into tall black leather boots that almost reach their knees causing the pants to billow out like a parachute. Without waiting for an invitation, they move past Apu and welcome themselves into the Teschners' home.

"Do you have a blanket?" one of them gruffly asks.

Mamička, without asking any questions, goes to the closet and pulls out a light blue wool—one which she mildly thrusts over to the man without enough force to accuse her of being uncooperative. A quick motion of his head gets the other four scurrying about the house, like mice running away from a looming cat. Cupboards, armories, and drawers are being opened, but not closed by the hands of these discourteous thieves. Personal belongings are swiftly rummaged through, the valuable ones plucked out in mere seconds. Violation seeps from all corners of the house.

"Over here," the young one shouts. His arms are already stacked with Mamička's fur coats, and he needs assistance in retrieving more items. Apu bought the black one for her twenty-seventh birthday when they had all their family and friends over for a dinner party in celebration of the event.

Methodically dismantling the house, another one swipes all the glass cabinets with Mamička's precious gold, crystals, silver collection, and Dresden and lace porcelain statues and sculptures. Into the blanket goes the one of the men walking in a park, a young ballerina, and a pair of birds. Janči turns his head not wanting to see the rest being lifted.

"I need another blanket," Janči is told. Without a choice, he fetches them another one that is stockpiled with more of their possessions. As hastily as they came, they leave, efficiently carrying with them things the Teschners have had in their family for decades, not just material items that can be replaced, but dolls holding sentimental value, birthday gifts from family who have passed away, and wedding gifts bearing loving inscriptions. In less than twenty minutes, they have left Janči and his family completely shattered. Fright resides in Opapa and Babka's eyes. Mamička is inconsolable. Apu takes her in his arms that are deflated of strength, bitter about not being able to protect his family as he once used to.

"They won't be back."

"It doesn't matter anymore. We can't do anything even if they come back. All we can do is sit here watching them while they take everything of ours."

"The main thing is we're all okay. They didn't hurt us." But the end of that sentence feels like it should have a comma, not a period.

―〰―

Slovak Fascists do visit their home again. Barging in, the self-righteous intruders take what they missed on their last looting, more jewelry, and the wedding bands melded onto Mamička and Apu's fingers are pried off. They even take the inconceivable—Mamička's piano. Systematically, they have all the man power required and the right sized vehicle waiting outside, already loaded with chairs, coffee tables, and cabinets from prior lootings. It's as if they had made a mental note on the first visit of what they couldn't steal, so they were able to plan better this time around. Days filled with music are abruptly coming to an end.

―〰―

The Jewish school is about twenty kilometers away, but that doesn't matter to Janči. He just wants to bring back some normalcy to his uprooted life; the commute, even through hail and snow, is an insignificant detail. The school runs from eight o'clock in the morning until two o'clock in the afternoon, taking up a large chunk of his day, keeping him occupied outside of home. Janči takes the electric street car to the train station in Trenčianské Teplá, and from there, the train to Trenčín every day, twice a day, by himself. Marta stays at home because the distance is too far for her to travel at that young age.

In a matter of time, carrying a star becomes insufficient, and one must be worn on the exterior of their clothing, decorating them with humiliation. Stars can be purchased, but in order to save money, Babka begins sewing these stars for them, using yellow material she finds in their house. Sitting in a chair in the living room, each stitch she takes with the hands that that cared for a multitude of relatives is another puncture wound in her dignity. In time, these stars are generously provided to the Jews, relieving Babka of her duty to sew them. Before going to school, Babka hands Janči a bright yellow star with the word *Žid* that she wordlessly attaches to his jacket.

"You can go now," she says in a voice barely audible. Janči looks down, unnerved by the sight of the star but not saying anything.

Outside, he catches too many eyes smoldering through the star on his chest. This bright yellow star becomes permanently affixed to Janči's wardrobe—a constant reminder of how people view him, a constant reminder of the insidious hatred.

Within the four walls of their home, supplies are quickly diminishing, prompting Janči's parents to ration the remaining food to sustain them for as long as possible. Even in their current predicament and amid the risk that lies outside, Apu does not hesitate to act as the head of the Khila, the Jewish community in Trenčianské Teplice. Resolutely, he puts two *pishkes* by the door, a white and blue metal money box with a slit on the top. *Keren Kayemet*[32] is written on one and *Keren Hayesod*[33] is written on the other.

Throughout the house, the doorbell chimes, echoing off the walls, a sound that has become more common each day. Apu opens the door with Janči squeezing in under his arm to get a better look at the middle-aged couple standing on the other side. A little bit of money is unquestionably doled out to these people who come to the house desperately asking for anything that can be spared as they try to live one day to the next, displaced without a place to call home anymore. Food, however, cannot be offered to the religious Jews as Mamička doesn't keep a kosher kitchen. Janči studies the man with the long brown beard who is extremely grateful for his father's generosity as they all always are.

"Janči, this is a time when education is not enough for you. Times are hard for Jews, especially the doctors and lawyers, so you have to learn some practical trade while going to school. Is there anything you would like to learn?"

Carefully appraising his options, Janči points out his technical inclinations toward electrical and radio work. Not wasting any time, Apu phones a man he knows and arranges for Janči to begin work as an apprentice, an apprenticeship that Apu has to pay for since Janči is underage to work for wages.

Every day, after school is done at two o'clock, Janči is to make the short twenty-minute walk to his new job, the electrical store, Electro Štrba in Trenčín across the square from his high school. Swinging the

---

[32] Keren Kayemet is the Jewish National Fund founded in 1901 to develop land in Palestine for Jewish settlement.

[33] Keren Hayesod is the central fund-raising organization in Israel, founded in 1920, calling on the "whole Jewish people" to do its duty to the land of Israel.

front door open, Janči is mesmerized by the irons, radios, iceboxes, vacuums, and chandeliers on display, waiting to be sold.

"You must be Janko," a presentable middle-aged man assumes walking toward him, his large green eyes twinkling. His thin lips, curled into a distinct smile, are almost obscured by a thick beard. Janči is amazed by his spotless skin and abundance of wavy salt and pepper hair.

"Yes, I am. Nice to meet you," he says, offering his hand.

"Well, let's get right to it. You'll be working in the back where all our repairs are done. Dodko Dotkozus has been working here for a while, so he can teach you everything there is to know." Janči follows Mr. Štrba out the back of the store and through a gate into the large workshop, which is in a standardized disarray of parts of pieces belonging to what were once functioning radios and appliances.

"Dodko, this is Janči. He'll be your apprentice."

A tall six-foot teenager comes forward. In order to properly make out his facial features, Janči tilts his head up. Brown hair recklessly falls over his tall forehead, framing intelligent blue eyes that seem to know more than his seventeen years. His slim physique detracts from his threateningly tall stature. His lips curl up into a large smile, cheerfully greeting Janči.

"We'll have lots of fun together, and there is definitely a lot to learn, but I'm sure you'll be an expert in a few weeks." Immediately, Janči is put at ease with his personable nature.

Mr. Štrba, seeing the two of them can handle it from here, takes his leave.

Dodko talks avidly about the work he does, his passion contagious.

"I can't wait to start," Janči exclaims, inspired.

"Good."

Thinking over the possibilities of his first day, Dodko is ready to start with something a little more advanced.

"Do you want to learn how to build a crystal radio today?" Shocked that this complex project will be his first undertaking, Janči readily accepts the challenge.

Before the hands-on work begins, a brief lesson is given to Janči on crystal radios which are essentially a diluted version of a real radio with fewer parts. Expertly, Dodko explains that it requires no power source, using only the energy of the radio waves sent by radio transmitters, a handmade antenna of wire and insulators that the human ear has the capability of picking up. Set out on the table is a wooden board which is to act as the receiver, a sewing needle, a pocketknife, crystals, earphones, and insulated wire coil for the antennae, many of the items purchased through his personal connections. Using a pocketknife which Janči pulls out from his pocket, Dodko instructs him to poke a small hole in the wooden board.

"The crystal now goes into that hole."

Leading by example, Dodko carefully puts the quarter inch sized crystal into the hole Janči carved. He then takes a piece of wire, attaching one end to the sewing needle and the other end to the wire coil. The second end of the coil attaches to the antenna. The needle touches the crystal perpendicularly, acting as a tuner for a radio station. The other end of the wire is attached to a pair of ear phones. A second length of wire is attached from the antenna hanging at the side of the workshop to the needle in the crystal.

"This is how the signal is received." They get a strong one from a radio station in Bratislava that Janči hears through the earphones.

"The longer and higher up the antenna, the louder the signal," Dodko explains.

Janči glances at the clock for the first time since he arrived and sees it's almost seven. The time has flown by and he doesn't even want to leave yet. He could easily stay for a couple more hours, but he can't. Dinner and homework are waiting for him at home.

"Wow, it's already time for you to go home," Dodko exclaims, just as surprised as Janči.

"Thank you very much for teaching me all of this today."

"Tomorrow, there will be more. See you then."

All the way home, Janči can't help smiling from ear to ear, ecstatic about being part of the grown-up working world.

Dodko is an enthusiastic and patient teacher, never rushing explanations and always clear with his instructions, guiding Janči through numerous electrical and radio adjustments.

"When fixing a radio, always remember to shut off the dials. People are only allowed to get state-approved radio stations. If they discover we're leaving other stations open, we'll get fined." Janči chuckles at the irony of the work he is doing on these radios.

Janči easily understands how everything works, knowing the correct answers before the questions are even posed. Mechanically, his fingers work with valves, tubes, capacitors, resistors, and wiring like they would with his pocketknife and a piece of wood. Within a few short weeks, just as Dodko guessed, Janči is able to repair appliances and radios on his own.

At home in his lab, Janči practices what he learned by building his own crystal radio. Piece by piece, a process he doesn't rush through, he creates a twenty-meter antennae which he attaches from the side of the house to the fence. He also devises a capacitor with two conducting aluminum plates separated by an insulating plastic material which stores energy in an electrostatic field. With the tuner, he is then able to get stations in Prague and Vienna, not just Bratislava.

1941—Janči's gray suit and constricting maroon colored tie will be left in his closet and their seats at *schul* will remain empty this year for Yom Kippur. Apu and Mamička think it would be very convenient for the Hlinka Guards to go to the synagogue, where all the Jews will be congregated, and send them straight to the camps. Alternate arrangements have been made which heavily weighs on Opapa.

Perched on the kitchen table is a basket of food Mamička has packed that will accompany them up into the high altitude that is to be their refuge for the next twelve hours, away from any potential harm. Etched in Apu's mind is the route they will take up the mountains today. Crossing streams, they step on rocks to get across, passing serene lakes and trudging through spruce trees. A slight clearing ahead marks the point they will settle into for the day.

The basket is unpacked, giving the children the illusion of a regular family picnic while escaping the reality that persists below. Janči warmly acknowledges this isolation among the mountains that have no eyes. Freedom, enclosed in this space and moment in time, allows him to do as he pleases, say what he wants, being completely carefree and fully wrapped up in these simple pleasures. They all relish in the warmth of the sun and savor the food—the way their Sundays used to be—except now, Babka is also with them. Janči and Marta lightheartedly run around, playing hide-and-seek behind the trees, studying the plants and animals, laughing without restriction.

Dusk begins forming on the horizon, slowly overtaking the dark blue sky, streaking it with scarlet and then a darker hue of midnight blue, indicating that nighttime is fast approaching. Darkness is their mask from recognition and their cue to exit.

It is only a matter of time before Conditoria Weil and Baračka are seized from Jančiʼs family. The uniformed fascist Nazi officers storm in one day, amid the buttering of pans, smells of delicious plum cake baking, and sprinkling of powdered sugar on vanilla cookies. Knowing the reason for their presence, Uncle Miki does not put up a fight, not wanting to endanger himself or his workers. One boorish Nazi Officer is stationed there daily, observing everyone hard at work, eating the desserts meant for paying customers, and shouting orders that don't make sense to the proper operation of the pastry shop. They learn to live with the intolerable setup, but it's something they never get used to.

A TRAIN RIDE, 1942

SADLY, OVER THE past two years, the number of students at the Jewish school begins to severely dwindle, familiar faces not reappearing, ominously leaving unanswered questions behind. It all ends for everyone in March of 1942, when the school ceases operations and the transports of Slovak Jews begin to concentration and extermination camps.

Apu learns that Fiorella's dad is taken to Auschwitz. Fiorella and her mom are spared that train ride due to their Italian lineage.

Uncle Miki receives notice that he is required to leave for a labor camp situated in Poland. Two days is all he's given to say goodbye to his family. Forty-eight hours can never be enough emotional preparation for an ordeal like this, but Uncle Miki makes the best of it, not wanting to create additional strain on his family. Janči and his parents go to the train station to say their goodbyes.

Usually, the train station evokes happy memories for Janči, like going to Beluša to visit Babka, or going with Jožka to see her family; but today, a menacing tone overwhelms it. Uncle Miki's ten-month-old son, Peter, lies in his carriage, a melancholy demeanor plastered on his face, sensing everyone's sorrow and adopting it as his own. Only two years ago, Uncle Miki had married Hela, and now their wedding bliss is being cut short with such an unnatural separation of newlyweds.

As the train becomes visible from afar, Uncle Miki, tall and striking, looks at all of them with optimism and declares, "I'm a strong man," pounding his chest. "I'm going to work, do what they say, and then I will come home. Everything will be all right, you'll see."

Hela wails, latching on to him, not daring to let go. Her sobs get louder as the train approaches. Miki holds her until he is summoned to get moving. Prying her off, he boards the train with his chest pushed out as if embarking on a European adventure. Through the window, he waves and blows kisses until the train is well out of the station.

Janči's family receives two postcards from Uncle Miki, saying things are good, but they can tell by the black lines covering his words, and the sentences that don't sound like they are from his mouth, that this is untrue. No more cards come from him after that. Miki ends up in Auschwitz.

After learning of Miki's tragic fate, Janči and his family officially begin living a life consumed by paralyzing fear. Each day, they anticipate the unavoidable notice of getting on a train; but as each day goes by, they are granted another day to live. Life continues, enclosed in their house, with mini excursions made only to get necessities, and even then, the most direct and discreet route is taken. Every action, they know too well, may be their last.

April—A public announcement is inexorably made that they are to be at the train station in three days, along with all the other Jews in Trenčianské Teplice, under the guise that it is solely for relocation purposes. Their fear of what is to come is inescapable, the truth more real now than ever before. Three days is all they have to say goodbye to family, friends, and their home. Janči tries to sort out how to best spend the next seventy-two hours, unsure if he'll ever be back.

Janči draws a card from the stockpile and adds it to his hand. The ten of hearts is what he is hoping for, but instead, a seven of clubs falls in his hand. To complete his turn, he puts the seven of clubs faceup in the discard pile, not confident enough with his hand to knock. Janči's trash turns into Apu's treasure as he quickly grabs it, puts another card in the discard pile facedown, and knocks on the table. Four sevens of all suits are exposed, demonstrating Apu's strong hand, which beats Janči.

"I was so close."

"Not close enough," Apu says with a wink.

Janči begins shuffling the cards for another game, trying not to think about what is to come tomorrow, keeping things as normal as possible, but their measly bags at the front remind him of what's about to happen.

"I know you're scared, Janči," Apu says concerned, sensing the shift in his mood. "We all are. We just don't know what to expect anymore."

"I don't like what's happening."

"Neither do I. But we have no choice except to do as we're told right now. I do promise you that we'll make it through." Taking artificial comfort in his words that seem devoid of truth, Janči nods and smiles.

That night, Janči's eyes absorb everything in his room, confident this is the last time he'll be seeing them. All the colors and shapes of his model airplanes are transformed into a permanent imprint behind his eyelids, so each time he closes them, they will be there. He smells his comforter, the scent of fresh air still clinging to it after hanging outside on the clothesline. His hand runs along his dresser. In his closet, he runs the softness of his favorite wool burgundy sweater against his cheek, unsure if he will ever wear it again. Taking one last look out his window, Janči takes in the forest, stretching into his backyard, his playground.

Janči has never been more distraught at seeing the sunlight peeking through his curtains, tempting him with the illusion of a promising day. Rather, this is the beginning of the end. Reluctantly, he gets out of bed as he normally would do, except this time, it's with the nauseating knowledge—one that consumes his every move—of where his family is expected to be in the next few hours. Not wanting to drag out the miserable goodbye with his personal belongings again, he puts on the clothes he picked the night before—a simple pair of trousers and shirt. Silently, he forces his feet to walk down the familiar hall that he has travelled countless times.

In the living room, the wretchedness of what is happening saturates each family member, the forlorn expressions not needing any clarifying commentary. Mamička holding Martuška's hands, Gypsy standing beside them, his tail between his legs keenly aware that something is terribly wrong, Apu, Opapa, and Babka tightly holding large sacks in their hands containing the "essential belongings" they have been given permission to bring. Practical items like blankets, socks, and warm clothes have been included among some valuable possessions that somehow remained after the robberies by the Hlinka Guards.

Uncanny stillness of the house unnerves Janči, only ever having known it to be bubbling with energy. Apu turns off the lights and holds the door open while everyone walks outside like a funeral procession. Behind them, he locks the door in anticipation of returning home sometime soon. Outside, they are met with mild temperatures, sunny skies, and a light wind gently caressing them as if knowing not to be too harsh.

"Come on, Gypsy," Janči beckons.

Gypsy eagerly leaps beside him, ready for their journey. Wishing this time didn't come, Apu approaches Janči, having to break the hard news.

"Gypsy can't come with us, Janči. We're not allowed to take any animals with us."

Janči stares at Apu in disbelief, unsure if he heard him correctly. How can his beloved pet be considered a "nonessential" item when Gypsy means everything to him? How can all these things—family, friends, and pets—keep being taken away from him so easily? How can this be allowed to happen? Knowing nothing can be done, he doesn't bother to protest. He picks up Gypsy and nuzzles close to him, whispering his last goodbye, tears blinding him. He can't let him go. Apu approaches and gently takes Gypsy from Janči's hand and puts him back on the ground. He squeezes Janči's shoulder, as if telling him it will be okay, and tenderly pushes him forward, so he doesn't hear the quiet whimpering behind them. In a state of shock, Janči does as he's told, too overwhelmed to comprehend the loss of his dog.

Closely walking together, with several other families around them, they try to drag out their steps to the train station, but the ten-minute distance doesn't allow them much extra time. Perilously, the train station stands ahead, what once evoked happy memories now darkly summoning the throngs of people heading in its direction. All three hundred Jews from Trenčianské Teplice have been ordered here.

White tops and red bottoms of the electric cars wait on the tracks, faces already peering through the several windows on the tram. In a somewhat orderly fashion, all of them, Janči, Marta, Apu, Mamička, Babka, and Opapa are herded on to a section of it. Seats still remain empty as they are one of the first onboard. As if going to school in Trenčín, Janči takes a seat by the window, the lacquered wood underneath him, and his family squeezes in next to him. It almost feels like an ordinary tram ride until he turns his head. Hlinka Guards are trying to fit as many people as they can into each compartment, their hands becoming more impetuous, grabbing anyone within arm's reach and pushing them in—not bothered about separating mothers from daughters or husbands from wives. Marta cries and clings on to Mamička's arm crazed with the thought of being torn apart. Outside the window, hundreds of Jews looking bewildered and distraught are continually piled into the cart until not a square inch of room is left between them. Janči catches a glimpse of Ali and his family getting on board, the standard grim looks plastered on their faces; but he is too far away, too many people between him and his friend that he'll have to wait until they reach their destination before he even has the slightest chance of speaking to him.

Incessant crying fills the car as families are separated, torn from each other like leaves from a tree in a strong windstorm. Managing to get his face to a window, Janči peers outside. A small dark speck dashing toward the train catches his attention, and quickly, at the realization of what it is, Janči's heart twists in pain. Gypsy is standing by the train car looking up at the window, barking loudly for a dog of his stature, mistakenly thinking his barking will save them from all of this. As the train struggles to a slow start, having been filled over its capacity, he runs alongside it. His endurance is a miniscule fraction of the engine and his barking quickly subsides as he runs out of breath, yet he still keeps running, forcing his small legs forward. Tears are trickling down Janči's face as he bangs his fist against the window, willing it to break open enough for him to scoop Gypsy into his arms. The train gains speed and Gypsy manages to keep up for a few kilometers using all his power to do so, but his small heart can't take it anymore. With his tongue hanging out of his mouth, panting hard, his little legs are no match for the speed of the train. He soon becomes a speck in the landscape and then vanishes completely. A guttural cry flees Janči who is unable to handle the emotional burden of losing one of his best friends. Apu gathers him in his arms while his eleven-year-old son cries.

The train begins slowing down after some time, the fear of hundreds crammed inside about to be realized. Janči's heart tremors at the thought of what's lurking outside. Barely able to catch the breath that lodges in his throat, he sees they are at a train junction, not a notorious camp. The breath of air dislodges itself and oxygen enters his lungs. Before his brain can register this encouraging situation, he is callously being pulled out of the car. Feet shuffling along the pavement and bobbing heads paint the landscape ahead. Blind to the course they are being led along, Janči continues along in the one direction. Heads begin ascending ahead, making it all too clear, on to another train they go. A ramp is placed by the entrance of each cart, helping the cattle prepare for slaughter.

Inside the new car, all the comforts of their previous one, like windows and seats have been removed. Janči reaches for Marta's hand beside him to offer her any reassurance he can. In the crowded mayhem of this transposition, Janči still hasn't seen Ali.

Hours later, they arrive in a small railway station. Bodies are pulled out of the carts into the fiercely bright light that hits Janči in the face with such force he recoils. Adjusting to the outdoors, he sees a sign, the block letters eerily spelling out Žilina. They are in northern Slovakia.

Positioned in front of them is a one-story, long, wooden structure filled with small windows, easily distinguishable as an old horse stable from the First World War with the caveat that horses are to be replaced with humans. Lifeless spirits drag their feet, one in front of the other through the masses. Soldiers stand along the perimeter, brandishing their threatening weapons. Watch towers are in position around the camp. Marta's head hangs down, not exuding the curiosity that is inherently in her character.

A registration line forms as if signing up for an extracurricular activity. All their belongings are confiscated and deposited in a heap of jewelry, fine cutlery, and picture frames with photos still inside illustrating a happy life—everyone's connection to their past severed, the trickery of being told they were only relocating was deeply insulting.

After their identities are recorded on the ledger, they wander through the stables, looking for an area to settle down in. Stone walls around them are two feet thick, the rest of the structure made of wood except for the concrete floor beneath them, sloping downward on a slight angle where the horse urine was meant to drain, now leaving a reeking stain. Hay has been spread around the floor, and using the blankets still in their possession, they lay them out, marking their territory and beds.

Janči has his eyes peeled, trying to make out Ali's figure in the throngs of people surrounding him. It feels like an impractical search with everyone beginning to look the same. A lack of energy stifles his will to keep up this quest, and he despondently yields to the idea of not seeing Ali tonight. Tomorrow, he will continue his hunt with renewed vigor.

Outside, the sun has disappeared, leaving them all in a cover of darkness, the sliver of moonlight coming through the cracks of the stone walls is the only light they have. Through the blackness, silhouetted figures slowly take form to the naked eye. Apu is not ready to rest yet though. Anxiety is pressuring him to find out any new information he can. Warily, he makes his way through the bodies lying on the ground to a cluster of men huddled together, talking in hushed tones.

Janči lies down into the prickliness of the hay irritating his skin. Chills slither through his body, the lone blanket he has is not warm enough to keep them at bay. Even with the body heat of thousands around him, his teeth continue to chatter. He stares up at the wooden roof, questioning if this is all really happening, and praying it is just a dream he will wake up from; but the overpowering smell of horse manure filling his nostrils, inescapably infiltrating every pore of his skin, harshly clinging to him, reminds him it's not. Unable to fall asleep, he sits up and gazes around, completely in awe at the sight. Sprawled around are thousands of exhausted people in tattered clothing. Some are speaking in serious hushed tones while children lie in restless slumber, tossing and turning. Women clutch babies firmly into their arms trying to soothe them with a rocking motion, staring out at a horizon that doesn't exist.

Small groups of unassuming men have formed, not caring to draw attention to themselves. Soldiers slothfully sit on chairs throughout the barracks, joking with each other, sending hoots of laughter through the tense air, rudely interrupting those who have managed to break away from all this with a little sleep. They sneer at those below them, ensuring all the while that their guns are prominently displayed.

Sleep does not come easily for Janči, jealous that it has for others. Eventually, though, his eyelids can't remain open any longer physically, and he succumbs to the sleep that softly eases him out of his calamity. Apu returns after Janči has drifted into a fitful sleep. For a moment, he watches his children, who have had to leave behind all their comfort and security, resentful of this enormous burden that has been unfairly imposed on them. Turning to Mamička in a whisper, he informs her of what he found out.

"Each week, they have transport trains come here that take people to Auschwitz."

"Oh, Dežko, what are we going to do?" Mamička asks in shock.

"I really don't know," he says, deflated.

Each day that goes by, new faces are being thrown into the oppressive stables while others are hoarded off, never to be seen again; their identities vanquished from earth as if they never existed, except only to the family they may have left behind. Janči and his family go through the motions, following all the orders snarled at them, like obedient dogs to their masters. Fortunately, with a lot of begging and money, they are able to sporadically buy a half day, and sometimes, a full day of freedom from the camp through its greedy commander. Mamička's cousins from Žilina are able to surreptitiously pick them up, feed them, and clothe them—a temporary reprieve from the stuffy communal living.

Thirty people have the use of one washroom that is sprinkled each day with white powder, a dismal attempt at killing bacteria. Only cold water is available. These deplorable sanitary conditions create a breeding ground for typhus. Everyone continues to wear the same clothes they had from the moment they arrived, the fabric fraying and tearing. Everyone just sits around, frittering away the strength in their muscles and sharpness of their minds.

Janči goes searching for Ali again, not finding him, but learning that another train left this morning with hundreds of people in it. Without his best friend and not wanting to think about what could've happened to him, Janči looks for something to do that will occupy his time and mind. Hammering and clangs of chisels and iron planes are emitted from an open doorway that immediately catches Janči's attention. Peeking in, he sees a large carpentry shop filled with levels, ripping bars, and hammers used to construct roofs for army barracks. A friend of his from Trenčín, Erwin, is already working in there, and knowing there is a need for more able bodies, wastes no time showing Janči how to build the frames using ten by ten pieces of wood.

"It's just a matter of hammering the pieces together accurately," he shows Janči. Readjusting the nail, Erwin's framing hammer bears down on it before his hand gets out of the way, his reflexes is not fast enough, forcing the nail through the flesh of his hand. A startled scream of extreme pain makes everyone around look up for a moment. Seeing it's just another small injury, they go back to their own jobs before any punishments can come their way. Blood pours out from a deep gash, the sight of it all too familiar to Janči. Erwin pulls out the nail, wincing in pain while Janči hands him an old rag lying close by. Erwin wraps his hand with it as tightly as he can, securing it with a knot. He then takes a new nail from his tool belt and finishes the frame he was working on, aware of the guard staring at his back.

For two and a half months, Janči goes to work in the carpentry shop each day, more vigilant about his hammering since the incident with Erwin. In a daze, three months has dragged by, winter converting to spring, the changing seasons meaning nothing to Janči anymore. The purpose of his existence has become to wait. And then, one evening, a solider yells Apu's name in the stables. They all look up from the cold ground, thinking the worst has finally befallen them.

"The Commandant wants to see you."

Apu knows better than to ask questions and just nods, following the instructions given to him. All of them are escorted to the Commandant's office, a small room, sparsely furnished with a simple desk and chair. A stocky man with a pronounced jaw line and wide nose is reading papers on his desk. Only when the soldier asks for permission to enter does he look up, a flicker of distaste visible in his frosty grey eyes. They all file in and stand as still as possible in front of the Commandant.

"Dezider Teschner. Is that you?" he gruffly asks Apu.

This is it, Janči thinks. Almost twelve years old and life is about to end.

"Yes, that's me," Apu replies, immediately standing straighter, unsure of what lies behind this questioning.

Looking down at the sheet of paper in his hand, the Commandant looks up with a sneer. "You are being granted a release. It seems you are a Jew who is economically important to this country."

Release—the word sounds bizarre to Janči. Momentarily unable to comprehend it's meaning, Janči stands stunned at the twist of events, thinking that just seconds ago, his family was counting down the days to their death. Divine intervention has answered their prayers and so has one of Apu's previous employers who managed to get him the status of being economically important. Elation pours into Janči's body filling him with a mixture of euphoria and relief. Apu is given the release papers—freedom being handed back to them.

Being such an important event for Janči, he expects to see a red carpet rolled out in front of him and trumpets playing a victory song, but it's actually very unceremonious as the guards open the gates and barely give a second glance back at the family who walks through them. Once outside the guarded perimeter of the barracks, they are truly liberated, almost four months later. No longer prisoners for a crime they never committed, they begin their trek back home to Trenčianské Teplice with the help of their relatives. The sun beats down on Janči's face, the scent of blooming flowers fills the air, and birds can be heard chirping in nearby trees. Spring has replaced the frigid air and heavy snowfall. Life is starting to flow back into Janči's cold veins.

Arriving on the familiar street, their pace quickens toward the front door of their home, but they stop short in their tracks. In the driveway sits a black Škoda never owned by them. Strangers have overrun their house, settling in with the belief that complete ownership over this property is undoubtedly within their rights. A man walks out the front door. It's Mr. Uhlar, one of their old Slovak neighbors who they lived beside for years on extremely good terms. Six gentile families have seized all their personal belongings that the Hlinka Guards didn't pilfer. Everything they have left in this world is no longer theirs. Janči longingly peers beyond the opened curtains into the living room, trying to will himself inside, shocked to see their paintings still hanging on the walls. Knowing there is nothing else they can do here, they turn their backs on the life they spent years building and living.

"We'll go find Uncle Robert," Apu tells them, taking charge of their dour circumstance. Flashes of happy summer months in Trenčín before the war wind their way through Janči's head.

They take the electric train to Trenčianské Teplá, and then the train to Trenčín—what used to be such a natural trip—and now they are averting their eyes from all those nasty stares. An old-fashioned entrance gate, wide enough to have let horses and carts through in the olden days, greets them in front of their summer home at number eight Pribinova. They walk through, uncertain about the outcome. Apu knocks on Uncle Robert's door. A socially awkward man pulls the door open, seemingly annoyed at being disturbed.

"Can I help you?"

"We're looking for Mr. Robert Weil," Apu states.

"He doesn't live here anymore," he replies at the absurd question with a barefaced answer. "They were all taken away."

"Thank you," Apu says while Mamička is already turning around, gripping the handrail as she tries to make it down the stairs without falling over at the stomach-turning thought of Robert, his wife Ica, and their two daughters, Agi and Eva, being sent to Auschwitz.

They don't bother venturing to their own apartment for refuge as they have seen a strange family living there already. Shunned from both their homes, their only option is to find a new one. Through word of mouth, they find a small house, owned by Mr. and Mrs. Tochten, near the Square of Santa Ana and a church. Apu is able to rent out a unit on the first floor. Inside is one bedroom where they all share a bed except for Babka who sleeps on a couch set up in the kitchen. The five of them share one washroom, but they still consider all of this a luxury no matter how cramped the living quarters are. Even though Babka lives with them, Opapa decides to relieve the strain of minimal resources and moves into a Jewish old age home down the street that gladly accepts him. The home, which only accommodates thirty people, is very long and backs on to the quiet of the forest. Opapa still manages to come over wearing a suit, even if it is always the same one, to eat dinner with them. Janči also visits him almost every day at the senior's home.

Eva and Babitza, the Hungarian refugees that Janči's family had taken in when living in Trenčianské Teplice, also live in a unit in the same house. Their parents play cards over coffee and tea while the four children find other ways to amuse themselves. In another unit of the house lives a cabinet maker with a workshop where Janči finds work in return for wood and access to machinery. Drawing plans and reading books, Janči attempts to construct a steam truck, applying the mechanics of his old steamboat—heating water and using dry alcohol tablets to create steam that moves the truck forward. When he finishes, Apu is amazed to see the truck driving along on the ground.

Work has eluded Apu except for a part time job as a bookkeeper for a mechanic with a large body shop. Mathematics is one of his strongest subjects, able to do complex calculations in his head that span two or three or decimal points. Here, he also goes for test drives in cars that are to be overhauled and resold.

Janči resumes going to Jewish school, now with a much shorter commute. Close to six hundred Jewish students used to pack into this school each day. Only two small classes remain with about forty students. Army trucks furnished with Slovak soldiers park in front of the school each day as a friendly reminder. Marta attends a Catholic cloister close to the apartment where nuns are her teachers. With her blonde hair and blue eyes, no one suspects she is Jewish. Janči enjoys the same ambiguous identity, relieved that harassment against him has finally subsided.

GLORIOUS FRUITS, 1943

AN ANNOUNCEMENT IS made that all Jewish men between the ages of eighteen to fifty are to report for duty at a designated location—a forced labor camp in Trenčín. They are required to support the war effort and contribute to the economic vitality of the country by building new infrastructure in Slovakia. Apu and Uncle Lajko, left with no choice, reunite in this cheerless circumstance and begin work; building a new railway station is their required duty: ties, underpinning, straightening, and digging, the list of exhaustive work. Being physically fit gives Apu an advantage at the amount of work that is being pressed upon him, preventing him from wilting under the heavy demands like others around him who pass out of fatigue, heatstroke, and dehydration. Uncle Lajko is unable to keep up with the drudgery, afflicted with a high fever and becoming very ill only a few weeks in. On the railroad, his superiors aren't concerned about his feeble state, only pushing him to work harder.

Compensation for this slavery is the unguaranteed prospect of staying alive. If one is blessed with survival, Jewish organizations will pay them a certain amount of money. If you don't survive, you don't get paid. Starvation rations are what the workers live on, their daily allowance including a slice of black bread the thickness of one's thumb, some margarine, and a miniscule cup of soup that periodically might have something floating around in it.

Each day after school, Ivor and Janči visit Uncle Lajko and Apu's job site, bringing an aluminum food carrier filled with hot food. Aluminum cups are used to eat the soups, potatoes, meat, and refreshing water to sustain their vigor. Mamička and Ilona take turns cooking meals for their husbands with the meager rations they receive.

Janči and Ivor see how sick Uncle Lajko is getting with each passing day. A fever is taking over, and now he is ravaged with a plethora of other flu-like symptoms. A dry cough hacks his lungs. He is barely able to move because of his aching body, lifting the food to his lips is taking too much effort, and without an appetite, it usually never makes it into his mouth. The boys refrain from feeding him, knowing his protests are a masked outcry of wanting to preserve his dignity. They bring blankets to ease the constant shivering wracking his bones, but the chills never subside. He is sinking into a depression no one can rescue him from. His heart is weakening severely. Cast off to the side on the dirt bank above the tracks is the shovel he is supposed to be digging with. The sight of Apu and Uncle Lajko at the labor camp makes Janči feel incredibly helpless and dizzy in a world that has gone crazy around him.

Two months later, the railroad project is completed. Released from their duties, both Apu and Lajko make it out alive and just in time, and no one knows if they would have lasted.

―⁂―

In May, it happens all over again like a broken record. The Hlinka Guard and Gendarmes come and pick up the family, including Opapa, from the small house that served as their refuge in Trenčín. Rounded up in cattle cars, everyone knows the routine all too well. It's a recurring nightmare that they're always awake for. Žilina, close to the Polish border, is back on their destination list.

Conditions at the camp are just as deplorable, even worse than the first time because the abundance of people has escalated, and many of them are malnourished. Two months pass as they each go through the repetitive motions of being rebuked, thrown meager food portions, erratically sleeping among the living and the dead, the reek of human decay nauseating. Mentally, they prepare for their own death, waiting for the transport that will take them to Auschwitz.

A guard approaches them, causing the hairs on the back of Janči's neck to stand up.

"Teschner," he announces, "come to the Commandant's office immediately. It looks like you have been granted an exemption," he says, reading the name off a list in his hand. By a God-given grace, Apu receives another exemption, still being considered economically important, giving them a second chance at life, the exemptions only issued by the Fascist Nazi President of Slovakia, Jozef Tiso, with the backing of a corporation. They hurriedly gather their paltry possessions and follow the soldier to the Commandant's office. Eyes full of envy and resentment follow them every step of the way, people wondering why this family gets to leave, why are they so special, what makes them better than us?

Back inside the Commandant's office, nothing has changed in the sparsely furnished small room, especially not the hefty, intimidating man.

"This exemption is for your family," he starts off right away. Looking down at the paper he lists all the names maintaining the convention of formality.

"Marta Teschner, Maria Teschner, Dezider Teschner, Jan Teschner, and Helena Teschner."

"What about Leopold Weiss?"

"He's not on the list."

"He's my father-in-law."

"He's not on my list."

Pleading for the reversal of time, Janči feels like he's been hit by a blunt object on backside of his head. Opapa's eyes glaze over, the tears

BECAUSE OF A FISHBONE

apparent but not yet falling while his grandchildren are still in front of him. Stiffly, he stands, maintaining the air of a distinguished man in a fraying and wrinkled three-piece gray suit that hangs off his shrunken body, a discolored white handkerchief tidily poking out of the pocket. Dark bags besiege his eyes, the lines around them deeper and more pronounced than Janči's ever seen them. "I'll be fine here," he says, trying to keep the children from worrying. Bending down, he embraces Janči and Marta, his arms unable to gather the protective force they once had.

"You two be good. I'll make sure to get out of here soon, so I can come home and be with you." Janči's chest painfully constricts by the tightening grip of panic around his heart, knowing well enough that he will never see Opapa again. He holds on even tighter in these last moments, unable to release because when he does, it will be forever.

Kissing each of them, Opapa rises to face his daughter and son-in-law. "Get your stuff and get out of here as fast as you can before they change their minds," he says, offering a weak smile. Mamička's knees buckle under her, and she throws herself into her father, burying her face into his chest to muffle her mournful cries. "Don't cry," he says, stroking her hair. "You'll just make this harder. Just go," he says, withdrawing from her.

With a final woeful hug from everyone, Opapa moves out of the way, allowing them to pick up their blankets, clothes, and morsels of food. Once his family is ushered out of the office by the guard, tears in Opapa's eyes have finally been given the cue to release themselves. He is escorted back to the harsh, cold barracks where he sits down on the ground, alone, waiting, his vision blurred by his tears.

Unsurprisingly, their small room in Trenčín has become occupied, and the only other place they can try to find shelter is Uncle Lajko's apartment block. An eerie silence is draped around his door. No one answers Apu's importunate knocks. Turning the door handle, it opens up to an empty apartment, stripped of all furnishings and personal mementos, only a bare grey carpet and taupe walls remaining.

One of the neighbors walks by, carrying brown paper bags having just finished grocery shopping, a cucumber sticking out at the top.

"They're not here anymore," she mildly informs them.

"Do you know where they went?" He's dreading to hear the expected answer.

"I heard to Novaky," she says as if speaking about the weather. With that, her key opens the door, and she walks into her apartment.

Shockingly, no one has declared Uncle Lajko's two bedroom apartment as their own, leaving it for them to move into. However, the strangeness of living there without Uncle Lajko and his family is not something they can get used to.

Starting from scratch, they begin to settle in with the little that they have. Apu returns to the mechanic's office, continuing his work as a bookkeeper. Even with the extra income coming in, their lifestyle becomes exceedingly frugal, limiting the amount of food they eat and what they eat, only able to afford rudimentary items like bread, jam, potatoes, and beans. Leftovers are never discarded, not even a spoonful, always eaten the next day or made into something else. The same goes for scraps of any material that can't be used for clothing anymore, worn to the core of its fiber. They become masters of resourcefulness.

In the storage room, neatly stacked along the wall are logs of wood for the stove in the kitchen. Janči carries one three feet long outside. He uses a saw with a large serrated blade to cut it into three pieces. An axe is then used to slice it into even smaller, more manageable pieces. In the crook of his right arm, he balances all the pieces as he makes his way back up the fifteen stairs leading to their unit. His left hand carries the saw. On the fourth stair, his foot missteps, and he ungainly tumbles backward, the blade of the saw breaking his fall, along with his upper front tooth. The loud thud echoes up into their unit and Mamička runs out to find her son lying on the bottom steps amid scattered wood, crying out in pain. Rushing down, she finds the broken half of Janči's tooth a foot away from him. She carefully puts it in her apron pocket and helps Janči to his feet, leaving the wood scattered where it is.

Janči rinses his mouth with water to clean the fresh wound. In a piece of cloth, the tooth fragment is wrapped up until it can be put back in Janči's mouth. Apu's friend, a dentist who works nearby, sees Janči and promptly fixes his tooth. A pin is used to attach the broken piece to the tooth still in his gum.

Although the times are dire, their generosity and kindness toward others in need doesn't wane. Several people who are still trying to escape the atrocities manage to make their way to Apu for solitude. A rabbi from Budapest is one of the first to arrive. After him comes one of Janči's former teachers from the Jewish school.

Next to the apartment extends a beautiful garden filled with an abundance of lush fruit trees, offering the ingredients for sweet jams. Peaches, apples, and cherries all leisurely dangle above, enticing anyone below to unlawfully sneak one off and bite into its juicy ripeness. The temptation becomes too strong for Janči who has to see and smell the glorious fruits on a daily basis. He calls on his friends, Bohush and Peter, the sons of a family who escaped the Czech Republic and now lives on the first floor of the apartment block. All of them are close in age and instantly bond over the foolish adventure. They jump over the fence, separating them from their neighbor's orchard, and quickly pick the biggest apples and apricots their eyes can spot. Once safely back on their side of the defense lines, they sink their teeth into a ripe peach. Immediately, the juice begins flowing out of it, the sweet nectar much tastier than anything found in their own garden.

The neighbor living opposite the orchard is Mr. Javor, a tailor who also raises rabbits in his backyard that live in small cages and then sells them. White, black, grey, and brown plush fur-covered bodies with large drooping ears race across the grass in confusion, digging burrows or gnawing on fresh root vegetables with their sharp front teeth. Seeing the boys standing near the fence, Mr. Javor grabs a brown rabbit off the ground by the scruff of its neck. With a swift twist of his hands, he breaks its neck with a fast snap and nonchalantly, holding it by its feet, brings the dead animal over to the boys. Janči's stomach lurches at the gruesome fate he just witnessed to something so small, innocent, and cute.

"Here," he says, handing it over, "your mom paid me for one. She said she's going to make rabbit soup." Janči lets Bohush take it, hiding his revulsion with a tight-lipped smile.

Boredom, being an easy affliction for Janči, urges him to join an airplane model club at the local high school. Every week Janči attends, he hides his Jewish identity by removing the star he is ordered to wear. Twenty boys gather inside a classroom and build model airplanes together.

Janči makes a new friend at these club meetings, Edvard, who is three years older and can converse in Slovak. Janči is unafraid to divulge the fact that he's Jewish to his close friend, who doesn't even blink at this revelation, having a father who is a communist and hates the Germans. After club hours, they visit each other's homes to continue building planes. Plane dynamics and physics calculations like wingspan are just a few topics Edvard teaches Janči. Janči absorbs it all, not letting one drop of his words spill. They pour over illustrated books on how to build various planes, carefully dissecting the images and instructions. Building planes such as gliders, biplanes, single-winged planes, and rubber wound propellers poses a challenge because all the required materials are not readily available. However, being very resourceful, Edvard always manages to find something. Melting an old toothbrush handle, he shows Janči how to mix it with acetone to produce the glue they need to put all the plane parts together. Propellers are carved to their exact size and then balanced. Thick sticks of balsa wood comprise the body of the planes with paper stretched and smoothed over it. An acetone-based lacquer is used to paint the onion type paper, one that dries fast, ensuring the paper does not become mushy. After flying a plane, Janči dips it in a jar of glycerin that Mamička has in the apartment to preserve the elasticity of the rubber bands as they become hard in the colder temperatures and are very expensive and not easy to obtain. A few weeks into doing this, he notices how soft his hands feel.

 Obsessed with this new hobby, Janči uses any spare time he has to craft new planes. Pieces of a plane lay scattered on the stoop—the body, wings, and propellers, a jungle of mechanics made of small pieces of balsa wood, rubber bands, glue, yarn, and paper—all of which need to be analytically sorted through. In the book is an illustrated version of what the final product should look like when he's done piecing it together. He picks up what is to be the main frame of the body—Janči's point of reference. The first creates a wing using the balsa and attaching it in place with glue and yarn. Quietly and contently, he continues on with his work in progress. Although it will still be about eight weeks before the plane is complete, Janči is already trying to figure out what color it should be once the raw wood is covered with paper to be painted or swathed in colored silk.

In 1944, Edvard and Janči's friendship disbands involuntarily when transports became more frequent, and Janči has to escape with his family.

CUCKOO CLOCKS, 1944

ON SUNDAY, AUGUST 27, hundreds of American planes and a few British ones speckle the sky, roaring through like a flock of birds, shaking the whole sky in their wake. Germans are shooting flak canons up toward the planes, outnumbered among their enemies but still resolute in shooting down as many of them as they can. On the radio, the latest news is that the German planes are turning toward Gőr, Budapest, and Bratislava.

The mild August day is too nice to be spent inside, so Janči takes Marta out to their backyard to fly the model airplane he just finished. Colder weather will be settling in soon, and before it does, Janči needs take full advantage of the summer days left.

"Janči! Marta! Come home now!" Mamička yells from their second floor balcony, seeing German trucks up the street. In hearing the familiar voice, Janči immediately notices something very different about it—it is satiated with panic. His worst fears begin to play out in his head as he has dreamed they would on many sleepless nights.

"Please don't let this be happening to us," he pleads to anyone willing to listen. Janči races to the apartment, pulling Marta along with him, his feet ferociously hitting the ground. A feeling of dread suddenly sweeps over him. The blood flowing throughout his body instantly freezes. Babka. She's not at home. She left early in the morning to have tea with a friend of hers down the street, her weekly Sunday ritual.

"Marta, go inside. I'll be there in a minute." He starts heading toward the street but doesn't get far once Mamička's arms physically pull him inside.

"What about Babka?" he wails. "We can't just leave her alone. I have to go and get her."

Amid his panic, Janči looks up to see Mamička desperately trying to control her own state of sadness and tears.

"Janči, it's too late. We can't do anything to help her. They're already halfway up the street. If we don't leave right now, they'll get us too."

'No!" he screams, the word uselessly flitting off his tongue. His dear Babka—the one who always makes him his favorite cookies and lets him eat as many as he wants, the one who always covers for him when he does something foolish, and the one who never runs out of love for her family. The possibility of losing another grandparent in these circumstances and in such a short period of time makes Janči's heart collapse, the constant pain always reminding him of what is.

On the back of the front door, a small bag of food with dry salami and bread hangs. It's been there for a couple of weeks, foreseeing this day. Money has been sown in the hem of Mamička's skirt. Two packed suitcases full of clothes are positioned in the closet, knowing this day would be here sooner rather than later based on the information Uncle Lajko managed to pass along from the labor camp in Novaky and that Apu was able to decode. There is a guerilla uprising in the Low Tatras that Uncle Lajko is planning on being a part of, and due to this revolt, the Germans are starting to occupy Slovakia, uneasy about the possibility of a Slovak attack against them.

Janči anxiously catches a glimpse out the window as they are rushing out, frantically scanning through the mob of people, trying to find Babka among those being forced onto trucks. Even if he did see her, Mamička is right; there is nothing they would be able to do. German soldiers are already up the street where her friend lives, but maybe she had enough time to escape. That is the only thread of hope he is able to hang on to.

Germans brandishing rifles are going door to door, yanking people from their homes and hurling them on to trucks. Some people with energy left try putting up a fight, but most don't, too frail and tired to try. Mothers are protecting their babies in the nooks of their arms, doing everything they can to keep the roughness of the soldiers from reaching the children. One little boy with tufts of curly brown hair is crying uncontrollably, trying to save his father from a beating, but he is powerless. Desperately, he keeps reaching into the air, grasping for his father.

"Let's go," Mamička screams. They all run down the stairs, almost trampling each other. *This is all just a bad dream*, Janči convinces himself. He'll wake up soon to find Mamička making a breakfast of *palacinky* with apricot jam. Apu is carrying Marta whose little legs can't keep the pace that is necessary to outrun the soldiers. They are running through the orchard which is surrounded by agonizing screams on the streets, pleadings for mercy, random gunshots, and soldiers barking their orders in gruff German. Janči tries to block it all out, but it surges through his eardrums, not allowing his mind to ignore it. Germans are strategically planted in the city, leaving only one way out—east of the Brezina mountain.

As they reach a meadow, the overhead roaring of a plane interrupts Janči's thoughts. They all look at each other in horror.

"Get down," Apu yells. Instantly, they drop their bodies flat on the ground melding into one with the earth as the plane swoops down. Luckily, it's only a Fieseler Storch which the German's use for short landing and surveillance, not hurtling out bombs and gunshots. Seeing no threat of partisans on the ground, it flies back up, leaving those who are trying to flee in a moment of calm. Unsteadily, they stand up, quivering at the close encounter to death they just faced. Like Bernie up at Baračka, they shake what mud they can off their bodies and continue on in fast-paced silence through fields and forest toward the protection of the mountains. Janči and his family quickly blend into the landscape with the foliage and mountains camouflaging their bodies. Occasional animal calls, chirping of insects and birds, and serene flow of rivers and streams cuts through the deep panting of their arduous breathing. For almost thirty-five kilometers, they run, trying to make their way to the partisans.

As daylight begins to dim, they manage to reach the road to the small village of Banove nad Bebravou, flanked by mountains. Haggardly, they walk through the village. A wagon filled with hay being pulled by a pair of horses passes in front of them. Without wasting a second, Apu yells up to the farmer.

"Please, sir, could you help us out? We're trying to get to Bánoce."

The Slovak pheasant curiously looks at them.

"Bánoce is not a safe place for your family to stay in. Germans are everywhere. You need to go to Uhrovec if you want to be close to the partisans. It's about ten kilometers north east of here."

Without any contemplation, he offers to take them there. Apu's eyes were filled with gratitude. He shakes the pheasant's hand and offers him money.

"I don't want your money. I just want you to make it out of here."

"Thank you, sir," Apu says, ignoring his request and placing money in his palm.

Janči lifts Marta onto the wagon. Apu helps Mamička up, and then the two men of the family jump on. The wagon starts off into the dusk on a bumpy road through the mountains. Hypnotized by the rhythmic jounces, everyone remains silent, fixedly staring out past the horizon, falling into a wistful reminiscence until the rising of a pink and orange gleaming sun emerges from beyond the span of the earth, promising a new day.

"We're here," the pheasant informs them. "But you still have to continue up the mountains and find a place there."

With nowhere to rest and safety being their number one priority, they continue further into the mountains until they feel protected enough by the imposing landscape. partisans walk the streets of this tiny village adorned with grenades, rifles, and machine guns from Russian and American soldiers who parachuted down with them. American and British pilots who were shot down seek refuge in this unknown land. Apu converses with them, trying to uncover more useful information about the war, Janči understanding most of the dialogue, his English lessons paying off at least.

Apu automatically begins looking for a place to rent, walking the streets in search of any postings of vacant apartments. An innkeeper's house appears promising from the outside, and Apu steps in ready to negotiate with the farmer who owns it. They cannot afford any of the asking rates and will have to barter for something less. Mamička is able to cook there, lowering the cost the farmer expected them to pay. Not spacious by any means but providing adequate shelter, their new abode is one room, resembling that of a motel room without a bathroom. They have to go to the outhouse for that.

Coincidentally, although never having lived in this village before, Apu bumps into several people he recognizes on the close-knit streets as many displaced Jews have landed in Uhrovec, seeking refuge. To his shock, a former neighbor mentions having seen Babka in Nové Mesto nad Váhom, just beside Trenčín, after the German convoy plunged in. It appears she had seen the trucks in advance, escaping before they were able to capture her.

"How do we get in touch with her?" he asks in a frenzied jubilation of this news.

"I can try to pass on a message for you."

"Tell her we're living here right now."

"I will do my best."

"Thank you!" Apu yells over his shoulder as he's already sprinting down the street to tell his family the wonderful news.

But just as quickly as their elation spurted, the grim news comes that Babka was caught and was deported directly to Auschwitz. Teased with the false hope that she may have been alive, Janči feels as if he's mourning her death for a second time, the grief in his heart never ceasing.

On another outing, Apu bumps into Arnošt, an old friend of his, a pharmacist who escaped from Trenčín. His unattractive features, extremely wide-set eyes, thin lips, and flaccid skin around his cheeks spurs pity when Janči sees him. Single with barely any money, although his clothes and shoes demonstrate otherwise, he has nowhere to live.

"You are more than welcome to stay with us. The apartment is very small, but we'll make room."

Arnošt is at a loss for words as his luck has finally changed.

———

Quickly, the village swells, absorbing more people, the overcrowding sending off alarm bells on the already scarce supply of food and nonexistent jobs. Needing to ease his unoccupied hands and ease the burden of Apu having to feed the entire family, Janči ventures out in search of something to do. He wanders into a blacksmith's shop on the same street as their apartment, a stone chimney jutting out from one side into the shop, and watches in awe as a piece of iron is being heated over a charcoal fire in the hearth where the man wearing a black apron uses tongs to grab the malleable red-hot metal.

Crafting horseshoes on the anvil, he hammers out the various angles and bends in his piece of metal. At the end of the hearth is a counter filled with tools and cooling pieces of iron. A tub of water is close by to douse the hot iron. In the back, low ceilinged workshop, guerilla rifles are repaired, hammered back into shape, bent from weeks of fighting in the field.

"Excuse me, sir."

The man looks up; his droopy bloodhound eyes examine the young boy.

"I was just wondering if you might need any help here."

"I could use help pumping the bellows. But I don't have much money to pay you with."

"I don't want money. I just want food."

Being a villager, the blacksmith has access to food and agrees to that form of compensation.

Behind the chimney, connected by a tunnel to the hearth are the bellows which pump air into the trough, bringing the charcoal in the fire to a high temperature. Janči watches as Mr. Raptoš welds a clip to the front topside of the horse shoe to prevent the horse's hoof from slipping on the shoe. Eight rectangular holes are then punched into each shoe for nails. These shoes will protect the cushioned area in the middle of the horse's foot. Once Janči learns to pump the bellows with ease using a foot pedal, he is given the additional responsibility of holding iron pieces in place after heating and hammering the sections that need it. He also hammers deformed rifles back into shape, making them usable again.

After his first week of work, Mr. Raptoš brings Janči to a horseshoe fitting. The shoe is attached by nailing it at an angle through the side of the hooves, the horse not feeling any of this because hooves have no nerves. The ends of the nails are dulled down, and the hoof and shoe are filed to make them even.

As a part-time gig aside from working at the blacksmith, Janči cleans and repairs rifles and machine guns for the partisans in return for food like bread, potatoes, and beans. Already knowing how to repair them from Mr. Raptoš, he is shown how to clean them by pushing a steel rod covered with a piece of flannel through the barrel of the gun.

On his way home from cleaning rifles, he sees a sign advertising cuckoo clocks. Inciting his curiosity, he ventures in. An old German man, Mr. Schweinert is inside. Janči approaches this white-haired balding man whose face is filled with wrinkles, showing his years of age. His glasses maintain the keen sense of his eyesight while he sculpts a bird that will come forward through the doors of the clock when it chimes. Janči asks if he could watch how the clocks are made.

"Of course, you can. I work better with an audience anyways," he says, grateful for the company. Readily, he places the bird down and demonstrates how the clocks are mechanically powered by a weight. "This stone goes up, and it has to be pulled down each day." The stone, hooked on a string, goes through the wheels and cocks of the inner workings of the clock. "See, it's not spring mounted as you may expect," happily explaining it all in his mother tongue of German which Janči is adeptly versed in.

Mr. Schweinert also makes small houses that measure barometric pressure. When the weather is nice and dry, a smiling man and lady come into view from two doors. When snow or rain is in the forecast, the man comes out on his own, holding up an umbrella. Rubbery and wrinkled sheep intestines of a yellowish brown color are used inside, determining the weather by expanding when humid and wet and shriveling when dry outside. Farmers supply the intestines, hanging them on a hook prior to selling them, weighing them down on the bottom with a stone in order to stretch the innards to their greatest length.

Both the cuckoo and barometric houses are carved beautifully and painted masterfully with colorful Slovak ornaments and pictures of pine trees. They are then hung on walls inside homes as pieces of art. In summer, Mr. Schweinert collects linden wood; and in winter, he spends infinite hours carving it into cuckoo clocks of all shapes and sizes.

A few days of watching elapses, and Janči is certain he can assist. Mr. Schweinert nods in agreement.

"Okay. I will pay you for your work then, but with food. Things like plum butter, sugar, and bread."

Janči leaves his work at Mr. Raptoš to take on this job and learn fresh skills of expertly painting and varnishing smooth wood. Before Janči is allowed to operate the antique-looking lathe, Mr. Schweinert explains all its parts from the bed, tool rest, and headstock to the spindle and tailsock, and how it functions from the automatic screw shaft and gear train to the pullies for the belt drive. All these new terms supplement Janči's vocabulary. Once satisfied that his new mentee is prepared, Mr. Schweinert shows Janči how to make wooden cog wheels on the lathe that cuts and forms intricate shapes and designs from a simple piece of wood. Cam shafts, the geared mechanism creating the impetus of the clock, are also constructed, looking like large wheels with teeth around the circumference, interlocking as they move around.

Spending day after day with him, Janči learns of Mr. Schweinert's solitary life. His wife passed away years ago, leaving him a widow. They never had any children, no one waiting for him at home each day after work in the house attached to the back of the workshop.

He comes into his workshop one day, carrying a loaf of bread. "I baked it myself at home. This one is for you."

From another loaf, he breaks off two pieces handing one to Janči. Taking a break from their work, they sit on a bench, enjoying the fresh bread.

"You must be wondering why someone like me doesn't care if you're Jewish."

Janči lightly shrugs, never having thought about it. Inching closer to Janči's ear, ready to reveal a secret, Mr. Schweinert explains his rationale. "I lived here between the Slovaks for forty years, and I never had anything against Jews. That's not my way." With a triumphant smile, he takes a large bite out of his piece of bread.

At the end of the day, Janči takes his loaf home, many others to come in the future, along with a bag of sugar for his family to share.

―⁂―

Building model airplanes becomes a hobby that is too expensive to maintain and evolves into one that is more feasible—building kites. Apu gives Janči some money to buy paper and fishing wire, restoring his ability to construct things at home. Branches from willow trees are used as sticks to form the body of the kite. Acquiring other tools, Janči starts building his kite, tying the branches together with fishing wire and attaching the paper. Completing it in the evening around five o'clock, Janči is anxious to go outside and test it as there is a perfect wind in the meadow, just like there used to be on the shores of the Váh river in Trenčín.

Clouds are starting to roll in, but that is irrelevant because the wind is still present for the small two-foot kite to make a run. Gracefully, it soars in the darkening air with ease. Pleased with his efforts of creating a functional kite, he confidently smiles to himself and begins running as the kite goes higher and higher above the village. Not wanting to stop, the kite splits through the fibers of the sky, the sturdy paper noisily fluttering in the air, the sound of victorious engineering.

Out of the corner of his eyes in the distance, Janči sees a group of twenty partisans running toward him from the village up to the meadow carrying their large rifles. As they get closer, Janči notices the rifles have a clear target in mind, him. If he runs, they'll shoot. If he stays where he is, he has a better chance of surviving. He stands there, trembling, waiting for the partisans to reach him. Most wear regular civilian clothes unless they've escaped from the Slovak army, in which case they have a uniform with a red star.

"What are you doing?" they angrily scream.

"I'm just flying my kite," Janči stammers out of his mouth.

"We thought it was a parachute coming down. We were ready to start shooting. You're lucky we didn't." Heatedly, they proceed to kick and punch Janči, who curls up on the ground thankful that the blows are not hard enough to seriously injure him but have enough force to teach him a lesson. "Don't do that anymore. We have enough trouble without you."

November—Artillery fire can be heard in the pinnacles of the mountains. Through the gorging valleys in between, the sound—as far as ninety kilometers away—reverberates as it winds around the crevices of the mountains and flows into Janči's ear. On a clear day or night, the sound is especially crisp. Assuming the Russians are getting closer, people feel the end to these murky days is near, but other news outside the village states otherwise—Germans are forcing the partisans higher into the mountains, a foreseeable attack dangling above them.

Aware of how comfortable he is in bed, Janči burrows further into the warmth of the duvet cover, not wanting to ever get out.

"Janči, wake up. We're leaving in half an hour."

Groggily, he climbs out of bed and wipes the sleep from his eyes, the thought of staying there all day is no longer a possibility. Awaiting him is a crucial job that will require all his strength. Choosing comfortable, durable pants and shirt that are able to withstand the dirt and digging, he is ready to start on this expedition.

Eggs are frying on the stove, splattering, popping oil into the air. "You're going to need your energy today," Mamička tells him while heaping the rare breakfast onto his plate. Janči takes a seat, Apu and Arnošt already at the table, consuming their hearty breakfast—fuel for the day.

Shovels and pickaxes are propped up by the front door—local farmer's tools that have been borrowed that are not in use during the winter months. Each of them takes what they can carry in their hands and in the bags on their backs.

Trekking up to the low Carpathian Mountains in the village of Kšinná is not easy in November, when large snowstorms threaten any progress. Trails replace roads, their destination inaccessible by car, making their legs the only means of transportation, burdened with the extra weight of the tools. Nine kilometers and almost three hours later, they arrive, and Janči is already wondering how they're going to get back if the exhaustion he's feeling now will only multiply after a full day's work.

"We need to start digging over here, below the roots," Apu points out. "It's by a small creek, so we'll have water. The creek runs down the hill to the village."

Hours into the digging process and a burning sensation travels through all the muscles in Janči's body, ones he's never felt before. Sweat pours down his back and face even though the air is frigid.

The next eight weeks are filled with the same laborious work through heavy snowstorms toward the latter end, leaving Janči's body in a constant state of pain. On their last day up, Janči rewinds a movie reel in his head that plays out the progression of what their hands accomplished—three men, slaving away each day to build a shelter that may save their lives one day. Standing inside the bunker the size of a tiny bedroom, even smaller than four square meters and less than two meters high, Janči looks at his hands in awe. They are covered in blisters and dirt, calloused, and his nails are chipped, but they helped produce this. A few sacks of potatoes, dried prunes, flour, beans, and bread rest in the corner. Bunk beds have been painstakingly constructed of tree branches. A small stove made of half of barrel is placed on the side of the entry, only to be used at night when no one can see smoke flowing out of the bunker. Apu comes over and puts his arm around Janči. "You did well. I'm so proud of you." Janči beams at the praise his father bestows on him and in that moment forgets the pain circulating throughout his body.

With a renewed sense of energy, the three of them climb out and cover the tiny entrance with branches and leaves. Falling snow will further disguise their secret entrance, purging all traces of them being up there.

Mamička goes outside to collect wild berries, apricots, and plums which she will cook into jam. Huge tarpaulins are laid out on the grassy sides of the road with a slew of sliced fruits neatly piled on them, drying in the sun. The smell is wonderfully intoxicating. Apples, pears, apricots, and mostly plums make up the plethora of eye warming colors radiating from the tarps, the proximal orchards are their source. Plum butter is the most preferred because of its high resiliency. It can last for ten years without spoiling if it's cooked properly.

Large copper kettles are placed in the field under the trees where plums are dumped in alone without any sugar, a fire lit under it. Frequently, a farmer slowly stirs the contents of one vat with a large wooden paddle. With the progressively more arduous stirring action, the consistency of the nearly black mixture becomes thicker and more viscous. Once cooked, the plums are sieved, separating the pits, leaving a pure and delicious jam. Jars of it already waiting in the bunker, a place they'll probably have to hide in soon.

Janči and his family sleep in their clothes each night, anticipating an inevitable attack, ready to run at any unexpected moment. Then one very early morning, it happens. Sounds of machine guns and mortar fire bombardment have the entire family springing out of slumber. Startled, Janči jumps out of bed, dawn still loitering in the sky. Glancing out the window, Apu sees Germans on the west side of mountain, shelling the village and partisans. Civilians are running in the opposite direction, Janči and his family speedily joining them, running for their lives; again, a journey that never seems to end. Someone is always chasing them. Again, left behind are all the items they've been able to amass over the past months. Mountains loom ahead, signaling their direction.

Aside from the mortar shells and machine guns unashamedly going off around them, a shallow, partially frozen mucky marsh, filled with slimy ribbitting frogs is their first obstacle. Without a second thought, knowing they cannot risk leaving tracks in the snow, they begin wading through the knee deep water, the weight of their sopping clothes slowing them ever so slightly. Janči is only wearing a pair of shorts, long sleeve T-shirt, and canvas shoes, most of which are already soaked through. Apu is carrying Marta, desperately trying to show leadership in a situation beyond his control. From all directions, a medley of bullets and bombs transiently whiz by them. Inexplicably, none of them make contact.

Keep running, Janči silently screams at himself, forcing his legs to move faster. *This can't be the way it ends*, he thinks. A loud explosion shakes him from his thoughts. In front of him, Arnošt falls face first on the ground with a sickening thud. A bullet has entered the back of his head, and a snarled mess of blood and brains is trickling out, seeping into the grass. Apu and Janči run back in the vulnerable open space to help him while Mamička and Marta run ahead and hide among the bushes.

"Please keep going. Don't let me hold you back. At least some of us can survive this," Arnošt mumbles. "I won't be able to."

His breathing becomes more shallow and forced. Apu, with his unwavering loyalty, lifts his friend and begins carrying him.

"Dežko, don't do this. You have a family you need to take care of, not an old man like me. Go, please, just go. I'll be fine here."

Despite his pleading, Apu keeps carrying him. A few feet later, another explosion sounds, and the instability of the ground is felt under their feet. A spray of machine gun fire propels its way toward them. An anguished wail exits Apu's lips. Spinning around, Janči sees Apu falling to the ground with Arnošt, clutching his stomach with ferocity, trying to contain a new wound, fearing it will come undone, spilling out vital organs.

"Apu," Janči screams and runs over. He does not believe this wounded man lying on the dirt is his father. *It has to be someone else*, he thinks, trying to convince himself of this. Apu can't get hurt now, not when they're so close to getting away. Blood is streaming out of his belly. Luckily, the shrapnel wound appears isolated to this one section, not anywhere close to a vital organ or vein. Amid the turmoil, Marta's wails supersede all other sounds. Mamička futilely tries to console her.

Janči eases him off the ground, and Apu hobbles along using his son as a crutch, continuing on without Arnošt. Apu looks back at his friend, lying on the damp ground, chaos swirling around him. With no strength left, Arnošt gives up trying to crawl, realizing it is useless. Life in him is slowly draining out, and there is no one left to comfort him. This man, who managed to come so far in his escape, will live the last minutes of his life utterly alone.

Gunfire ricochets everywhere around them, bouncing off trees into the air, prolonging the deadliness of each bullet. Crossing an undetectable marker, the gunshots wither into the distance, and Janči and his family make it out of the torrent of shells in one piece.

Janči's keen sense of direction guides them to the safety of their bunker, three long hours up the mountain.

"It's right over there," he informs his parents and points toward the other side of the forest where he, Apu, and Arnošt spent laborious weeks. Apu is unable to move at the imperative speed, his shirt sodden in dark red, the color travelling to his pants, the flow of blood not appearing to have subsided. Mamička grabs the other side of him, and together, they help him with Marta leading the way. At the entrance of the primitive bunker, the leaves and snow that once covered the passage to this secret underworld have been brushed aside.

"How can someone be in there?" Apu asks incredulous, unable to hide the lethargy in his voice.

"I'm sure it's fine." Janči assures him.

Lifting the door open, Janči signals for Marta and Mamička to start the descent, and they do, carefully taking each step. Janči grabs Apu under his arms and slowly helps him down the unsteady ladder into the familiar dwelling, practically carrying him down. Adjusting his eyes, Janči sees five people crammed into the small space.

"What are you doing here? This is our bunker!" Apu yells.

"Not anymore. We were here first," a male voice informs them.

Anger swells in Janči. How do these people think they can come here and take over their bunker after he and Apu spent countless hours digging and hauling things here for their family?

"You have nothing to do with this bunker," Janči screams, unleashing all his pent up rage. "We built it, and we're staying here."

The shape of a large blob slowly comes into focus. With the heavy gait of a very fat man, he saunters over. Janči is puzzled how a man of such large proportion made it into the bunker without getting stuck along the way. Once the features on his face are distinguishable, the view is disconcerting. Bright red cheeks that match his hair and the pugnacious face make him all too recognizable as their butcher of Janči's parents from Trenčín, with whom they had unthinkingly shared the secret of their bunker.

"You can't stay here. There's not enough room. Can't you see?" He points out to them in a matter-of-fact tone, his three daughters and sister frostily staring back.

"Can't you see my father is badly injured? This is our bunker, and we're staying." The bunker built for four now houses nine.

Mamička tears some fabric from her skirt and wraps it around Apu's waist, gently putting pressure on the wound, careful not to inflict any additional pain. Apu clasps his hand over hers, a simple motion communicating so many unspoken words. Their eyes meet and lock. Their thoughts travel back in time to their wedding day at Baračka and then back to the present moment, silently acknowledging the unfathomable course their lives have been diverted on.

Ballet is what brought the two of them together many years ago. Mamička took ballet with Ilona Pulitzer, Uncle Lajko's girlfriend, and they grew to be close friends. Ilona introduced Mamička to Apu in 1927. Apu was twenty-seven and Mamička was five years younger. When he saw Mamička dressed in her ballet costume, gracefully moving like a swan on the dance floor, he instantly fell in love. Irresistible to him, she had a captivating charm that took hold of him, and he couldn't shake it loose. Not wanting to risk losing her to anyone else, he proposed shortly thereafter. Two years later, they were married.

Mamička, the only child of Ella and Leopold Weiss, a well-off couple, was always immersed in arts, culture, and the best education. Apu's life growing up was a stark contrast, living in a small village with little money. Not discouraged by their financial circumstance, his parents had a strong desire for him to get a good education, so they moved to Košice where Apu was born. In Hungary, the medical university would've been his first choice to study at, but it limited the number of Jews who could attend to an insignificant percentage, using the *numerus clausus* rule as an excuse. Apu wasn't accepted despite his aptitude. As second choice, he studied at the University of Berlin in 1920 where he completed his Doctorate in Organic Chemistry.

As night falls, Mamička boils water on the small stove, maintaining somewhat sanitary conditions, and tears apart Apu's undershirt, using it to clean his wound. Janči watches, his eyes getting drowsy and then closing fully. After miraculously falling asleep for a brief interlude, Janči's eyes open and try to adjust to the darkness. Someone is snoring very loudly. Unsurprisingly, he sees the blubbery mound intermittently rising with each breath and expelling the raucous noise. Mamička and Marta have also stolen a moment to nap, but Apu is still awake, leaning against the wall, his legs outstretched in front of him.

"How long have you been up?"

"I can't sleep. The pain is keeping me awake aside from other things," he says, motioning his head toward the grumpy butcher.

"Is your stomach very bad? I can go find a doctor."

"No, Janči. I'll be fine," he said, knowing the impossibility of the proposed task. Although the bleeding appears to have stopped, pints of blood have already been lost, never to be recovered.

"Janči, try to get some sleep. You'll need to have energy for me."

Janči nods and tries to tune out the snoring in order to gain the rest he'll need.

A stream of light pours in as Janči opens the bunker pulling the tarp aside. He climbs out with Apu in tow and instantly gets a headache from the bright light penetrating his eyes. Astonished, they realize that they are not the only ones up here. Six other bunkers surround them within a one-kilometer radius. People are crawling out of their depths to talk with each other; partisans clad in army gear and other Jews trying to escape the terror going on below. One of them, looking like the commander or someone of significance is saying something to a crowd of men. Janči walks over with Apu to hear.

"Every three days, we will need a volunteer from each bunker to come with us to Kšinná to get food supplies. We have made arrangements with some farmers in the village to exchange food for money. We're going down today, so I need people from this bunker to come with me if you want food."

Apu and Janči look at each other and then to the butcher who has managed to heave himself out of the bunker.

"You go," the butcher instantly says to Apu.

"Are you crazy?" Janči yells. "He can't even walk ten feet."

"This isn't a sanatorium."

"You go," Janči spits his words at this evil man who doesn't even flinch.

"I'm not going anywhere. Why don't you go then since your dad is so useless?"

"He's not going," Apu forcefully interrupts. "He won't be able to carry all of the food with him. He's only fourteen years old."

"It's okay Apu. I'll go. I can do it."

"Are you sure?" he hesitantly asks, wishing he didn't have to see the day where his son would have to do work he should be doing.

"Yes. I helped you build this," he says, motioning to their bunker, "didn't I?"

"You did. If you feel you can do it, then go. But be very careful, and if you get too tired or can't carry the food, then don't."

"Okay."

Janči turns toward the partisan, ready to face his duty. Curiously, the partisan looks at the small boy.

"Are you sure you can do it?"

"Yes," Janči replies confidently, squaring his shoulders.

"Okay then. It looks like we have our team."

Ten partisans and civilians are ready in the early evening to trek down to the village.

"We must go through the creek, not to leave any traces in the snow."

Feeling like an expert at walking through water, Janči marches forward, the ice cold water momentarily shocking him. Soon, numbness overtakes his skin making him immune to the severe cold. Once through the creek, the troop wades through hip deep snow, each step more strenuous than walking through water, the density of the snow unwieldy to human legs pushing through it. The snow is the largest hurdle for Janči, being the smallest one working through it. Weakness in his muscles and the shortness of breath from his heart pumping too hard slow him down. He doesn't dare show he's lagging, not wanting the brave partisans to think he can't handle this duty or disappoint Apu. He sums all his energy to barely keep up in his canvas shoes that are drenched, not wearing proper boots like the partisans.

As the snow becomes shallower, ice makes the seven kilometer downward journey even more treacherous, its expanse surrounding them, shimmering in the dusk. In these subzero temperatures, everything freezes at night. Janči's foot slides on a slab of ice, causing him to come crashing down, luckily landing on his bottom, the best cushion his body can offer. An outstretched hand of a partisan helps him up, and they continue on.

Once on stable ground, Janči contemplates the risk of going to the village Kšinná for food, having learned no one can be trusted anymore. He can't be sure the villagers haven't been informing the Germans of their visits. But reality sinks in. Feeding himself and his family outweighs all risk, making up the decision for him on this matter.

The bottom of the mountain gives way to a road where small houses are outfitted in colorful roofs. The group splits into three smaller ones, each one going to a different house in the village. Inside the one allocated to Janči's group, a sweet old lady sits them down at a large wooden table and offers them hot bean soup with sausage, on the side, a slice of freshly baked bread that is still warm. Tearing it apart easily, he dips it into the soup, soaking up the broth like a sponge, the softness of the bread sinfully delicious in Janči's mouth. His core finally feels traces of warmth as the hot, thick soup with kidney beans makes its way through his system. Fried potatoes and sausage follow, filling his cells with the fuel they'll need for the trek back. Each bite is relished, while others around the table scarf it down, unable to control their hunger. Resistant to leave the warmth and comfort of this house, Janči continues his slow forkfuls, stretching out the time as much as he can. Linden tea is served afterward while they laze by the fire. Janči believes he has arrived in heaven after eating only plum butter, tree bark, and frozen apples for so long. This meal is fit for a king, and Janči desperately wishes his family were here. Lounging by the fire, Janči's warms his feet and somewhat dries his water logged shoes, uninterested in engaging in the conversation around him.

"We have to start heading back," one partisan announces, thanking the lady for the food. Janči's backpack is laden with food, the weight of it on his shoulders almost causing him to topple backward, making it apparent why strong men were required for this expedition. One loaf of bread alone is five pounds, add to it the beans and potatoes, and it feels like Janči is carrying Marta like he used to up the mountains. Dreadfully, he thinks to the uphill battle awaiting him. Coming down took two hours, and he can only imagine what it will be going back up. Around them sprawls the dark December night, extinguishing any life form from the human eye. Janči's body, warm only moments before, is assaulted by a blast of frigid air, the temperature outside having drastically dropped. His body temperature plummets, and the snow seeps through his dry sneakers, drenching his frost bitten feet in ice water. A severe numbing sensation enters his feet again making it feel like he's walking on two blocks of ice. With the weight of the backpack, his body is rapidly losing energy. Over exertion causes pain, which slows him down. One of the young partisans, Tomaš, notices his struggle to keep up.

"Janči, you follow me. If you need any help, just let me know."

Janči moves behind him, the last in their row, and watches in awe as this six-foot tall man with broad shoulders swiftly moves up the mountain with the ease of a monkey. Janči studies the automatic rifle he is carrying, a hammer-release mechanism allowing the firing of one shot only at each pull of the trigger. Tomaš turns around.

"I know your mom from Trenčín."

"Really?" Janči asks, surprised at this revelation.

"Yes. She was friends with my parents."

"She's in the bunker with us."

"I know."

"What were you doing before in Trenčín?"

"I was an electrical engineer."

Janči responds with silence, but Tomaš doesn't seem to mind.

On their continued ascent, Janči's vision starts to blur, and his heart doesn't feel like it can keep pumping this hard. His chest is constricting, and the air isn't getting to his lungs fast enough. Shivers begin and his palms start sweating. Dizziness enfolds him, and he can no longer see or hear anyone because he has fallen too far behind their steady pace. The last thing he feels is his entire body submerged in the freezing creek, the shock jolting him awake.

Not hearing footsteps behind him any longer, Tomaš immediately turns around to see the vast emptiness. His eyes quickly scan the area, and he begins backtracking through his steps in the snow, stopping at the creek where he finds Janči's unmoving body, but his eyes were blinking. A bluish hue has taken over his skin tone. Promptly, he lifts Janči up and pulls him on to the side of the creek out of the water. He takes off his jacket and wraps it around the young boy.

"What happened?" Janči asks dazed.

"I think you fainted. You're okay though, just very cold."

Tomaš helps him up.

"I'll take your backpack and you hold on to my belt. That should help you make it back up."

Gratefully, Janči grabs a hold of his belt and uses it as support all the way up the rest of the mountain.

Tomaš takes Janči back to his bunker which he shares with a few other partisans to give Janči a change of clothes. Inside, a fire burns, heating the bunker. Regaining warmth to the extremities of his body, Tomaš brings Janči bread with plum butter.

"You need to get your strength back."

"Thank you," Janči says and ravenously eats the food.

"I think I can change back into my clothes now. They should be dry."

"No, no. Just keep what I gave you on."

"It's okay. I'll just put my clothes on."

Tomaš shrugs indifferently.

"Okay, but now we should get you back to your family. They're probably wondering where you are." The two head over to Janči's bunker. Before Janči goes in, Tomaš hands him a jacket.

"You'll need this." The quilted Russian army coat is heavy with warmth that once protected a soldier who succumbed to his battle injuries.

"Are you sure?" Janči asks, hesitant to take it.

"You need it more than anyone else."

Janči puts on the coat, feeling the bulk of the quilted material. "Thank you, Tomaš."

He smiles and gives Janči his backpack of food, one he earned for the struggle.

"Do you need help carrying this down?"

"No, I think I can manage."

"Okay then. Goodnight, Janči. See you tomorrow."

"Goodnight."

Janči makes his way down into the bunker, finally with some hope that things will be all right. Mamička sees him coming down and immediately notices that he doesn't look well, even in the dimness of the bunker.

"Janči, what happened to you? Are you all right?"

"I'm fine, Mamička. Just a little tired. Look, here's all the food I brought us."

"Which you'll be sharing with everyone here," the butcher barks. Janči glares at him disgusted by his self-serving manner. The food gets passed around to the hungry group, each portion rationed and much of what Janči brought set aside for the long days to come.

Apu's condition is deteriorating with each passing hour. He can barely move anymore and doesn't say much. He just sits, staring blankly into space. Cases of dysentery caused by unclean water and resulting in bad diarrhea spread like wildfire through the bunkers. Microorganisms are released to infect their digestive systems and inflame their intestinal lining. Urgently, Janči clambers out of the bunker with barely enough time to dig a hole a safe distance away. Cold wind hits his buttocks; the luxury of toilet paper is a thing of the past. He resorts to freezing foliage that has fallen on the ground, the most unappealing way to go to the bathroom.

Days go on like this, each one becoming more unpromising. No end is in sight as to when they'll be able to leave. Germans continue to occupy the valley below with Ukrainian and Slovak fascists. Four weeks pass, and on one night, something in Janči changes. He is lying on the hard ground, floating in and out of sleep, when a sudden sense of urgency seizes him. Immediately, he wakes Mamička, gently shaking her out of sleep.

"Mamička, we can't stay here anymore. We have to leave."

"Janči, what are you talking about? We have nowhere to go. This is the only place we're safe for now. And how can we move with Apu like this?"

"I have a terrible feeling something is going to happen, something bad. We can't wait here anymore. We have to go."

"But where, Janči? Tell me where."

"We can go back to Trenčianské Teplice, to our house."

"Okay," she warily agrees, not wanting to argue further and especially not wanting to get in the way of her son's intuition. "We'll leave in the morning."

Neither of them asks Apu for advice. His delirium is eclipsing his state of awareness, and his mumblings are becoming more incoherent and illogical. Janči's unexplainable ominous premonition doesn't fade but grows more compelling. He remains awake the rest of the night, the rush of his swelling adrenalin preventing him from sleeping. Beside him, Apu restlessly sleeps.

At six o'clock, Mamička gets up, and they gather the few things they have. Marta gets bundled up as best she can to protect herself from the bitter cold outside. Janči takes Apu on his shoulders and Marta by the hand while Mamička carries their scanty belongings. Without a word to their ungrateful roommates, they leave the bunker hoping to never come back.

Apu has lost a significant amount of weight, but Janči still has to support a hundred and forty pound load. Getting back to Trenčianské Teplice means they first have to go up the mountains and eventually down the other side. Boy scouts training has paid off for Janči as he knows exactly which direction to take his family. Navigation has become a sixth sense for him, able to get anywhere. Climbing higher, the birch forest turns into pine and then spruce. Tree bark helps Janči figure out which way is north, the appearance of moss showing the direction of humidity and lack of sunshine. Now he knows which way to walk to get to the city. At night, he lets the stars lead him through the deep woods. Mamička puts her complete faith into her son's expertise. Blowing snow swirls around them, blinding the way and hindering their pace. Daggers of biting wind slash their face. Five hours later in the early morning, after climbing and hiding in trees and shrubs, they reach the peak of the mountains, about a kilometer from their bunker. One kilometer isn't very far, but in the snow, cold, and wind, with a child and a wounded father, it feels like an eternity. Collapsing for a moment, Janči sits in the snow to catch his breath. Fear and exasperation fill Mamička's eyes who doesn't know how they'll survive, all alone at the top of mountain, fighting the bitter elements of nature.

"Don't give up," Janči warns. "We'll make it. We just have to keep going."

She nods with frozen tears in the corners of her eyes. Janči puts a protective arm around Marta's shoulder, wishing he could erase all of this from her ten-year-old mind. She shouldn't have to live through this. She should be at home, playing with her friends or on the piano. Not here. Not like this.

"What's going to happen to us?" his sister asks, echoing Mamička's thoughts.

"We're going to be fine, Marta. I promise," Janči assures her. She weakly smiles and stares out into the unknown distance as the wind whips her hair around, and the snow beats harshly down on her face.

Gunfire and explosions suddenly erupt, loudly vibrating through the still air. Instinctually, they all duck behind the trunk of a fallen tree, taking cover from any bullets that may come their way. Perking up his ears, carefully listening to where the sound is coming from, Janči realizes the gunfire is not within proximity to them. He peers over the tree to investigate. Down the mountain, through the birch trees that have lost all their leaves, he mutely watches as German SS guards in blue and green, Slovak Hlinka guards in blue, and Ukrainian soldiers on horses are shooting throughout the entire area of their bunker. That not being enough, they also discover the hidden bunkers and drop grenades into them as if playing a game. Partisans are shooting back with their rifles, unwilling to go down without a fight, but a jet of bullets from the enemy is no match for them. Being shot at point-blank range, the bullets penetrate every partisan trying to fight back. Like dominoes, they each topple over and fall to the ground. Janči feels an infinite cavity of guilt open around him and suck him in. He is unable to help Tomaš as Tomaš once helped him.

Civilians hiding in bunkers like the butcher and his family won't be safe for long; many of them already shot dead while trying to run away. Giddily, the soldiers continue pulling open the underground homes and plunking down grenades. No one will make it out of there alive. Until they are certain everyone has been killed, the soldiers won't leave. And Janči escaped with his family.

They don't move that entire day. Covered in snow, they remain lying in it, a cold bed without covers or pillows. No energy is left in any of them to keep going at this point, the scene played out below sucking them dry. Their fingers and toes are dreadfully frostbitten, a gradual dark discoloration of the skin and formation of blisters taking place. Burning sensations from the intense cold transform their limbs into complete numbness. The next night, they continue walking in snow up to their knees, with Apu back on Janči's shoulder, the additional weight cumbersome. At night, the mountainous forest morphs into a threatening batch of shadows—darkness and noises that keep them on edge until day breaks. Janči stops to pick wild apples and bark from a tree. Although frozen, they manage to work their teeth through the fruit right down to the core. If the core wasn't so hard on their teeth, they would eat that too.

Another day goes by, and they are still walking, not fully grasping the expansiveness they must cover to reach Trenčianské Teplice. Janči does not feel the cold anymore. Only his visceral need for survival remains. Something in the distance catches their eyes. Getting closer, they find sacks of rice and sugar on the ground. Finally, someone has listened and answered their prayers. Their mouths salivate, ready to quench their dire hunger. A familiar smell hits their nostrils, and immediately, Janči knows. German's have already been here, pillaging the area and pouring kerosene all over the precious food. No one else can lay claim to it anymore. A renewed sense of despair hits them with the brutal reality of their situation.

An architecturally unsophisticated log cabin used by wood choppers and lumberjacks in the summer stands several feet away. As long as no one is in it—and it's a risk they're willing to take—the cabin could provide shelter from the cold and snow. Mamička and Janči tirelessly work on opening the door that is either locked or frozen shut. On the ninth forceful pull, it gives way and opens with a groan of displeasure at being disturbed. Inside, a few small windows line one wall, keeping it fairly dark. A loft is situated at the top of the room with a small stepping ladder attached to the floor. Janči climbs up and finds matches among axes and chopped wood. Against another wall is a fireplace and hearthstone, and Janči is able to start a fire. They huddle around defrosting themselves.

"Look what I found," Marta's voice yells from the corner, dragging a sack on the floor toward them. "There are some potatoes in here! And over there is some canned meat!" she exclaims with joy. Excitedly, they bake the potatoes and warm the meat over the fire—their first meal in three days. Apu sits leaning against the wall, unable to participate in the excitement, not understanding what the jubilation is all about. Mamička feeds him first. He doesn't eat much, either not realizing how hungry he is or not having the strength to chew, or maybe it's a combination of both. Gradually, his eyes close into sleep. Dividing the remaining food, the three of them make sure each bite lasts minutes, unsure when they'll eat like this again. Knowing how unforgiving hunger pains are, they cannot bear to shove any precious food down their throat. Silently, they chew and stare into the fire, each one recounting the past days in their mind. No words are left to fill the air. No more promises can be made without knowing if they can be kept. Janči's eyes start to feel heavy as he drifts off into a peaceful sleep with the warmth of the fire and his family surrounding him.

Another day accosts them, and they gather their belongings and continue on, determined to reach Trenčianské Teplice soon. All the food they ate last night has raced through their system, leaving them famished again. Janči rips barks off a tree—the only sustenance they can find—and passes it around for all to eat. He helps feed it to Apu who has difficulty chewing and swallowing it. A mouthful of snow washes down the coarseness.

Without much food in his system, a bad case of diarrhea claims Janči's insides again. Mamička and Marta suffer as well. Without any proper medication, the only substitute they can rely on to prevent dehydration is snow. With everything coming out of their system, they all feel weaker than ever before, Apu barely able to hold himself up anymore.

From a short distance away, they hear voices. Hurriedly, they lie low in a snow bank behind a large tree trunk. Remaining still, silent, and hidden, they pray the hostile voices approaching won't discover them. Janči puts his hand over Apu's mouth to quiet his incomprehensible speech and moans of agony. He feels awful for having to do such a thing, but they can't risk being discovered. Apu would understand.

Janči pictures his bare hands digging a tunnel in the ground for them to crawl through away from these men who are apt to hear the loud palpitations coming out of his chest. Deep, gruff voices get closer, speaking Slovak. Janči and his family remain immobilized in their spot. Another stroke of luck comes their way as the voices and crunching of boots on the snow pass, fading into the stillness of the forest. Although it is deadly silent, they stay where they are, soaked through to the bone, teeth chattering over blue lips. Only when they are fully confident the men are gone, they get up and keep going, finding shelter among trees at night where they huddle together for warmth and trekking purposefully during the daylight hours.

With the sun still rising, creeping up from behind the horizon, the sky is glowing pink and orange, promising a new day. After only a few hours into their morning journey, they happen upon a narrow path. At the bottom the trees clear way to two picturesque stone houses engulfed by snow in the middle of a meadow. Smoke wafts out of one of the chimneys.

"Let's go knock on the door and ask for help," Janči tells Mamička.

"I'm not sure if that's a good idea. We don't know who lives there. Think of what might happen to us."

"It can't be worse than what's already happened to us."

She sighs. "You're right." With her acquiescence, Janči marches to the door and knocks, praying someone kind will answer.

A petite lady in her forties with a black kerchief tied around her head opens the door. "What can I do for you?" she asks in Slovak, her face full of genuine sincerity. Janči is relieved he can speak to her in his own language.

"Could you give us some food and possibly help us rest a little."

Without a moment's thought, she pulls the door open wider. "Of course, I will help you." She looks behind Janči and sees Apu hanging off Mamička's arms. Immediately, she rushes out and helps carry him in.

"Michal, come here, I need your help!" she yells to someone in the house. A man with the same-sized frame comes out of the hallway sporting the overalls of a farmer.

He quickly acknowledges them and then helps the lady take Apu to the outhouse, the strength of this couple's arms deceiving. They delicately bathe him, using lukewarm water at first, not wanting to shock the frozen skin. Michal brings out disinfectants they use to clean the wound, redressing it with proper bandages.

Amidst the shuffling around their house, the two families are able to exchange names. Michal, Maria, and their daughter Olga Skultety all live here. Mamička informs the Skultetys of their situation. They grimly nod, admitting it's not the first story they heard like this. It's something they never get used to hearing and still can't fully comprehend.

Janči's turn in the bath comes shortly after—a slice of heaven on earth complete with smiling angels. Mrs. Skultety notices the Janči's frozen toes and the lice swarming his body. She *tsks* in pity, preparing socks and blankets for all of them to ease their frostbite. Warm water caresses his sensitive skin, the ice slowly melting from his body and dissipating in the bath. He luxuriates in the bath, disregarding his fingers which are shriveling.

Mrs. Skultety rejuvenates them with chicken soup, hot tea, and a burning fire—genuine concern for their well-being found in her kindhearted eyes. Choked up inside, tears tickle Janči's eyes. Finally, he feels again, for these fleeting moments, that he is a human being. Mr. and Mrs. Skultety are the only ones in a long time who have treated him as nothing less. Janči looks around their home. Inside, the stone walls are just one room. All the rest of the living and sleeping space is communal. But it is very comfortable and cozy, especially with the warmth of the fireplace. For Janči, it's a small slice of paradise, a place he could stay forever.

"You cannot stay here in the house," she informs them. "But I do have another safe place for you to stay. Finish eating, warm up more, and I'll show you."

With several Jews and partisans already hiding in the basement and underneath the floor, the barn is the only other alternative Mrs. Skultety has to protect this fraught family. Around the house across another path is the weathered A-shaped barn. Inside the square barn, cows roam around. Between the wall and roof, there is a small space that Mrs. Skultety fills with hay and blankets, an attempt to add an element of comfort to these living conditions. This becomes their new home.

"Please be quiet so no one knows you're here. Just lie here and don't worry about anything."

Each day, for one week, Mrs. Skultety and her husband make daily visits with food and water. Sleeping most of the days away, the four of them live cramped, submerged in the smell of cows that dwell on the farm, listening to the clucking sounds of chicken and nay's of horses outside. Apu's delirium is getting worse, and he has developed

BECAUSE OF A FISHBONE

an extremely high fever. He continues rambling incoherently, no one understanding the intelligent man. His mind has left him, leaving his body behind. Janči cradles him in his arms.

"I love you, Apu," he tells him, hoping he can hear and comprehend those three simple words. "You can make it through this. We all will. And then we'll be back at home in our house, and we can go on more walks in the forest and skiing in the winter. We'll go to the park on Sunday's again. Mamička will pack all that delicious food, and Jožka will come too." Janči continues to talk, recounting all his favorite moments of the past that he shared with Apu, believing things will get back to how they used to be. He talks until his mouth goes dry and his eyes close into sleep.

Apu's state of semiconscious hallucinations wakes Janči who has no concept of time, living in the darkness between these two walls. Mamička hurriedly gets up. "I'll be right back," she tells Janči. "I need to get Mrs. Skultety. Maybe she can help Apu."

Janči watches Apu, listening to his strangled communication which gets softer in the passing seconds. Then all is quiet. Noticing with horror that Apu's chest is not moving, no rise and fall of the breath of life, Janči swallows his panic and tries shaking him awake. Nothing happens.

"Wake up, Apu, wake up."

Marta is now awake and coming to the realization of what is happening and shakes him vigorously as if the momentum will infuse life into the still body.

"You can't leave us, Apu. You can't leave us," Janči pleads, holding Apu's face in his hands, tears falling freely. Quietly they cry, a piece of them dying along with Apu. Anger, denial, sadness, fear, and loneliness ambush Janči all at once. Instantly, life has lost all meaning. *This can't be happening,* he thinks. "Apu isn't really dead" are the words he keeps repeating in his head, denying this moment in time, the magnitude of it too much for him to handle. He feels as if his body and mind are shutting down, unable to cope, his heart not accepting the reality he is facing. Mamička returns, minutes too late, hurling herself on to her dead husband and silently screams in heartbreaking anguish. The true sound of her feelings is being contained, kept inside by the fear of being heard.

December 16 is the day Apu died, a date to be branded in Janči's memory forever. Just when he thinks he can't possibly have any tears left, another special memory of Apu comes to mind, and they flow uncontrollably again, the internal grief finding a way outside. He remembers their summers in Trenčín, particularly one walk the two of them took as they always did. Apu was teaching him along the way, pointing out the Trenčín Castle built in the eleventh century. Janči recalls looking up from the town below which lent an excellent vantage point to the imposing structure. They then walked through the town square for a treat of walnut tarts, the southwestern end of it flanked by twin golden towers of a church and the single brilliant white tower of one of the city gates.

Thinking back to these seemingly commonplace moments, he realizes their significance in the big picture of life. It is these moments, as simple as they are, that make life worth living. He questions what the point of all this is now, and how he can possibly move on without Apu by his side for guidance and support. A deep-seated yearning for Apu rips through Janči—one that can never again be fulfilled. At only fourteen years old, he is already half an orphan. And now he needs to take on the responsibility of being the man of the house. He has to take care of Marta and Mamička because no one else is around to do so. Janči decides that although he was given the name Janči Alexander Teschner at birth, he will honor Apu by assuming his Hebrew name, David.

Mrs. Skultety brings some medicine she scrounged up for Apu after Mamička visited her in a panic. Entering the barn, she sees it is too late.

Mamička takes money out of the hem of her skirt. "Please, take this money and give my husband a proper burial in a Jewish cemetery."

"I won't take your money," she says, placing it back in

Mamička's palm. "You don't worry. I will bury your husband. You just try to survive."

Olga rushes breathless into the barn, carrying a small sack of food. "You need to go and save yourselves because the Germans are coming up the valley. We can already see them from the top of the mountain."

Used to hasty exits, they take the food, socks, and blankets Mrs. Skultety offers and get directions toward Trenčianské Teplice. Janči now realizes they have to leave Apu behind, not sure if they will ever know where he is buried.

Before Mrs. Skultety pulls the blanket over Apu's face, Janči commits the wide-angled arch of his eyebrows, the bridge of his nose, his strong jaw, the curve of his lips, his thick light brown hair, and the serene look on his face to memory.

Mamička tells Janči to take the boots off Apu's feet and replace them with his canvas ones. "Take the jacket, too. He won't need any of it anymore," she solemnly whispers.

Janči pulls the boots and jacket off Apu's cold, dead body. Olga removes her own outer coat and gives it to Marta, both of them the same age and size.

After eighty more kilometers of arduous trekking through the mountains and dense forest blocking out the daylight, Janči notices a large hole up ahead which he curiously approaches. As soon as he looks in, bile surges up and spills out of his mouth into the snow. In the hole below lie bodies of dead Jews, all who have been recently shot, their bodies freezing into blocks of ice. The snow is lightly falling on them, steadily accumulating. Soon, it will be like they never existed, vanishing into the blanket of white that covers the mountains. Among those buried is a face Janči recognizes. It's a friend of his, the son of a local veterinarian. He is only two years younger than Janči, and his life is already over. Shot dead. In a hole. All these people were probably hiding somewhere in the mountains and got caught. *Why did they get caught and not us?* Janči wonders.

They don't have any choice but to continue along, even after witnessing this horror. They can't even stop to give these people—sons, daughters, mothers, and fathers—a proper burial. A little more fortune comes their way. They find a primitive hut where lamb and goat shepherds stay, who freely invite them to spend the night. Blankets, beds, and even some food are offered, giving the Teschners the greatest gift— another bearable night in the forest.

The next morning, they head out again on a seemingly endless journey. All the food they took from the Skultetys' eight days ago is long gone. For the past six days, aside from the food in the hut and cabin, all they've eaten is tree bark and frozen apples. Cramping and nausea take over their stomachs, but at this point, they can't feel it anymore. Janči is astonished they survived all these long, arduous days dealing with cold, snow, starvation, dehydration, exhaustion, insomnia, and the list goes on. But now, on this eighth day, as if someone knew there wasn't much resolve left in them to keep going, they arrive in Trenčianské Teplice, right next to Baračka. A layer of white snow plasters the landscape, but even still, they can tell where they are without difficulty. An indescribable sigh of relief leaves their lips and the three of them walk through their home city wearing grubby, torn, and tattered clothes that cover their backs. Pieces of what once used to be a shirt or pants are hanging off various limbs. A blanket that was cream now looks brown and is wrapped around Janči's shoulders. Workers walk toward them who have finished for the day and are heading home to their warm houses where there will be food on the table and a happy family waiting. Some of them sneer at the sight of Janči, Marta, and Mamička. Their sarcastic laughs echo in Janči's head.

"The three kings are coming before Christmas," they tease, ignorant to the fact Janči, Marta, and Mamička are one of them, understanding the language being used to insult them. This is how Janči figures out it is December 23.

"Ignore them," Mamička says to them through gritted teeth. "They are a bunch of idiots." Janči smiles at this remark, rarely used to hearing Mamička use any kind of profanity.

"Let's go back to our house. We can talk to the superintendent and offer to sign the house over to her. I'm sure she'll let us stay then, at least for a while."

In the direction of their sorely missed home is where their feet usher them. Even though Janči can still remember everything so clearly, it seems like ages ago that they were there. Guns and bombs continue to erupt in the valley, marking the Russian's advance, but all is quiet and still in their backyard, which they walk across with trepidation. Opening the side door, they walk down to the basement, hiding under the stairs for the time being.

"I think I hear her coming down," Mamička whispers.

A moment later, Mrs. Antal stands in front of them, shock visible in her beady eyes. "What are you doing here?" she asks gruffly, not the warm welcome they were expecting.

"We'd like to hide in the basement until the Russians get here. They're so close already. We'll give you the house and sign it over to your name," Mamička explains. "We just need a safe place."

"I don't need you to sign it over to me. I own this house now, not you." She pauses for a moment, examining the family.

"I'll be back in a few minutes, you wait here." Her small, bulky frame waddles back up the stairs.

"I can't believe this," Mamička says, ready to cry, taking Marta into her arms.

"It's okay," Janči tries reassuring her. "Maybe she went to see if she can find a place for us to stay."

They wait in silence, wondering. A few minutes later, Mrs. Antal is back with a Hungarian officer by her side. Fear and anger rises up inside Janči seeing this officer. Outrage at what Mrs. Antal does subsides once he sees Mamička conversing with the officer in Hungarian, hoping she'll make an ally out of him.

"This is now the Hungarian Army headquarters. It's not your house. Unfortunately, I can't do too much to help you because this bitch has already phoned the Gestapo in Trenčín and so I have to send you to jail. I don't want to do this. I only fight soldiers, not civilians. I don't care if you're a Jew or Catholic. It doesn't matter to me, but she left me with no choice right now. All I can do is promise I'll do my best to make sure you won't be hurt."

Two soldiers escort them to the local jail, their holding area before being shipped to Trenčín. A lone cell stands in the room. As soon as the jail guard opens the door to let them in, he instantly recognizes Mamička.

"Mrs. Teschner, what are you doing here?" the middle-aged head waiter of Baračka rhetorically asks, incredulous. Before Mamička can say anything he continues. "Don't worry. I will make your life easier here.

"You know, your Uncle Geza's lady friend, Ženka, is in the city. Let me call her for you. I'm sure she'll come and bring you a few things like clothing and food."

Like a miracle, Ženka, a gentile, really does come, meeting them in an arranged hotel room where she bathes their frost bitten toes, rubs sulfa cream into Jančí's body to ease a rash that is developing, feeds them food she brought, and gives them functional clothes. Even though their heads are still lice-infested, washing their heads with kerosene is the only way to kill them. At least, they feel clean.

After a day of this luxury, the Gestapo pick them up and take them back to the jail for three more days. Then a phone call from the Gestapo Headquarters puts the three of them on the electric train to Trenčín. Everyone on the train gawks at them, the family flanked by a soldier on either side standing guard as if one weren't enough. Around noon, they arrive in Trenčín and are whisked away from the railway station where they travel by foot guarded by Hungarian soldiers.

Their eyes passively watch the sights, architectural delights going by. On one side of the gate tower, restaurants and shops speckle the narrow streets with people going about their lives that have not been disrupted. In its vicinity close to the main square, is Štúrové Námestie, the twentieth-century synagogue, easily distinguishable by its light turquoise cupola. Jančí remembers going there with Apu and Opapa, the interior main dome always leaving a lasting impression.

Unable to take any pleasure in the architecturally splendid buildings, their eyes vacantly scan the landscape. All of it is irrelevant while they are on their way to jail which ironically is inside the beautiful Art Nouveau hotel Tatra located by the foot of the castle cliff in the city center, right at the entryway to the pedestrian-only town square. In the rear of the hotel is an inscription telling of a Roman victory over a range of German tribes in the years 179 AD. Jančí knows this because Apu used to take him during summer vacation in the afternoons to the restaurant inside the hotel. Apu would sit with his friends over cappuccino or read the newspaper while Janči sipped on a soda. Now it's been converted into Gestapo headquarters.

They are led to the dark and damp basement where the wine cellars used to be. It now houses one tiny jail cell. Immediately, the questioning begins.

"Where are you coming from?"

"Where were you hiding?"

"Do you know of any partisan activity?"

After obtaining all the information they can get in two days, Janči, Mamička, and Marta are disposed of and put on a train going to Sered transitional camp in the south western side of Slovakia where people end up working for Germans or are forwarded to Auschwitz.

Each person must be registered upon arrival. Today's date, December 29, is inked on top of the page. With meticulous pen strokes, personal information of each Jew is transcribed in a ledger as if keeping track of bank accounts. Germans oversee this meticulous collection of information, ironically written out by the hands of Jews, creating a reference file on everyone entering their camps. Once their identity is documented, they are moved into barracks where they are kept together. Exhausted at the day's turn of events, they lie on the bunks and sleep through to the next morning, not wanting to deal with the new roadblock thrown in their path.

Waking up the next morning, Janči forgets where he is, disoriented at his new surroundings. The faint smell of hay and manure, the drab walls and the rows of bunk beds, remind him too quickly of where they are. All of the hard work and effort trying to escape just landed them in here, the exact place they were running from.

Two effervescent ladies with tireless spirits approach Janči's bed and ask him to come to the kitchen with them. Although slightly guarded, he yields to the request, following the women with Mamička and Marta behind him. A small cake minus the impractical frosting and decorations rests on the counter. Breaking out into song, the middle-aged women sing the well-known verses which Mamička and Marta merrily join in clapping their hands.

"Happy birthday to you. Happy birthday to you. Happy birthday, dear Janko. Happy birthday to you." The two women from the Jewish Committee who read over the registry each day saw that today, December 30, is Janči's fourteenth birthday. Janči cries completely moved at this simple gesture. He makes a wish that doesn't take any time to think of. These five minutes of his life have reassured him again that good people still exist in the world he lives in.

Whittling time away these past few days, without anything to do causes Janči to become agitated. Getting up, he wanders through the camp in pursuit of a resolution to his idleness. Fortunately, his army coat from Tomaš allows him to mill about as he pleases. Hunting with a trained eye, he scopes the area for any work he can do.

A group of men are walking close to the fence of the perimeter of the camp. Their tools catch Janči's attention. These are men that have been given work to do. Drawing near to the leader of the group, Janči asks whether there is any work for him. Always in need of more skilled workers, Janči is told he can assist in building doors and windows for houses. He is directed toward the carpentry shop where the materials are. He works there for two weeks.

After finishing work each day, Janči heads back to the barracks where Mamička and Marta are. "Here," he says, pulling out sour dough bread with strawberry jam from inside his jacket, his compensation for work in the carpentry shop. Gratefully, they take the food. Huddling in a corner, they covertly eat, taking small bites, chewing quietly, internally vocalizing sighs of enjoyment. Devouring the last crumb, they leave nothing to prove the existence of their meal.

Going to sleep on full stomachs sets the three of them adrift into pleasant dreams of Baračka, of Bernie, and of gypsy music. The three individual dreams connected by a string of shared memories are shattered by an earsplitting yell.

"Everyone up! Now!" shouts a Hlinka Guard.

Butts of guns hit the helpless elderly who are barely mobile, let alone able to stand at attention on command. Unsure of what is happening, Janči, Mamička, and Marta scramble up, not wanting to prompt any unnecessary beating. Funneled out of the barracks, they are herded into cattle boxcars in the glacial January winter. Once the doors close, a hundred people are left standing with no room to sit, in only the clothes they were wearing inside the barracks. Next to Janči is a window with a steel grate. There is no glass on it, allowing air to reach the inhabitants inside.

Once a day, during the precarious train ride, when it comes to a halt at some geographical location, soldiers open the door and throw in a bucket of water. Everyone lunges toward it, wild like rabid dogs. Instincts for survival cause them to scratch each other's eyes out, to choke those in their way, because they are dying of thirst and desperately need water to live. Janči stays in the corner away from the animalistic chaos that will claim a life quicker than starvation, huddling with Mamička and Marta, stunned at how things are unfolding before him. Nothing warm is given to the passengers to eat. A hundred people cannot survive on this water alone. Many succumb to death as their malnourished bodies give up. Amid the feeding frenzy, the train starts up again and begins navigating the tracks to another destination pulling the cattle wagons filled with the living and the dead.

Three days elapse in this portable hell and lavatory, counting by all the sunrises and sunsets. Cold, dry air from outside and lack of water makes Janči's throat feel like sandpaper. Miniscule icicles begin forming on a grate next to Janči; the collective breathing yielding vapors that condensate and freeze. Subtly, he breaks them off, giving Marta and Mamička their own, which they all chew to quench their dehydration. Clustering together with another young lady separated from her husband and Marta wedged in the middle, the four of them try to keep warm, unable to sit with the mass of standing bodies around them while the cold air claws heat out from their bones.

Janči stares outside the grate that has become his personal porthole, seldom blinking in his dazed state, watching the land roll by, barren in one section, forested in another, or civilized on a different stretch. People go about their daily lives as usual, walking to the grocery store for bread, chatting with a friend over a cappuccino, and buying a newspaper from a kiosk, selectively unaware that the trains going by are carrying human freight. Distinguishable Polish names appearing at train stations startle Janči, the first one he's seen after getting used to rhyming off the Slovak ones for two days.

Drawing in a breath, he whispers to Mamička, "We're in Poland." Mamička's eyes enlarge, unmistakable fear clouding them over. Not wanting to disturb the fragile conditions of those around them, they keep this information to themselves.

Abruptly, the train stops after a few more kilometers, and within minutes, the doors are slid open.

"Raus, Raus,"[34] is shouted by the SS Guards.

Janči, fearing the worst, follows the mill of people toward the door with Marta and Mamička behind him. Taking a few steps down, he's

---

[34] *Raus* means "get up" in German.

finally standing on solid ground without the jarring motion he has gotten used to, an odd sensation of being stable. Behind the clouds cowers the sun, shielding itself from what lies below, sparing the prisoners headaches from bright light. A few meters away, the ominously open metal gates of Auschwitz welcome all the passengers fortunate enough to still be alive. A large sign above the menacing entrance to the main camp eulogizes the merits of work, *Arbeit Macht Frei*,[35] as if trying to blunt the effect of captivity.

Drab grayness touches everything in sight, from the sky, the walls, the double electric barbed wire fence, to the people, including the numerous SS guards who patrol the area. Hundreds of barracks clutter the property, each one filled with close to a thousand Jews, the sordid stench of human rot inside. A network of wooden beams support the ceiling and several three-tiered bunk beds line the floor. Janči wonders, yet again, when all of this will end.

Barely moving from the bed assigned to him, Janči tries to avoid the disease and unsanitary state spanning each footstep, not yet forced to go anywhere or do anything. Only one day into their stay and he hears one guard lividly shouting to get outside immediately. Janči almost falls off of his bed hearing those words. *This is it*, he thinks. Just outside and around the corner, such a short distance—the place where it will all end.

Astonishingly, through some divine intervention, they are led back to a train and loaded inside. Reversing its direction back toward Slovakia, the locomotive pulls away from death. A murmur of confusion rises around the walls of the boxcar, everyone relieved at being spared the horrors of Auschwitz but still uneasy about their unknown destination.

"The Russians must be getting closer," a man declares, optimistic about the westerly direction the train is moving.

---

[35] "Arbeit Macht Frei" means "work makes one free."

For five days, the train travels through Poland to Bohemia under the German Protectorate, a trip that would normally take three days, but with all the railroads bombed, untimely side rails are the only substitutes. More space fills each cart, a result of discarding the deceased. Janči resumes his position and watches the signs go by again, Czech changing to German.

Theresenstadt is the final stop where there is no turning back. They are escorted to an old colossal stone fortress which Maria Theresa, the Queen of Austria and Hungary, had built. Old houses and barracks that are hundreds of years old surround the perimeter of the fortress.

Janči notices Mamička's slow pace and tremulous walk. Beads of perspiration line her forehead, the effort of walking wearing her down, a sure sign that illness is coursing through her body. Immediately, they are all put in quarantine for one week, a safe guard to ensure no one is riddled with disease like typhus.

Thirty people fill one large dorm-style room with three-tiered bunk beds until given the all-clear of being contagious. Janči takes the top bunk, Marta the middle, and Mamička the bottom. Across from them lies French Prime Minister, Léon Blum.

Once Janči, Marta, and Mamička are released from quarantine, they are separated from each other without warning. Steering them into different anonymous groups, the soldiers make no attempt to inform them of where they are being led and whether they will see each other again.

Janči looks behind him and sees Marta walking away with a group of children her age. In another direction, Mamička faintly walks with an assembly of women, everyone split into clusters of similar demographics. Where are they going, he wants to ask, but knows he is in no position to do so. Their backs are the last thing he sees before turning around and being commanded to walk somewhere else with several other teenage boys. His feet only want to follow Mamička and Marta, but they can't.

They are taken to barrack L414, or more pleasantly called "The Youth House." All properties in the camp are systematically numbered, not by street number, but through a coordinated, seemingly more complicated process. Janči remains in the large three-story house for a few days, expectantly waiting for an opportunity where he will be granted work. He doesn't have to wait long.

"Everyone, stand in one line," orders an SS guard. All the boys jostle into a neat row for questioning. One by one, questions are flung on each boy ranging from where they came from, who their parents are, what their skills are, and the list goes on, the boys trembling with fear, worried at what type of response their answers will elicit. Next is Janči. Still donning the quilted army coat, Janči appears much larger than his actual fourteen years. The soldier in charge takes a step over to Janči, coming face to face with him. Without the cordiality of preamble, he instantly begins his line of questioning.

"How old are you."

"Sixteen."

"What kind of work are you able to do?"

"Electrical," Janči says assertively, the jacket giving him the conviction to do so.

"Go stand over there," he orders, pointing to a corner where only one other boy nervously stands. Janči takes being in the minority group as a good sign, silently thanking Apu for his sensible advice on learning a trade.

Janči is transferred from the Youth House to work at the Electro House, a two-story house used as a boarding area for all electricians. On the second floor, he receives his own room with a window overlooking the railroad where trains pass through, carrying their latest transports.

A phone sits atop a desk for his night shift when all he does is sit by it in case any important calls or emergencies come in. Although he is appointed to the night shift, Janči is on-call twenty-four hours a day. Twenty people are always on call at the Electro House.

Additional warm civilian clothes are provided to Janči, including undergarments, pants, sweaters, and a blue coat, resembling that of mechanics, for the times he visits area hospitals for work purposes. Putting on an ordinary shirt feels almost strange, having gotten accustomed to the Jewish star on ragged clothes.

A special pass card with his name and occupation listed as electrician is also issued, allowing Janči to move around the campgrounds and beyond the barracks. It is with this golden ticket that people answer his questions, and he is able find out where Mamička and Marta are. Mamička is working outside the camp, and even with his pass card, he is unable to see her.

But he immediately goes to visit Marta in the children's home. Janči walks into the large three-story house to find Marta in her group, learning how to create long brushstrokes on their paintings. Handfuls of children of varying ages intently practice on the pages set in front of them.

Willy Groag, the head of their group, a young mellow artist about twenty-five years old, inspires creativity within these children through painting and drawing. Marta feels right at home with these activities, revitalizing her fond childhood memories with Mamička on cold winter afternoons. She looks up and sees Janči, immediately putting down her brush and running over into a big hug that is waiting for her.

"Janči! What are you doing here?"

"I came to visit you."

"Come see what I'm painting," she excitedly says, not finding his visit at all unusual. Willy smiles at Janči as he walks into the group to study Marta's artwork.

"Wow. I see you haven't lost your artistic touch." Marta blushes at this compliment.

With his special pass, Janči regularly visits Marta, bringing her and the other children food that is hidden inside his jacket.

A civilian German named Karl is delegated to Janči's group to ensure everyone is properly doing their job. Janči is slightly taken aback when he sees the red, white, and black Swastika armband prominently displayed, not having worked in such close proximity to someone wearing one.

Janči becomes an electrician's apprentice for a Jewish-German professor and an engineer from Dresden, Professor Hans, who teaches Janči about radio and medical apparatuses. Upon seeing Janči's passion and proclivity for the electrical trade through his swiftness in repairing a broken radio, Professor Hans has no qualms in taking Janči under his guidance. A separate building houses the large workshop all the electricians use with access to quality electrical equipment and tools. Janči and Hans have their own workspace, the only two specializing in the repair of medical equipment. A broken ECG machine sits atop Professor Hans's table that will serve as Janči's first lesson. Pulling out a milliamp meter, pliers, an Ohm meter, a volt meter, and an oscilloscope, Janči stares in wonderment of the gadgets he's never worked with before, enthusiastic at getting his hands on them. Professor Hans first goes through the basic steps in fixing the machine gorged with tubes, valves, and dense wiring. Once Janči has mastered the elementary steps, Professor Hans proceeds to more complex instructions.

Restoring such medical instruments from the German army hospitals, some located as far east as Dresden, along with overhauling German telephone lines are the weighty tasks Janči is expected to assist Professor Hans with. Their small team of two competently carries out all the duties assigned to them, always smiling and laughing at the inside jokes they share about their trade, ones only the two of them understand. Over a short period of time, they become close friends who scheme together.

Karl drives Janči and Professor Hans in his beat-up old blue pickup truck to the hospitals that are in need of having instruments refurbished. Any pothole they cross is cavernous, no matter how small, as the car bangs them around inside its compartment, unable to absorb the shock of imperfect road conditions. Once at the army hospital, although suffering a mild case of nausea and minor headache, Janči inspects the valve in front of them. Without a second glance at it, Professor Hans loudly declares it's broken and pulls it out. He motions for Janči to bring him a replacement. Inconspicuously, Janči takes the malfunctioning valve and carefully puts it in his canvas workbag. Back in Hans's workshop, the valve, one that is in fact perfectly functional, is taken out of Janči's bag and put in a pile of other good valves that have been procured in the same manner, all amassed for the purpose of building a radio. With enough valves at their disposal, they are able to create a shortwave radio. Hollowing out a loaf of bread, their secret hiding place, they slide the radio in. Sitting around the loaf of bread they tune the radio to BBC. Professor Hans offers Janči a wink when the well-known jingle comes on. Other times, if the signal is strong, they are able to do their work listening to Beethoven's Fifth.

News reaches Janči through his contacts at work that Mamička has not been at her assigned location for the past few days. A surge of alarm sweeps over Janči who frantically begins asking the women who know her where she is. One after another, they shake their heads without any useful information to offer. Finally, an answer is found.

"She's been taken to the infirmary. She was too sick to stay here. I think she's in the Lazaret Hospital. It's only a couple kilometers from here." Janči's heart resumes its normal pace but not enough to quell the panic of how ill she's become.

On his next outing with Professor Hans, he will insist they make a stop at the infirmary.

After getting a few hours of sleep at the end of his shift, Janči has a gnawing need of being close to his family. He goes to visit Marta again, the only family he can see. Donning his civilian clothes has bought him the freedom of moving around within the camp, even without his pass card, no one stopping to question who he is and where is he going. To soldiers, he appears like a regular person, not a Jew in a work camp. These outings made him nervous at first as he always waited from someone to stop him, but they never did, and his comfort level increased with each visit.

On their way home from another hospital, Professor Hans and Karl agree to stop at the infirmary for Janči to briefly visit Mamička. Entering the large room with ten-foot high ceilings illuminated by a few scant bulbs, he makes his way along the wooden floor, passing all the cots standing side by side until he reaches hers. Seeing how pale and frail she is reminds him of the time she gave birth to Marta. She smiles, delighted and surprised by the company of her son.

"How are you feeling?" he asks, sitting next to the bed, taking her hand.

"I just feel very tired all the time. That's all. They thought it would be best for me to come here than stay in the camp."

"I think they were right."

"At least I can rest here. How are you and Marta doing?"

"I saw her. She's happily painting away in that house. And I'm good too. We go to hospitals every day and fix the machines inside. The work is interesting, and the people I work with are very nice to me." Mamička smiles, comforted that her children are happy and safe.

"I have to get going. They're waiting for me outside. But I'll be back as soon as I can."

"I know you will. Send my love to Marta. I love you, Janči."

"I love you too, Mamička," he says, bending down to give her a kiss on the forehead.

Before leaving, Janči pulls the doctor aside.

"How is she really doing? She tells me she's fine, but that's because she doesn't want me to worry. I can see she's not fine."

Understanding Janči's genuine concern, the doctor uncovers Mamička's real medical condition.

"She has complained about not being able to see well and that black spots also appear in her eyesight. Her blood pressure is high. It's not diabetes though. I've diagnosed it as being an outcome of all the stress and poor conditions she has been through. She is also lacking vitamin C, and I truly don't know what to do about that. I can't give her tablets or anything similar because I'm not allowed to. Is there anything you can bring for her from the camp?" he asks.

"I'll see what I can find," Janči tells him, determined at curing Mamička.

He speaks to Hans immediately after.

"I don't know, Janči. It looks like the war is coming to an end soon, and there's nothing left for anyone to buy, not even the Germans."

The next day, Janči tells the doctor he's having problems finding anything.

"See if you can find some rhubarb somewhere and bring it here," the doctor says.

"How am I going to bring rhubarb there?"

"I can't tell you, but all I know is it has a lot of

Vitamin C, and it will help your mother so much."

Wheels are spinning in Janči's head. Finding rhubarb shouldn't be too difficult. Germans love rhubarb, and there are fields full of it all over. The challenge is smuggling it into the infirmary.

Back in the Electro House Janči feels he can ask Karl for help.

"The doctor said my mom is lacking vitamin C. He can't give her any and wanted to know if I could bring something."

Mulling over the request, he is unhopeful. "I'm not sure where you can get anything. It's so hard to buy things with the war."

"The doctor recommended rhubarb." Karl's eyes light up.

"Of course! Be ready half an hour early tomorrow, and don't forget to bring your electrician's pliers."

Janči does as he's told and is ready early the next morning. Karl wraps rubber bands around the bottom of Janči's pants while he stands there confounded.

"We'll do this fast so no one suspects anything. Let's go."

The two of them climb in the old pickup truck and drive out to a field filled with rhubarb.

"Do it fast," he emphasizes again. "I'll wait here and keep our eyes open. If I whistle, come back."

Janči jumps out of the truck and runs into the field. With his pliers, he clips some leaves and stuffs them in his pants. Now it makes sense to him why the rubber bands are at the bottom—to prevent the leaves from falling out. In a matter of minutes, Janči is back in the truck, out of breath but ecstatic at his loot and at not getting caught while stealing it.

"Nice job," Karl congratulates him. "We'll go to the hospital now, but it has to be quick." At the hospital, the doctor hustles him into the kitchen where nurses cut up the rhubarb, making it easier for Mamička to eat.

Back at the Electro House, a bag of potato and carrot peels is handed to him, leftover scraps from the soldiers' meals. Janči chuckles to himself knowing the peels have more nutritional value than the actual vegetables. The potato peels have been cooked in water, but are still gritty, old, and black. He eats them without a second thought, not in any position to be picky.

Ghetto money is also given out by the Jewish Committee who allocates it to those in need to purchase food like dried onions and carrots. A warehouse has been set up in the camp where people go to get these basics—their own grocery store. Janči has to go to the committee and line up to receive this money while the clerks record everything in their books.

―⁂―

Show camps have also been launched, spearheaded by the commandant SS-Obersturmführer, Karl Rahm, who struts around in his polished black boots and impeccable white gloves, aiming to prove the exemplary situation artistic Jews are in at this camp.

A German filmmaker makes a movie of this grandiose exhibition, Janči doing the lighting and electrical work for it. Shots of the artists painting duplicates of the Mona Lisa and various Matisse masterpieces are filmed. The narration describes how talented they are, and the images don't deny that claim. Himmler puts a stop to the release of this film because the public should never be able to see how artistically talented the Jews actually are.

Royalty is still invited, like the King of Sweden and Denmark, and so is the Red Cross from Switzerland, to see the how masterfully these artists paint and draw, the finished pieces proudly sitting on display as if in a prestigious museum. Food stands are erected, and buoyant music drifts through the delusional ambience. Ironically, on the opposite side of this camp are people going hungry and crematoriums for the prisoners who perish from starvation, illness, fatigue, or what is considered to be wrongdoing. Piles of their personal belongings, glasses, shoes, dentures, and gold teeth pulled from the mouths of dead bodies, and clothing don't make it into the crematorium, too valuable to be burned. This part of the tour is not offered to any royalty.

Other barracks on the compound, also not part of the tour, are filled with hundreds of women hunched over at tables, an assembly line in a factory, methodically slicing sheets of transparent stone, a glasslike quartz with a knife. It is from this material, not real glass, that the windows are made. The military also uses it for spark plugs because of their quality electrical insulation. Inhaling this substance on a daily basis is a health hazard for the workers as the fibrous crystals enter their lungs, diseasing them, eventually making breathing difficult, but the women are given no choice.

In April, the transports are endlessly coming in from concentration camps in Hungary and Poland, carrying people who have miraculously been spared a torturous death and granted a second chance at life. Descending the train stairs, they all contain the same apprehensive and puzzled look, uncertain of how they are still alive, waiting to discover that this is just another cruel joke, and they'll be thrown back on a train in moments for the real punch line. Several barracks that act as a holding area are filled with eighteen thousand former Jewish prisoners.

Up on the second floor in Janči's room in the Electro House, shutters cover the windows. A transport is coming in, the reverberations along the train track giving it away.

"Close all your shutters, and don't look out the windows," an SS Soldier orders all the workers as he always does when transports arrive. Janči does as he's told but still doesn't understand what they are trying to hide from him as he's seen it all, yet his curiosity gets the best of him and he peeks out his window.

Below are the notorious transports, illuminated by streetlights. People are lying in open boxcars covered with frost, a large number of them are still and frozen to death. Movement can be detected both on top of and below the dead, the living still trying to survive. Janči's stomach churns at this scene, and he quickly closes the shutter and slides down the wall to the floor burying his face in his hands.

—m—

Danishes are handed out on Friday's as part of their remuneration. For an additional reward, they are given chocolate bars if they work longer hours than expected. Janči always works nine or ten hours a day and qualifies for this additional treat.

After much anticipation, on the following Friday, the large Danish makes its way into Janči's hands. Prune jam filling overtakes most of the six inch diameter of the pastry. Last week, it was filled with cheese. Distressingly, he appraises it, remembering what he saw below his window only a few nights ago. With the picture of people dying of hunger etched in his mind, he is unable to bring himself to eat the Danish. He wraps it up in tissue paper and puts it safely aside on his bedside table. The sun flits away, taking with it the light. Streetlights turn on, compensating for this loss.

"Shut your windows," the SS barks the invariable order again.

Janči listens carefully as the lights go dark on the second floor. When the train has come to a stop, he gently opens the window a crack and begins tearing off pieces of the moist and sticky Danish. Bit by bit, pieces get thrown out of the window into hungry mouths below as if being showered with sweetness from the heavens above.

Stealing a look outside, the Danish doesn't have the effect Janči predicted. These once civilized people are killing each other for a morsel of food, scratching, hitting, pushing, and kicking anyone standing between them and the Danish. Swiftly, Janči shuts the window with trembling hands, squeezing his eyes shut, trying to shake the vision out of his head.

Still disturbed at what happened, Janči confides in Hans the next day about what he did and saw.

"Don't give them food. You're not doing them any good because they can't eat food after such a long time of being hungry."

All the food Janči amasses at the Electro House, especially chocolate and sardines, he takes to Mamička in the infirmary or to Marta. Marta shares it with all her friends in the youth home.

The next time Janči gives food to the Jewish prisoners again is toward the end of the war in April on different terms since his job is to help them. When they arrive on the trains, they are dressed in better quality civilian clothes. No more uniforms are being distributed to the prisoners. Various Red Cross organizations like the Swiss, Swedish, and Danish arrive with food, helping everyone survive till the end of this. They already got so far.

Toward the middle of April, Mamička's health improves to the point she is able to leave the infirmary. But it only takes a few weeks in the camp for Mamička to degrade again, and she is sent back to the infirmary.

A sense that the end is near is palpable, and the radio soon confirms it. At the end of April, an uprising in means the Russians are getting close.

Lying in bed, Janči tries to think of what this all means. He can't imagine freedom anymore, believing it was just a thing of the past. Could it be that he'll have the chance to stroll the streets of his home again without having to worry about being thrown on a train and sent to a camp? Shooting outside his window disturbs his thoughts. He jumps up unsure if the firing is from enemy guns and discreetly glimpses outside. American soldiers riding in jeeps and tanks with white stars are steadily moving around the barracks. Tea and crackers—part of their aid supply—is distributed to the hungry.

While they foray in, helping those in need, a conference with Roosevelt, Churchill, and Stalin takes place in Yalta. A decision is made among the leaders to divide Europe into East and West. The Elbe River becomes the dividing point that originates in northwestern Czechoslovakia then traverses through most of Germany, finally flowing into the North Sea. This river scrapes by Theresenstadt, putting Janči and his family on the Russian side. The American army is ordered to move out as the territory is no longer under their protection. Again, this leaves a void that the Germans hastily fill, casually shooting bullets into groups of children and adults, all while the American and Czech flags still blow pensively in the breeze without any soldiers to defend them.

After this display of indifference to human life, Janči refuses to go back to the Electro House, fearing he will end up among the dead. There is no one who could ensure his life would be spared from German bullets. Cautiously, without drawing any attention to himself, he heads in the direction of a five-hundred-year-old house. This is one place where he had to work while on duty at the Electro House. During the day, while he was fixing things inside, the owners were at work, giving him the liberty to explore the house. Finding a tiny attic, it became his secret tool receptacle. Now he winds up back inside, sneaking in when luckily no one is home, then crawling through a narrow space leading up to the attic, where he stays hidden for as long as necessary. He unpacks the little food he snuck under his jacket, unsure of how long he'd be here. Unable to stand with the ceiling being so low, he just sits on the dusty floor in the darkness, no windows to offer him light. In solitude, he can't escape his thoughts that keep reverting to Mamička and Marta, praying they are both safe. At least with Mamička in the infirmary, the thick stone walls will protect her from any German mortars. Alone and helpless as bullets intermittently go off outside, screams heard too frequently, he slinks down, waiting for it all to be over, his chances of surviving in the attic much longer being very slim.

On May fifth, two days after crawling into the attic, the floor vibrates, and loud rumblings sound through the walls. *It must be more tanks*, Janči thinks, *but whose?* And then the shooting begins. Getting on his knees, Janči edges his way out to investigate. By the doorway, he sees the red stars of Russian tanks and soldiers coming from the east side on the same road as the Americans came but from the opposite direction. Making sure his eyes aren't deceiving him, he watches for a moment longer; and then feeling it is safe, he steps outside into the fresh air his lungs have missed, his cramped legs begging for a good stretch. Relief and elation tinges the air as everyone rushes out from all corners and crevices, like ants scurrying out of invisible holes, embracing each other, still in disbelief that they are alive. They survived. They have been liberated.

Powdered milk, rice, and sugar are supplied by the Russian Army. In bulky caldrons, they cook the rice, keenly serving it to the emaciated victims. Janči doesn't touch any of the food as tempting as it is, hearing the wise words of Hans ringing in his ears. These bodies are unable to metabolize the food properly, having eaten barely anything in months. It is a shock to their system, the boost too hasty in such a short span of time. Many end up becoming sick from it.

Janči sets out to find Marta, walking toward the Youth House. It stands abandoned with no one inside. Thwarted but refusing to give up hope, Janči scours the campgrounds, searching in all houses, rooms, and bushes. He concentrates on everyone he walks by, not wanting to pass Marta by mistake, worried she might be wandering around, looking for him. Still, there is no sign of her. At night, he finds an empty bed in one of the barracks and sleeps. He needs the energy to continue the search tomorrow. Two days after the liberation, he coincidentally walks by a band of young girls encircling an army truck. He thinks some of them look familiar, and then it dawns on him that they are from Marta's youth home. His walk turns into a run, the optimism that Marta is among them pushing his legs forward. And then he sees her in the crowd, barely perceptible through the taller girls, looking lost and scared even amid her friends.

"Marta!" he howls, unable to contain his emotion. Seeing Janči, she breaks down in his arms, not daring to let go of him. For the past few days, she thought she'd been orphaned by her family, left to carry on by herself, the idea paralyzing her.

"It's okay. Everything is okay now. I'm here," he soothes. Her crying continues, and Janči lets her cry for as long as she needs. After she has calmed down, Janči takes Marta to the infirmary to find Mamička. No major damage has been done to the façade, but the conditions inside are worsening. No skilled doctors remain, and supplies are depleting. Nurses point them in the direction of Mamička's room where they find her lying in bed, unharmed. The three of them embrace for a long time.

German power in Czechoslovakia ultimately ceases on May 11, 1945 when Russian soldiers liberate Prague. Only twenty thousand Czechoslovakian Jews survived out of 277,000 before the war began.

GOING HOME, JUNE 1945

UNTIL THE END of June, they remain in Theresenstadt, waiting to receive their identification cards with their names and addresses that prove they were released from the concentration camp. This makes them eligible for food like peanut butter—which Janči finds to be extremely peculiar, always sticking to the roof of his mouth—and clothing distributed by the United Nations Refugee Agency. Free seats on the train to Trenčín are also filled instantaneously, everyone impatiently wanting to get back home. Railroads are being repaired from the succession of numerous bombings, causing a one-day train ride to take five days while the train circumvents the wreckage of snarled metal and caved-in bricks.

Uncle Lajko is still alive and head of Jewish Community Services in Trenčín. With his connections, he manages to track down Janči, Mamička, and Marta, euphoric at discovering he has surviving family. Uncle Palko, who also joined the partisans with Uncle Lajko, is alive as well, but his toes and fingers had been amputated during the war, a result from deep and serious frostbite. Discharged, he returns to Trenčín and reunites with his family. Uncle Geza also turns up in Trenčín, ready to take back Conditoria Weil and Baračka.

Uncle Lajko's family mission begins by arranging to have all their lives put back together while he prays for the return of his own son and wife. One month later, Ivor appears, unexpectedly materializing from thin air, still tall but skeletal, weighing much less than a thirteen year old should. He recounts the story of a stranger who shared her scanty food rations with him that saved his life. Mamička gives him all the butter they get on rations, trying to fatten him up, and he does.

Across the river on either side of their house, the walking bridge and long double railroad bridge were both blown up by the Germans before the Russians came, leaving scraps of metal in smithereens. All the houses in the area suffered terrible damage after the bombing, forcing everyone to move out and abandon their freshly dilapidated homes, a ghost town being born in their mass exodus.

Amid the rubble and devastation, Janči and his family search for their home in blocks of crumbled walls, piles of crushed bricks, broken pieces of glass, and bent metal. Personal effects, couches, drapes, tables, chairs, and iceboxes poke through, hanging on to be rescued. On a treasure hunt, they scavenge to see what is theirs, locating the exterior frame that still bravely stands, even though all the inner walls have collapsed and windows have blown apart as if a natural disaster swept through. Picking through the mounds of debris, the task seems futile, progress never appearing to be made. Fortunately, even though the upper part of the apartment block is demolished, the lower level where their unit is still intact.

Very little of the furniture recovered is usable, cabinets, coffee tables, and dressers written off, but what remains of bed frames and their dinette set is dusted off, the layers of wood recovering some of their sheen. Further scrubbing, scouring, and sanding brings the grains in the wood to life, restoring them to their brilliant finish. Colored fabric on the couch is coated with a permanent stain of brown age in severe need of reupholstering. Amazingly, they find some of their old pictures, the previous owners never bothering to take them down. Lying ramshackle is the flower room with flowers that withered and died, the dust blocking out the sun, the collapsed bricks not supplying water. Rearranging usable furniture, discarding the pieces damaged beyond repair, and hauling bricks up off the floor and tossing them out the window, the room begins to take on the semblance of a home. Even with the renovations, they continue living in their apartment in the areas not being worked on.

Before long, they move into their old dining room as the warmer summer months of July and August arrive. Remaining in Trenčín is a decision that is easily made by the three of them, none of them eager to face the bad memories that still haunt them in Trenčianské Teplice and a house with owners unwilling to relinquish the property.

Relearning their bearings, they go to the city; and with the help of Uncle Lajko, they look for brick layers and mason workers to plaster walls which they purchase using money granted by the Jewish Community given to Jews starting over. The American Jewish Congress also sends them parcels with clothing. Mamička hires brick layers to reconstruct their apartment, and as each brick is laid, each piece of their lives is slowly being put back together.

An American pilot shows up at Uncle Lajko's one day with a dog eared envelope in his hands. He solemnly passes it over to its owner. Looking down at the letter as if tainted, Uncle Lajko shrinks away from it. It takes him a moment while his mind grapples with what might lie inside. Finally, he opens the envelope. In permanent ink, the words contained on the paper narrate that Illona is in the hospital and hopes to be home soon. Uncle Lajko cries out in happiness, jumping up and down like a child, hugging everyone around him. He can't believe how fate kept him and his wife alive through all this, and miraculously, they'll be reunited soon enough. Days of waiting for his wife turn into months, and Uncle Lajko comes to the heartbreaking realization that Ilona is never coming home, dying, they speculate, from typhus before she makes it.

During these summer months, Marta and Janči are out of school, giving them time to readjust to a place they were once so accustomed to, a place tarnished by events that can never be undone. Walking home from an afternoon in the city, Janči watches the new wave of forced labor workers repairing the railroad bridge. Now that the war is over, fascists from the Slovak Republic are made to repent through manual work. Outfitted in dowdy coveralls, grime stains covering his sweaty face, grunting at the intensive work his body is obliged to do, Mr. Dubček—Janči's old teacher—is among them. The tables have turned. He heaves a shovel into the dry ground, hauling it back out with barely any dirt inside. Limping over to another area, barely able to manage his crutches and shovel; he tries for a softer plot of land. An awkward large cast surrounds his right leg from an accident a few days earlier, when one of the heavy traces from the bridge fell on his leg and broke it.

Recognizing Janči, he tries to make conversation. Janči continues walking straight past him, ignoring his effort at atonement. Although it may not be the appropriate thing to do, it's not in Janči's heart to forgive Mr. Dubček for what he did. Beating children with rulers and sticks solely based on their religion is not an action that can be absolved—not in this lifetime.

During the renovation of their home, the three of them visit the village of Kšinná, specifically Sebenove Lazy, in the mountains, in search of the Skultetys to thank them for all they did. From villagers, they learn that a traitor in the village notified the Germans that the Skultety family was hiding Jews and partisans in their house. Spared from being shot, the Skultetys were taken away, possibly to a worse fate, and their house and livestock were set on fire. People still hiding in the basement saw the bright orange flames, inhaled the acrid smoke, and felt searing heat getting closer to their skin. Climbing out of a window, their heads revealed the Skultetys' secret. A slew of bullets from German guns stopped them in their attempted escape. Everyone hiding in the basement died. Janči and his family stop looking for the Skultetys after hearing the shocking news. Gravely, they go back home.

Once all the cleaning and renovating is complete, they are left with a complete home, part old and part new, one they can call their own again and safely lay their heads at night without being cramped among thousands of panicked people or with the smell of manure suffocating them.

Waiting in line, groceries are bought with their ration cards, stamped when given bread, butter, milk, sugar, or ham. Wood for the stove is also purchased, inspiring Mamička to start cooking again. Taking zealous requests from her children, the first proper meal of bread dumplings and ham is laid out on the table. Sitting around the four-person table they salvaged, they delightfully eat, reminiscent of the old days, except Apu, Babka, and Opapa aren't at the table with them as they should be, the conversation empty of their stories and voices.

Even though things are finally getting back to normal, Mamička's health is waning again. Although her complaints of pain, lack of energy, and dizziness are sporadic, her children know she is only trying to conceal its gravity. Still haunting her each day is the anguish of losing Apu, a piece of her dying the day she lost him, a piece that will remain gone forever. She is sent by her doctor to Smokovec Sanatorium high in the Tatra Mountains to fortify her health. Up there, she can put some weight back on and relax; however, she never stops worrying about her children whom she always writes and whom she misses dearly.

In the fall of 1945 Conditoria Weil and Baračka are finally recovered, rightfully reclaimed by Uncle Geza after a long fight with communist Slovaks who stole it during the German occupation and refused to give them back.

Chocolate is unavailable at this time, not part of the rations given out to people but essential to run the restaurant and pastry shop, or else how could they make chocolate tortes, ice cream, and chocolate nut cake. Uncle Geza brings five-kilo bricks of chocolate wrapped in brown paper off the black market and hides them in the basement of the apartment block in Trenčín, to be used as required. Every week, he takes one brick from Trenčín to Baračka, risking the fine he could face if caught. He asks for Janči's and Ivor's help one day in transporting the goods. Agreeing to be coconspirators, the following Sunday, Ivor and Janči tie a carrier to the back of their bikes which adequately holds the five bricks of chocolate they each have.

"I think we're ready," Janči exclaims, feeling the giddiness of their past summer days going on a journey to visit Babka.

"I think so," contagiously catching the feeling. "This should hold."

Dark clouds begin rolling in just as the boys have taken off on their twelve-kilometer adventure. Drizzle hastily turns into sheets of rain, limiting their range of vision. Slick road conditions are no match for the grip on the bike tires that are too bald to sustain balance and skid out of control on a curved road in front of a police station. Bricks of chocolate fall out of the overturned carriers that snap off without the support of string, littering the ground. Crouching down, they swiftly collect all the bricks in their arms, one on top of the other, heaving them back into the carrier they reattach, praying the police don't come out and see their illegal trade. Vigilantly, they ride the rest of the way, sopping wet, but with all the bricks intact.

Letters routinely arrive from Mamička describing her hopes for them to be happy and successful, making sure they're eating enough, doing well in school, and taking care of each other. There are reminders for them to behave properly and help their uncles when they can. Letters addressed to only Marta contain complaints from Mamička that Janči doesn't write enough. For the two months she's up there, Janči doesn't see her, satisfied she is doing well after reading her letters. He doesn't worry about not visiting her, focusing all his time on working and taking care of Marta. And he's right. Mamička comes home strengthened and in higher spirits.

Uncle Lajko remarries a nurse from the partisans named Irenka, who had been hiding under a false name. Her husband was killed in a concentration camp, but her son, Peter, survived. The two of them move into Uncle Lajko's house.

A malevolent aura surrounds Irenka the moment she takes up residence in Uncle Lajko's house. However, Uncle Lajko is immune to it, but Marta, Ivor, and Janči feel her wrath. They see it in her unkind eyes that barely make eye contact with them, that only lovingly dote on her son. The nastiness, shortness, and sarcasm in her tone when addressing them leaves a sour taste in their mouth, causing them to avoid the exchange of any words with her.

Janči and Marta hesitantly visit for dinner; and only upon Uncle Lajko's insistent request do they go. While they eat, her scornful eyes bear into the unwanted children who are taking up space in a house that now belongs to her. She takes every opportunity she has to remind Ivor of this. Peter, uninterested in what his mother thinks, struggles to be included in the games Janči, Ivor, and Marta play.

In one year, Janči finishes high school and passes all his exams, opting to continue his education at an industrial trade school, learning electrical theories. The school is where the old Jewish school used to be. At this point in his life, Mamička thinks it's a good idea for him to find a job. A distant cousin of hers, a famous radio technician, Mr. Berger, lets Janči work for him, building and repairing radios. Janči eagerly accepts the exciting job offer, now making money on the side. Classical music starts to grow more on him more—an influence of Mamička's—and while fixing and testing radios, he listens to it, humming along to operas, operettas, and classical music like *Eine Kleine Nachtmusik* by Mozart.

He also bumps into his old friend, Edvard, who is currently studying aeronautics and engineering at the University of Bratislava. They get together on weekends when Edvard is home and work on model airplanes.

Janči works at Baračka every weekend, helping out Uncle Geza. Still not getting enough of his family's old business, he also frequents Conditoria Weil during the week after school, both to work and to eat lunch or dinner, making up for lost time. After eating, he goes to his second job with Mr. Berger until seven or eight in the evening; earning more money than he knows what to do with until inflation hits and the currency isn't worth a penny. Janči carries it around in a basket, trying to buy something, anything, just to get rid of it.

Returning to his hobby of building model airplanes, Marta becomes his assistant in flying gliders. Janči holds it with a long rubber bungee, stretching the bungee as far as possible. Marta holds the other end and shouts "release." Janči lets go of the bungee and the plane takes off. Only one person is needed to fly a motor-driven plane.

Zionist feelings are adopted by Janči, not seeing any positive future in his home country, the place that once held the only future he knew. Anti-Semitism still lingers, the weak economy and lack of necessities still remaining the fault of the minority of Jews left, blame just as easily being doled out as it was before. Janči has more than he can take of it all. Signs are pointing to a communist regime taking over the current democratic one as the Russian army stationed in Slovakia is exerting pressure for one. Americans are stationed in the southwestern part of the Czechoslovak Republic because of the east-west division. Both Janči and Marta desperately want to move to Israel but are unable to talk to Mamička about it because they know they could never leave her alone.

Janči joins a group of surviving Jewish youth, going to club meetings every Friday; they happily sing, socialize, and talk politics. On weekends, they meet each other for walks through the mountains where Janči brings a portable radio he constructed. Through Apu's old connections, he managed to obtain the radio tubes manufactured in the United States, smaller than traditional ones; and with lots of coils and wiring, he crafted a functioning battery-operated radio the group members love him for. With other youth groups, they take trips to different cities and engage in a social life they haven't had in a very long time.

Until the beginning of September, Mamička is relatively active, meeting with old friends, Maria Fried, who remarried and takes care of the apartment. Abruptly, she weakens again, unable to walk and being constantly dizzy. They take her to the Jewish hospital in Bratislava, hopeful of successful treatment like the one with Janči's hand years ago. She has to remain there for several weeks.

The slush and snow of November doesn't make the two-hour train ride any easier for Janči who visits Mamička twice during the month she is in the hospital in Bratislava. Her blood pressure remains dangerously high, problems with her kidney continue to exist, her complaints about seeing black spots in front of her eyes doesn't go away, and dizziness still racks her head and body. Under the wool blanket, her body shrivels, her weight being shed as easily as removing clothes. Hollows appear in her lackluster cheeks, and her collar bones become apparent, protruding from her taut skin. But then, toward the end of the month, by another miracle, she gets better again and is able to go home.

During his free time on weekends, Janči takes Mamička on walks around the city, citing the same facts Apu and Opapa taught him. Outings to the castle and cherry orchards are on their agenda as are espressos at local cafes, reintroducing her to an active lifestyle and prodding her with cheerful memories. As much as she can do, she willingly does, wanting to get back to her old habits of entertaining guests, visiting her friends, and spending time with her children.

In a matter of weeks, just as everyone was getting accustomed to this new routine and having her mom, Mamička winds up back in the Jewish hospital in Bratislava, taking a very quick turn for the worst. After examining her, the doctor immediately tells Janči and Uncle Lajko there is not much more that can be done to cure her. She has worsened beyond their control.

"The best thing for her is to be close to home and her family. You should take her to the hospital in Trenčín, where you can all visit her frequently. Sadly, I don't think there is much hope that she has a lot of time left."

Through the winter of December, Janči visits Mamička each day after school or work, staying until nine or ten each night. Simply, he holds her hands, and they talk. They talk about everything—how Marta is doing, how the apartment is faring, how Uncle Geza is managing with the restaurant, how Uncle Lajko and Ivor are getting along, Janči's own work and school, and direction he plans on taking in life. Each evening, she looks forward to these conversations, bored of lying in bed or shuffling down the corridors. This is her only connection to the world beyond the dutiful inquisition of nurses and the sterilized walls of the hospital.

One night, a month into her admittance, the doctor on duty stops Janči before he goes in to see Mamička, noticing his gloomy expression.

"Cheer up, she feels well. She might be okay."

By her bed, Mamička echoes those sentiments. "I feel so much better today," she tells Janči, taking his hand. "Jančika, my son, stay with me tonight."

"Mamička, you're feeling all right. I will come tomorrow and see you again."

Janči keeps his promise and heads over the next day, a slight bounce in his step.

"How do you feel today?" he asks. "You look good."

"I feel good, and I have more energy lately." She pauses for a moment. "Will you stay with me tonight?" she asks again.

"You're doing so well I don't need to. I will come tomorrow morning, I promise you."

First thing early the next morning, Janči goes over before school starts. As he walks down the hall to visit Mamička, a cluster of nurses sympathetically look at him. Ignoring their stares, he continues down the hall. Before reaching her door, Mamička's nurse, wearing a uniform with a black bib, black blouse, and white collar stops him and motions him to sit down in the chair in front of her room.

"Janko, we're very sorry to tell you this, but your mother passed away last night."

Janči gapes at her big white hat with wings covering the sides of her face, a garment that is intruding on their conversation, making her words seem comical rather than serious. His eyes then shift downward to the ground, the nurse giving his hand a reassuring pat, although he's not quite sure what she's reassuring him of. It takes a few minutes for her words to make their way to the core of his understanding. Unmoving and emotionless, he sits in the chair until the truth finally hits him with intense velocity. Mamička knew that would be her last night, and she was reaching out to her son, wanting him to be there so she wouldn't be alone. *But she was doing so much better*, Janči thinks. How could he have known? And Mamička forced herself to make it through the first night, so she could ask him to stay with her again, and he didn't. She died December 16, 1946, exactly two years after Apu. The death certificate states she had complications with her kidneys.

Janči's love and sorrow for Mamička runs deep, but a shell has grown around his heart, hardening each day of his life since they were taken on the train. It doesn't allow for any emotion to touch him, protecting him from a loss he can't handle. He doesn't know how to properly mourn anymore. Immune to crying and dried up inside, Janči continues the mundane motions of life, going through the grieving process on his own terms.

Mamička's funeral is held the next day. There is no snow on the ground. Janči dresses up in a black suit. The rabbi cuts the collar of his shirt, symbolizing the tear within his heart. A simple service is held for the small congregation of family and friends. Immediately after, Janči runs home, changes out of his suit, and goes to work, a place he can forget everything and focus on the scientifically explainable things in life like electronics. Nothing has been arranged to sit Shiva as he remembers was done when Omama died, giving Janči no reason to stay at home, alone, surrounded by painful memories.

"Janči," Mr. Berger says, stunned that he has shown up for work, "go home. Relax."

"No, I can't. I'm better off if I work and forget everything."

Janči learns that the Glen Miller Orchestra is coming to Prague from America. He asks Mr. Berger, who has a lot of connections in the industry, to send him as the sound technician for the show. It would be good for him to get away now, especially since Marta has moved into Uncle Lajko's. Mr. Berger mulls over his request, not asking any questions, knowing the reasons behind it. With a few phone calls, Janči is sent to Prague on his new assignment, a new level of responsibility given to him at only sixteen. Setting up the sound systems and doing sound checks are part of his duties, and he pulls it off flawlessly. Janči is there for the New Year of 1946 and returns in the beginning of January 1947. Arriving back home, excited at sharing his experience with Mamička, the reality hits him full force. Mamička is still gone.

Irenka has thrown Marta out of the house, and Uncle Lajko is unable stop her. A youth home in Bratislava takes her in, preparing her to leave for Israel, now that nothing is keeping her here. Janči doesn't blame her for wanting to leave. He sadly realizes there is no place that feels like home anymore, even their apartment in Trenčín where he's living. After the exhilaration of the orchestra, it's not a lot to come back to.

Uncle Geza moves in with Janči, not wanting him to be alone. Uncle Lajko also arranges for Szivesi Neni, an old Jewish widow, to move in with Janči to help around the apartment. She lives in one of the several empty rooms, spending her time cooking meals and doing laundry. Janči takes an immediate liking to her genial disposition as she does to him, treating and loving him like her own son.

Over time, Janči's reluctance to go over to Uncle Lajko's increases, his visits quickly become a thing of the past. It's now February of 1947, and having just received yet another invite, Janči forces himself to accept through gritted teeth. He mentally prepares himself to painstakingly endure the witch of the house in order to see his uncle and cousin. After a brief conversation with Uncle Lajko and completely ignoring Irenka, he and Ivor go outside to escape the stifling friction.

They head out to the backyard to fly a new glider that Janči just finished building. Peter follows them, watching in amazement as the plane flies high above. Wanting to be included in the fun, he runs after it, in the hopes of catching the plane, losing his balance on the descent of his jump. He innocently falls into a rosebush in front of him. Blood runs down one finger that was pierced by a rose thorn. The minor injury is bandaged up, but redness begins spreading across all his fingers. Peter is taken to the doctor who changes the dressing, but sees it is only getting worse. His hand becomes paralyzed, and then he has trouble moving his neck, the severity provoking a wild rage in Irenka who takes her precious son to the hospital. After running some tests, the doctor comes back.

"I'm sorry to tell you this, but the boy has been diagnosed with Tetanus. The thorn that pricked him was covered with manure which caused him to get blood poisoning. There is nothing we can do. There is no cure for this disease"

"This is all your fault," Irenka spits at Janči. "You pushed him into the rosebush. If it wasn't for you, he'd still be okay."

A week later, Peter dies and is buried. During the funeral, Irenka coldly stares at Janči, in between sobs, icicles forming in her eyes that the tears cannot melt. All Janči keeps hearing from her afterward like a broken record is "if you didn't fly that plane, he'd still be alive." He and Ivor are banished from Uncle Lajko's house by Irenka. Janči has had enough, fully recognizing he has nothing left in Trenčín anymore.

A NEW LIFE AWAITS, SPRING 1947

JANČI AND IVOR begin working with other youth on the *Trat' Mladeže* Youth Railroad running through the mountains in Slovakia. For the Jewish Brigade of Chavia Reich, made up of sixty males and females, the labor is very intense. The youth are told they are working toward rebuilding a nation. Janči finds this comical since it's a communist ideology, but they aren't living in a communist country—yet. Blasting away rocks in the mountains to make room for the railroad tracks to be laid, Janči is exhausted every single night for that month, and the cold weather that sets in at night makes it that much worse.

Janči and Ivor decide to leave Trenčín and go to a youth home over three hundred kilometers east in Košice and join the youth movement, preparing for their ultimate migration to Israel. On the date of their departure, Uncle Lajko solemnly looks at the two boys he raised. They are now big enough to handle the large suitcases beside them.

"You know I want you to stay. This is not how I wanted things to end up." Janči tries to understand the tough position his uncle is in.

"We know, but it's time for us to move on. It will be good for us."

"I know. You're both old enough to make your own decisions and do what makes you happy. I expect you'll stay in touch. Let me know how things are going over there."

Twenty boys and girls, aged sixteen to eighteen, live in a two-story, twelve bedroom youth home with a long balcony, where the arrangement by the management of the movement is that they all have to work and support themselves with the money they make—a prerequisite to moving to Israel, where everyone needs to be able to work in some industry. Passports are issued to the youth by the Czechoslovakian Interior Ministry Office of Immigration in Bratislava, these travel documents are easily obtained in the country that is still democratic.

Largely unaffected by the war, streetcars in Košice still run, and people attend the opera. No matter how often he walks through the city, Janči still finds the sights spellbinding, especially the massive medieval square, dominated by the Gothic Saint Elizabeth's stone cathedral. Green and yellow tiles cover the tapering crossing tower and steep roofs on the exterior. Completely enchanted, he often veers inside, allowing the velvety light sieving through the nineteenth-century stained glass windows to wash over him. Over the north and west portals of the cathedral are stone carvings that are works of art. On the north end is an astounding intricately carved stone staircase. Viewing it is a religious experience in itself.

Finding a job in Košice is still difficult as they are limited in number. The Jewish community always manages to arrange something for members of the commune though. One of Janči's friends works in a mill, milling metal and steel, preparing machine equipment, while others work in export companies packing things. For seven months, Janči is set up with a job, working for a painter who paints posters and stage backdrops for the opera, theatre, and movies. Formerly a partisan, Tibor is left with no hands, both amputated because of severe frostbite. Intrigued by the stumps that once used to house hands, Janči reticently glances at the two stubby fingerlike shapes that protrude from the elbow. Amazingly, a stick is attached to one of them, and it holds chalk. It is this contraption that Tibor uses to create his masterpieces. Janči is empathetic to such limitations, knowing the feeling of having an apparatus become an extension of yourself.

Tibor deftly draws the outline of characters on huge advertising posters as large as ten feet by six feet, voluptuous women, handsome rugged men, and unsightly antagonists. Landscapes, home interiors, and churches set the scene on backdrops for the various acts in the operas. Prior to putting chalk to paper, Tibor attends the dress rehearsals to fully absorb all the details that make his paintings come alive. Unable to mix paint or fill in the sketches anymore, Tibor relies on Janči for these tasks. While scrupulously painting in the pew of a church for Tosca's future engagement at the theatre, Tibor hears Janči humming along to *Rigolleto* or *Fiagro*. Janči secretly yearns for a ticket to see an opera and does his best to vocalize this desire to Tibor. Not wanting to deprive Janči of such an experience, Tibor willingly gets him an extra ticket for *The Barber of Seville*.

"Here, Janči, this is for you," he says, motioning to his shirt pocket. Janči removes the envelope and looks in seeing a ticket to the performance.

"Thank you."

"You deserve it. You've been such a great help. And you need to experience the opera after doing all these paintings for it."

Living in a communal residence, they are governed by the tenet of sharing everything which leaves Janči facing the enormous dilemma of sharing one opera ticket with eighteen people. Mulling over the options, he formulates a plan that works in theory if carried out properly. Janči asks Ivor's girlfriend, Haviva, to devise a small leather pouch.

"What for?" she quizzically asks.

"You'll find out soon. Can you do it or not?"

"Sure, that won't take long."

When the pouch is ready, Janči tests it by placing a heavy key in it to see how far down the weight will drag it. Once assured of his brilliant strategy, he then lets the rest of the house in on it.

Passing through the *Hlavné námestie*,[36] Janči observes people walking about, browsing in shops, sightseeing or just spending time soaking up the charming surroundings. Ruling the center of the square is the grand neo-baroque style *Štátne divadlo*,[37] lavishly built inside and out in 1899 by an Austro-Hungarian firm. It is one of the town's key highlights, fronting a serene park which Janči walks through. Benches, Victorian style streetlamps, trees and grass flank the cobblestone walkway with various planted flowerbeds adding a dab of color to the green landscape. High quality ballet and drama performances are part of the repertoires here, fodder for a culture fixated on the arts.

By the front doors, the loud hum of animated chatter drenches the air, making up for the bland dark-colored attire on the patrons, navy dresses dotted with small flowers, and ordinary black trousers—nothing inspiring catching the eye. Old acquaintances catch up with each other at this periodic meeting, and longtime friends reunite. Clutching his ticket, Janči enters, and the ushers in black striped suits with epaulettes warmly greet him, recognizing him from his work with Tibor. His seat is on the fourth balcony, the highest one in the theatre.

Inside, the theatre is opulently decorated with plaster ornaments, the ceiling playing out scenes from William Shakespeare's famous tragedies *Othello*, *Romeo and Juliet*, *King Lear*, and *A Midsummer Night's Dream*, painted by Vienna's master artist P. Gastgeb. Janči takes his seat as anyone normally would, not arousing any suspicion. A few empty seats are available in his vicinity. As the singing begins on the lyre-shaped stage,

---

[36] *Hlavné námestie* is the Main Town Square.
[37] *Štátne divadlo* is the State Theatre.

Janči puts his ticket stub into the pouch that still contains the weight of the key, smoothly opens the window beside him and throws the pouch down to his friends waiting below. Act one begins, a group of musicians and a poor student serenading the window of Rosina in a public square. Within minutes, Haviva is sitting beside him, just in time to see Figaro enter, deserving of the first chance at seeing the opera because of her role in making the pouch. The pouch is thrown back down the window. At the end, six of them manage to watch the opera from one opera ticket, the thriftiness of the Janči's idea inspiring them all to do it again when the opportunity arises, and it does.

Janči is voted by members of the commune to be their leader and manage everyone. With the responsibility of ensuring they all do their work—cooking, cleaning, sweeping, creating a work schedule—Janči doesn't have time to continue his job with Tibor. All the money everyone earns is put into one account for necessities like food. A secretary and treasurer are also elected to keep the place functioning optimally. Clothing and food are still scarce, and the commune is hungry and irritable. Wood and coal for heat are nonexistent in the house. Nobody wants to go out and work, the cold impeding them. Lots of Jews are already leaving for Israel, and Janči can't force the people in the commune to get out of bed, let alone do any work. He writes to the head of the youth movement, explaining the problem and asking for suggestions.

"Well, we can't really do anything to help you. You just have to try to get them out to work" is the unsupportive reply he gets. Each night, he makes phone calls to arrange work for them somewhere the next day, but none of them go. Taking the problem into his own hands again, Janči visits the local pharmacist.

"I have a problem," Janči tells him. "I can't get anyone at the commune out of bed to go and work. We need the money to buy food, but all they do is complain about the cold and being hungry. No one wants to do anything about it. I thought you might have something that will get them moving."

The pharmacist smiles mischievously. "Wait here," he says as he goes to the back, shuffles around for a few minutes, and comes out with a small package.

"This will definitely get them running," he says with a smirk. "Just use a very small quantity of it. Next time you make hot chocolate, mix a little bit of this powder in. I promise you, they'll get up very fast." Janči smiles and takes his powdery concoction back to the commune.

On the weekend, Janči tells the cook, Esther, a friend of his, what she has to do with the powder.

"I was told it will get everyone up very quickly." Liking the idea already, she takes the hot chocolate off the shelf, provided to them by the UNRA,[38] and begins boiling water.

"There's some freshly made hot chocolate in the kitchen," Esther yells to the comatose house. In minutes, the group comes out of the woodwork, hot chocolate only prepared a few times a month, in search of the incentive that got them out of bed. Plain white mugs line the counter, each one filled to the brim with the dark drink that has been spiked with the secret powder. Janči and Esther watch as they all guzzle it down, galvanizing their plan. Once the empty mugs are put back on the counter, no one offering to help with the cleaning of them, they all scuttle away, back into the burrows of their warm blankets.

"So now what?" Esther asks. "We gave them the stuff, but we're left to clean their mess."

"I don't think there was supposed to be instantaneous reaction. Just wait and see what happens," he says playfully.

---

[38] UNRA is the United Nations Relief and Rehabilitation Administration Agency.

"Okay. In the meantime, help me wash these dishes." Esther washes, and Janči dries with a green and white checkered rag, the house around them motionless again. Once all the mugs are washed and put back in the cupboard, a stampede of feet begins. Janči and Esther look at each other incredulously. Doors are rapidly slamming shut and fists frantically bang on them, trying to break down what stands between them and the toilet. "Let me in" are the only three words that pierce through the air in the house. Sitting down on the couch, Janči and Esther enjoy their own untainted hot chocolate while the spectacle continues. Sixteen people frantically try to dethrone one of the two bathrooms in the house. If one is occupied, they rush down the circular stairs to the other one.

"The pharmacist did say this would get them up very fast." And they begin laughing hysterically, almost spilling their drink. Janči later finds out that the powder given to the commune is also given to horses to make them relieve themselves.

A secret mission funded by the Jewish Agency and United States hear about Janči's aptitude in navigation. Based on this information, they recruit him to work for them. He is stationed at the borders of Hungary and Poland, transferring teenaged Jews through the mountains and across the borders into Czechoslovakia, still not controlled by a communist regime. From there, the teens go on to Vienna and then Italy, where they board ships to Palestine.[39]

A month later, once exempt of this duty and ready to leave the Youth House, Janči and Ivor return to Trenčín one last time before their own

---

[39] Palestine was to be declared an independent state of Israel on May 14, 1948.

trip to Israel, saying a final goodbye to a tearful Uncle Lajko, Palko, and Geza. Irenka stiffly stands there, unflinching.

Italy is the first stop for Janči and Ivor, with seventy other young Jewish boys and girls. Initially, they stay in an old Italian army camp from the Second World War in Trani. Staying in a barrack this time doesn't invoke the fear and distress it once did. Now it is a transition point to something better, not worse—a renewed chance at life. They are informed that in two and a half months, they will be able to board the ship to Israel. With all that time to spare, there's no better thing for them to do but travel around Italy.

Carrying only a backpack, cigarettes, and some silk stockings for their lucrative trading value, Janči and Ivor venture out into Italy, travelling around to all the cities they've only read about and seen pictures of. After the war, the Italians are desperate for anything, unable to afford much, working in Janči and Ivor's favor. Two cigarettes get them a room to sleep a night. Silk stockings get them accommodation and food. Ice cream, still in abundance, is a daily indulgence they always splurge on. Each day, the hardest decision they face is selecting from a wealth of flavors—chocolate, pistachio, tiramisu, raspberry, hazelnut, lemon, coffee, the list never ending, each description more tantalizing than the one before.

By ship, they journey up the Adriatic coast, lounging around on the beaches, over to Venice, where they take a gondola ride through the canals and feed an assembly of pigeons on the Piazza San Marco. In Florence, they are captivated by the Duomo; in Rome, they visit the Coliseum and Roman Ruins, and they do a brief stint in Napoli. A whirlwind tour brings them back with deep bronze tans to the port city of Bari for their departure, their turn to board the ship *Galila*, taking them to Israel on April 9, 1949, eighteen years after he was born, where a new chapter of his life will begin.

At night, they sleep under a deck unless it is occupied by others who claimed the coveted spot sooner, in which instance they sleep atop freight covered with tarpaulin. The gentle sway of the ship, the sounds of the waves lapping, and the warm, salty Mediterranean air coalesce into the ultimate outdoor sleeping conditions, renewing a sense of vitality within Janči.

Unsure of what to expect at his destination, he can only hope he will survive whatever life throws his way. And in the midst of any turmoil, he needs to cherish the happy memories of the past, the only possessions he has to take with him into the future. Most of his family is gone, not being given the new chance at life that Janči has been granted. He must take it for them and rebuild his own life, keeping their spirit alive. They are the ones who made him come this far.

After one week on the ship, dealing with bouts of seasickness and barely eating, the food offered to them looking very unappetizing, the port of Haifa comes into view from a far distance. Marta is already on this land somewhere waiting for him, fervent on escaping the past.

As the ship inches closer along the water, Janči enjoys the freshness of the early morning. Then there it is—the first thing in Israel that Janči lays his eyes on. Rising out of the water is Mount Carmel, its slopes blending in perfect harmony with the city—his new home. As if intentionally painted in to add even more contrast to the vivid landscape, Janči can't ever remember a time he was so awestruck by the splendor of such a beautiful deep blue sky.

AFTERWORD

JANČI MET HIS wife Ruth in Israel and married her in 1953. She passed away in 1992. He currently lives in Toronto, Canada with his two children, Ronit and Eitan, three grandchildren, Ryan, Ashley, and Hunter, and one great-granddaugther, Ella (named after Omama Ella).

Marta currently lives in Toronto, Canada, with her husband Ezra. They have two sons, Yigal and Gil, and five grandchildren, Karl, Elise, Samuel, Scotty and Daniel.

Uncles **Lajko, Palko, Geza** and **Irenka** have all passed away.

Uncle **Turi**, and Aunt **Kamila** and her husband all perished in Auschwitz in 1942.

Uncle **Adi** perished in Krakow, Poland, while searching for his wife in 1942.

Ivor married Chaviva and had two children. He worked as a factory manager at an asbestos company in Nahariya, Israel. In 1994, at the age of sixty-two, he passed away.

Fiorella currently lives in Trieste, Italy and is married with three children. Her mother, Maria, remarried a Czech engineer after the war.

Skultetys were honored by Yad Vashem as the Righteous of the World. They have passed away. **Olga,** their daughter, lives in Bánovce nad Bebravou, Slovakia.

Dodko(Dr. Jehuda Suss), immigrated to Israel after the war where he attended university and became a nuclear physicist.

Esther lives in a kibbutz in Israel.

The Teschner family in Trenčianské Teplice, 1935
Apu, Mamička, Marta and Janči

Omama, Opapa and Janči at
Baračka, 1931

Mamička and Janči at
Baračka, 1931

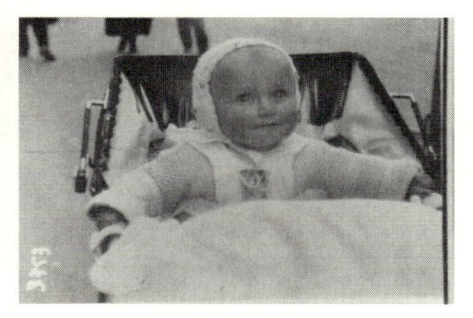

Marta, 1934

Baračka

Trenčianské Teplice

Janči's house in Trenčianské Teplice

Pastry Shop
Opapa with uncles Adi (left), Geza (right), Miki, Turi and aunt Kamila, 1933

Opapa with his friend, famous Austrian writer Roda Roda and his wife at Baračka, 1934.

Marta, Mamička, Opapa,
Apu and Janči, 1934

Apu in Basel,
Switzerland, 1933

Zelená Žaba swimming pool

Marta and Janči, 1935

Restaurant Kursalon, 1936.
Dr. Szephazi (left) playing chess with Ondrej Šrobár (right) and Uncle Palko (in tuxedo).
Caricature by then famous Sors

Janči's classmates from the Jewish school in Trenčin, 1940-1942

Mamička (right) with friends at
Smokovec Sanatorium, 1946

Mamička and Marta,
Trenčin, 1946

Mamička and Janči at park
in Trenčianské Teplice,
1946

Building a summer camp in the mountains with Esther, 1947

Janči (bottom) and Ivor (top) at summer camp, 1947

From left: Ivor, Uncle Lajko, Irenka and Janči,
before leaving Trenčin

Uncle Lajko

Janči and Ivor, 1947

Janči, 1948

Marta, 1948

Ivor, 1947

Fiorella, 1947

Blasting rocks at the Trať Mladeže Youth Railroad

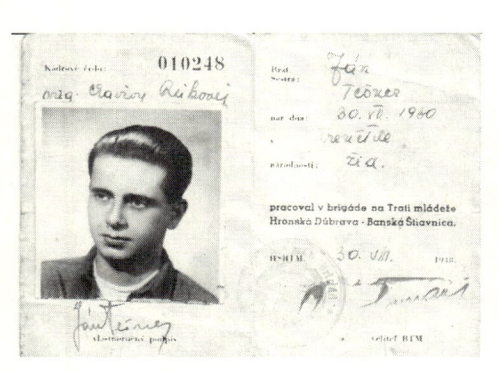

Janči's ID from Trať Mladeže, 1948

Loading trolleys with blasted rock

Camp Trani, Italy, 1949

Ship *Galila,* Bari, Italy

Janči and Ruth meeting Michal and
Maria Skultety, 1989

The barn where Janči and
his family were hidden
by the Skultetys

Burned house
of the Skultetys

Janči and grandson Ryan in Trenčin, 1995

Edwards Brothers Malloy
Thorofare, NJ USA
September 13, 2013